FIRST STEPS TOWARDS SANSKRIT

First Steps Towards Sanskrit: Language, Linguistics and Culture is an accessible first introduction to this ancient Indian language.

Complete beginners are introduced to the language from scratch. Key terms are explained clearly and there is an extensive glossary to assist the reader who is unfamiliar with the terminology of language learning. By the end of the book, learners will have grasped the basics of the language and be prepared to engage readily in an introductory college or university course or through private study. The addition of cultural, linguistic and historical notes will appeal to learners with diverse interests, ranging from religious studies and philosophy to yoga and comparative or historical linguistics.

The book includes references to classical and modern European languages. Parallels are also drawn with Indic languages where these are relevant, particularly as concerns the writing system. No knowledge of any language other than English is, however, presupposed. This book is ideal for both self-study and in-class use as a primer or core text for pre-sessional courses.

Anil K. Biltoo is an Honorary Fellow of the Chartered Institute of Linguists and has taught Sanskrit for many years at the University of London. He is currently teaching at King's College London.

FIRST STEPS TOWARDS SANSKRIT

Language, Linguistics and Culture

Anil K. Biltoo

Routledge
Taylor & Francis Group
LONDON AND NEW YORK

First published 2022
by Routledge
2 Park Square, Milton Park, Abingdon, Oxon OX14 4RN

and by Routledge
605 Third Avenue, New York, NY 10158

Routledge is an imprint of the Taylor & Francis Group, an informa business

British Library Cataloguing-in-Publication Data
A catalogue record for this book is available from the British Library

Library of Congress Cataloging-in-Publication Data
A catalog record for this book has been requested

ISBN: 978-0-367-34386-6 (hbk)
ISBN: 978-0-367-34385-9 (pbk)
ISBN: 978-0-429-32543-4 (ebk)

DOI: 10.4324/9780429325434

Typeset in Times New Roman
by Apex CoVantage, LLC

CONTENTS

ACKNOWLEDGEMENTS

The present work is dedicated to the many hundreds of Sanskrit students and to the University of London staff whom I had the pleasure to teach whilst at the School of Oriental and African Studies. Their patience and dedication to the study of Sanskrit went from beyond mere curiosity to a search to find meaning in a challenging but beguiling language. My former students are too many to name. Thanks are due, however, to Celeste Cronin, whose humour and diligence were a source of encouragement, not only in the teaching of the language but in the writing of this book.

Thanks are due, also, to my elder sister Bi and her husband David for the gift of food and 'fur therapy' (a Great Dane and a French Bulldog) when such therapy was most needed. Lockdown in the time of a pandemic would have been less endurable had it not been for both food and fur. I am indebted to Rosie McEwan, Editorial Assistant with Taylor & Francis, for her understanding when it proved necessary to extend the submission date for the manuscript, following a year that would not be wished on anyone and where not even food and fur could revive the Sanskrit muse.

Finally, I would like to acknowledge the reader, for having demonstrated such extraordinarily good taste in getting hold of an introductory text on Sanskrit. It is heartening to see that there is still interest in Sanskrit and that the modern world has not condemned it to obsolescence. Teaching students for more than a decade has informed me as to what an introduction to Sanskrit should look like, what it ought to contain and what might tactfully be omitted for the sake of clarity. Any mistakes are mine alone and I strongly welcome all comments and suggestions.

Anil K. Biltoo
akbiltoo@yahoo.com
Hampton Court
April 2021

INTRODUCTION

Introductory remarks

Sanskrit is a captivating language. It has long been the treasure of linguists for whom it represents a linguistic fossil, like a fly trapped in amber, reflecting a form of speech which existed before the Common Era and has remained unchanged and unchangeable. For an untold number of others, Hindu, Buddhist and Jain, it lies at the core of their religious tradition, since the literatures of these religions find expression in Sanskrit or in one of its sister languages (the Prakrits) of which the best known is **Pāḷi**, itself the language of a large and important body of texts.

There are many other people, neither linguists nor Hindu, Buddhist or Jain, for whom a knowledge of Sanskrit is something worth acquiring. Students of ancient languages and cultures are drawn to Sanskrit, many of them with an ability to read Greek or Latin (or indeed both). There are also the students of comparative literature for whom Sanskrit offers endless opportunities to explore the human condition in any number of texts ranging from remote antiquity (starting with the **Ṛgveda**, c. 1500–1200 BCE) to the later **Upaniśad**s and the twin epics of India, the **Mahābhārata** and the **Rāmāyaṇa**.

For practitioners of yoga, Sanskrit represents the language in which their philosophical practice is explored. It is the language which gives voice to the principles of yoga – the thing which literately brings the mind and body together (from the verbal root **yuj**: *to unite, conjoin*). The various postures

DOI: 10.4324/9780429325434-1

of yoga, the **āsanas**, all have a Sanskrit name, highly illustrative in terms of how they are formed. The **suptavīrāsana** posture, for example, is easily comprehensible with only a small amount of Sanskrit at one's disposal. It is the posture in which one lies like a sleeping warrior: **supta** (*sleeping*), **vīra** (*warrior*), **āsana** (*posture*).

Even if one is not a linguist, or a Hindu, Buddhist or Jain and has neither an interest in classical studies and comparative literature or an inclination to practise yoga, Sanskrit still has something to offer such an individual. Sanskrit requires concentration and a disciplined mind. It is methodical, rigorous, complex. To study Sanskrit is to immerse oneself in a mass of verbal roots, an enormous working vocabulary and a writing system much more principled in its design than the Phoenician alphabet from which the Greek, Cyrillic and Roman alphabets evolved. For all who come to the study of Sanskrit, for whatever reason, a rich and rewarding experience awaits. **Svāgataṃ** (*Welcome*).

The present work is intended as an initial guide to Sanskrit, aimed at those who wish to explore the language, its linguistic affiliations, its origin, writing system and structure. The language is presented in terms of its cultural significance as well as its structure. For those contemplating further study, the present work is ideal. It does not in any way presume to replace textbooks currently available, of which there are a fair few. Suggestions as to further reading (Chapter 10) will mention a number of these along with publications that are good to consult on various topics. It is important for the learner to be prepared to read widely around the language. Sanskrit, divorced from any context and studied simply as a language system, may have yielded its treasures to philologists in the past, whose chief concern was to the investigate the language much as a laboratory researcher might do with the contents of a Petri dish. For the contemporary learner, this approach is unlikely to be the favoured one. Information about Sanskrit literature and ancient Indian history is abundant, and the Internet has made much of this information accessible.

The present work aims to introduce the reader to Sanskrit in gentle, manageable steps which discuss the context in which the study of the language is relevant (Chapter 1). It includes an exploration of a transliteration system which allows the reader, from the outset, to tackle the sounds of Sanskrit without first having to master the writing system associated with it (Chapter 2). The sound system is then introduced in sufficient detail to allow the reader to gain confidence that the sounds being uttered are accurate (Chapter 3). Thereafter, the writing system – the **Devanāgarī** – is introduced, allowing the reader to connect the sounds of Sanskrit with their visual representation (Chapter 4). In the subsequent chapters, a knowledge of both the pronunciation and writing system of Sanskrit are used to ease the learner into the reading of Sanskrit words (Chapter 5) and, subsequently, to investigate the structure of the language (Chapters 6–7) and sound changes (Chapter 8). In Chapter 9, the reader is presented with verses in Sanskrit. These are explained in detail, permitting the reader to see how Sanskrit expresses ideas.

Use is made of a transliteration system throughout, so the reader can keep checking the transliteration against the Devanāgarī as the eye slowly and naturally adjusts to the latter. Where the transliteration is used, it appears in bold typeface. If a word is bolded in the main body of the text (section or table headings aside), it represents Sanskrit, hence the fact that the words **Upaniśad**s and **āsana**s were indicated in bold apart from the final *-s*, which does not represent the Sanskrit plural. A Sanskrit term, once used, is not repeatedly bolded, since that would unnecessarily distract the eye. By contrast, vocabulary items and examples from Sanskrit are bolded throughout (apart from the index). Certain words are so frequently encountered in texts related to Sanskrit that their everyday spelling in English is used. The word 'Sanskrit' is the obvious example; another is 'Prakrit'. It seems undesirable to refer to these as **Saṃskr̥ta** and **Prākr̥ta** in the body of the text. The same practice is applied to the modern languages of India.

Words and phrases from all languages other than Sanskrit, when used to illustrate examples, are in italics, as are translations or the titles of publications. Italics also indicate individual sounds (e.g. *sh*-sound) where English spelling is used to identify them. The alternative to this would necessarily have involved the reader learning the International Phonetic Alphabet – which is hardly to be expected of those coming from disciplines other than linguistics. The Devanāgarī appears throughout in a larger font, for the sake of legibility, addressing a frustration frequently voiced by learners of Sanskrit: *'I can't see the letters clearly. They're too small'*. Underlining is used to emphasize or highlight a word or part of a word. Finally, a <u>preceding</u> asterisk indicates unattested or non-licit forms. This is a convention in linguistics and a useful one to employ.

No knowledge of any language other than English is presupposed. Whilst there are frequent examples of words from other languages, as and when they serve to illustrate particular points, it is not assumed that the reader will have a speaking or reading ability in Latin (or Greek, or Lithuanian, or any other language). Pronunciation tips refer to 'English', pure and simple, in preference to the more customary 'Received Pronunciation' (RP), occasionally still defined as 'BBC English'. This is because terms 'RP/BBC

English' tend to bring to mind a particular pronunciation which has moved away from everyday norms and represents, certainly for speakers of British English, an unnatural and archaic pronunciation.

The present work does not rely on recordings for the simple reason that there is no fixed standard for Sanskrit pronunciation. In any event, those who promote Sanskrit as a spoken language very frequently bring in features from their mother tongues. Sanskrit classifies its sound system in a way which is rigorous enough to allow the reader to grasp the pronunciation of any given phoneme. The reader ought not to feel that the ability to mimic spoken Sanskrit is necessary. That is absolutely not the case. The voice which the reader possesses is more than sufficient.

How to use this book

The present work is intended to be read in the order in which the chapters appear. The reader who has some understanding of Sanskrit or can make headway with the Devanāgarī is urged not to skip through chapters. These follow in a logical sequence. Many of the points made are followed up in later chapters. There is a clean division as regards the aspect of the language under investigation. First comes the sound system, then the writing system, then the formal grammar. This is a natural way to proceed, given that the utterance precedes writing, both in terms of historical language development and in the way in which people acquire their first language. The reader should allow for a pause for consolidation between chapters, ensuring that the information has been absorbed and retained before reading further.

A good place at which to take a longer pause to consolidate fully is the end of Chapter 5. This represents the halfway point in the *First Steps Towards Sanskrit*. It is the first of two steps. On reaching that point, the reader is strongly recommended to comb through Chapter 1 to Chapter 5, picking up any points that were missed in the first reading. The aim of the author is to make the path towards a knowledge of Sanskrit as effortless as possible. The style is not overly dry and there is no assumption made that the reader would have to remedy any lacunae in understanding by going to other sources. That said, the chapters beyond Chapter 2 are informationally rich; and new information merits a rereading. The second step (Chapter 6 through to Chapter 10) requires the reader to have taken the first step securely.

For the reader who has the time to explore Sanskrit resources on the Internet, these are an excellent source of information on such things as font variation within the Devanāgarī (This is something which the reader is urged to investigate, after completing Chapter 4 or Chapter 5). It is not difficult to find examples of mantras or verses in Sanskrit, and accustoming the eye to fonts that are different to the one used in the present work will stand the learner in good stead. As illustrated in 4.4.2 and 4.4.3, certain fonts are easy to read; others, less so. Importantly, the Internet also allows the reader to hear a range of different voices reciting Sanskrit and to see the extent to which the cursory transliteration of Sanskrit is to be avoided. Just as all roads lead to Rāma, excusing the dreadful pun, every exploration of Sanskrit leads to greater familiarity with it.

1

THE SANSKRIT LANGUAGE

1.1 Linguistic background

Sanskrit is an Indo-European language. This means that it belongs to the same family of languages as do, for example, English, French, Spanish, Italian, German, Russian, Persian and the languages of northern India. The list of languages classified as Indo-European is long, for if German is Indo-European, so too are Dutch, Danish, Norwegian and Swedish – and all the other languages that are also categorized as 'Germanic'. From the outset, there is a need for clarity as regards various terms. When linguists talk of a 'language family', they refer to the concept that languages are related. The relationship is predicated around the concept that related languages have a common ancestor. So far, so good; but a language can have several ancestors: some are recent and are well documented, others go back to a point in remote history and have left behind no written records. If one takes Italian as a case study, the following propositions can be made and are all equally true:

'Italian is an Indo-European language'.
'Italian is descended from Latin'.
'Italian is a Romance (or Italic) language'.

It does not, however, follow that English is an Indo-European language and must, as a result, also be descended from Latin. Here, the concept of a language branch is important.

DOI: 10.4324/9780429325434-2

When one investigates the relationship between languages within the Indo-European family, one rapidly encounters the term 'branch'. It is often the cause of confusion, in that many sources conflate family with branch whereas these concepts are quite distinct. Modern Italian is descended from Latin, as has been asserted. Both Italian and Latin, as distinct languages, belong to the Romance branch – not the Romance family. The relationship between these two languages can easily be shown, since there is ample historical evidence attesting to the changes that took place from early Latin, through to Latin in its classical form (the form taught in schools), followed by the Vulgar Latin of later centuries, when Rome as an imperial power had collapsed. Thereafter came the formation of the early modern dialects of the Italian peninsula which gave rise to the modern dialects, many of which still exist (Ligurian, Venetian, Sardinian, Sicilian, etc.). All the dialects identifiable with Latin, including Latin itself, are Romance languages (if defined according to a branch) and Indo-European (if defined according to the language family).

The Indo-European language family can be divided into one of a dozen branches, of which Romance is only one. Going roughly from west to east (and excluding the Americas), these are as follows:

Branch	*Representative languages (not exhaustive)*
Germanic	Icelandic, Norwegian, German, English
Celtic	Irish, Scots Gaelic, Welsh, Cornish, Breton
Romance (Italic)	Portuguese, Spanish, French, Italian, Romanian
Slavonic (Slavic)	Slovenian, Czech, Polish, Russian, Bulgarian
Baltic (Balto-Slavic)	Lithuanian, Latvian
Illyrian	Albanian
Greek	Greek
Thracian	Thracian (Extinct)
Anatolian	Hittite, Luwian, Palaic, Lydian (All extinct)
Armenian	Armenian
Indo-Iranian	Persian, Pashto, Panjabi, Hindi, Bengali, Sanskrit
Tocharian	Tocharian (Extinct)

The precise number of branches within Indo-European is not subject to universal agreement, since there are languages of which little is known and on which archaeology has yet to shed light (Often, the evidence for these languages takes the form of words and scraps of data preserved in other languages). Within the branches themselves, there is also disagreement as to distinguishing between language and dialect. It lies outside of the scope of the present work to investigate the arguments surrounding the issue of language versus dialect. Suffice it to say that the issue is often far from clear, even with present-day linguistic varieties. Despite the fact, for example, that there is a high degree of intelligibility between Norwegian, Danish and Swedish, these languages are not referred to as dialects. The issue, ultimately, is a political one. Norwegian, Danish and Swedish are recognized as languages of three separate nation states, irrespective of the fact that they show greater linguistic similarities with each other than is the case with many of the so-called 'Hindi dialects'. The last word on this matter is best provided by Max Weinreich, a linguist who devoted his life to the study of the Yiddish language. According to Weinreich, *"a language is a dialect with an army and a navy"*.

Sanskrit is an Indo-European language belonging to the Indo-Iranian branch. As the table on the previous page indicated, the Indo-Iranian branch (which may further be split into two sub-branches: Iranian and Indic/Aryan) includes not only languages of South Asia but those spoken on the Iranian plateau and in Afghanistan. This will be important to remember when investigating the origin of Sanskrit (1.4). This branch contains a great number of modern languages which, taken together, are spoken by over a thousand million people, from eastern Turkey (Kurdish) to the China/Myanmar border with India (Assamese). No other branch of Indo-European has as many speakers except for Germanic, courtesy of English in its role as the global language.

The Indo-Iranian branch has left important literary records from before the Common Era, with Avestan, Old Persian, Middle Persian, Bactrian and Sogdian on the Iranian side, and the Prakrits on the Indic (or Aryan) side. The oldest representatives of this branch are Avestan and Vedic Sanskrit, which served as the liturgical languages of two religions: Zoroastrianism and Hinduism, respectively. Whilst knowledge of Avestan has been kept alive by priests in a dwindling community of Zoroastrians in Iran and amongst the Parsee community, largely resident in the Indian state of Gujarat (and also in diaspora), Vedic Sanskrit is chanted daily by many hundreds of millions of Hindus.

One frequently hears and reads the assertion that the modern languages of India are all descended from Sanskrit, but this is simply not the case. Sanskrit was reserved for cultural activities and was not the language of everyday speech. The latter function was served by the Prakrits (language forms literally *fashioned by nature*). Three major Prakrits can be identified, descended from an Old Indic language which, for want of any other contender, is stated as Vedic Sanskrit. **Apabhraṃśa** refers to a transitional phase between the Prakrits and the older forms of the modern languages. Sanskrit had no linear descendants. She was the spinster sister of the Prakrits, with her mind set on higher things.

	Vedic Sanskrit		
↙	↓	↓	↘
Sanskrit	Mahārāṣṭrī Prakrit	Śaurasenī Prakrit	Māgadhī Prakrit
↓	↓	↓	↓
No descendants	Apabhraṃśa	Apabhraṃśa	Apabhraṃśa
	↓	↓	↓
	Marathi	Hindi, Gujarati	Oriya, Bengali

1.2 The 'discovery' of Sanskrit

Stating that Sanskrit is an Indo-European language leads to the obvious question as to the evidence supporting such a statement. Often, languages are related if speakers of one can understand speakers of another without having formally acquired each other's language. It was noted that Norwegian, Danish and Swedish exhibited just this type of mutual intelligibility. So too, speakers of Spanish and Italian claim to be able to understand each other without too much difficulty. The same is, however, not often heard as between Spanish and French, or Italian and French. In India, something similar occurs. Speakers of Urdu and Hindi have little difficulty understanding each other (as long as the language register is of the everyday variety as opposed to technical). That seems analogous to the Scandinavian situation. As for speakers of Panjabi and Hindi, or Gujarati and Hindi, there can often be a high degree of intelligibility, although this is not guaranteed (This is more indicative of the situation as between speakers of Spanish and Italian). Situations such as these would tend to indicate that speakers are able to understand a great deal of the core vocabulary and grammar of certain other languages. This is a good starting point in an investigation of Sanskrit's credentials as regards membership of the Indo-European language family; but first, it is necessary to look at how Sanskrit was 'discovered' by Europeans, since this goes to the heart of the matter.

Although not the first European to identify similarities between Sanskrit and some of the languages of Europe, the accolade for first having posited a substantive linguistic connection goes to Sir William Jones, a judge serving in Calcutta in the 1780s. Jones's interest in the languages and cultures of India was such that he established the Asiatick Society – ultimately to become the Royal Asiatic Society of Bengal – in 1784. The aims of the

Society were to explore a broad range of subjects relating to Asia, but it is clear, from the number of manuscripts it collected, that the Society placed great importance on the exploration of the languages and literatures of India. In 1786, Jones gave a talk to the Society which has been hailed by linguists as signifying the starting point of the systematic study of language relationships which led, in the first instance, to comparative linguistics and the evolution of Indo-European studies. It is not out of the question to suggest, therefore, that Sanskrit is responsible for the creation of linguistics as a recognized discipline.

The talk that Jones gave in 1786 contains what is possibly the longest sentence in the English language and certainly one of the most momentous in terms of the impact it had on the study of Sanskrit. The talk in question is worth reading in its entirety, no less for its detail than for the fact that Jones displayed an extraordinary insight in having hypothesized connections between language that were subsequently proved to be correct. Jones asserted that Sanskrit showed too many similarities with Greek and Latin for such similarities to be coincidental. From there, he suggested that not only did Sanskrit, Greek and Latin appear to be related but, so too, *"the Gothic and the Celtic* [. . .] *and the old Persian"* (The term 'Gothic' would eventually be replaced by 'Teutonic' then 'Germanic' – the latter corresponding to current usage – whilst the term 'Celtic' has endured). As for Jones's instinct regarding *"the old Persian"* being related to Sanskrit, that too was proved correct. Strangely, however, the connection was only established once the cuneiform writing system used for Old Persian monumental inscriptions had been deciphered. That did not take place until the following century.

Sanskrit had a significant impact on the intellectual thought of Europe in the period following the Age of Enlightenment, which culminated in the French Revolution. The term 'Romanticism' is often applied to this period, although one may suggest that there was nothing particularly romantic about the rise of the nation state and a period of expansionism which saw the British and French vying for hegemony within Europe as well as further afield. European scholarship as regards Sanskrit was initially dominated by the British, who had access to source material from India. Along with Sir William Jones, mention should be made of Charles Wilkins (who had helped Jones set up the Asiatick Society) and who was himself a scholar of Sanskrit. Wilkins produced a translation of the **Bhagavadgītā** in 1785, with Jones's translation of a work by the foremost dramatist in Sanskrit (**Kālidāsa**) following shortly thereafter: *Sacontalá; Or, The Fatal Ring: An Indian Drama by Cálidás* (1789). Then followed the *Sanskrit Grammar* of Henry Thomas Colebrooke (1805). Sanskrit captured the imagination of poets such as Johann Wolfgang von Goethe, but it was in Sanskrit philology that German scholarship excelled. Franz Bopp published his *Detailed System of the Sanskrit Language* in 1827 and the groundbreaking *Comparative Grammar of the Sanskrit, Zend, Greek, Latin, Lithuanian, Gothic, German, and S(c)lavonic Languages* (1833–1852). The latter has remained a key resource in comparative linguistics and Indo-European studies.

1.3 Cognates

The moment that speech communities are in contact, languages are subject to borrowing. Often, borrowed items are easy to spot. The majority of English speakers would doubtless identify *pizza*, *kebab*, *tikka masala*, *sushi* and *coffee* as borrowings, even if they might be unclear as to the actual origin of the words in question (*Coffee*, for example, might be identified as having come from the Italian *caffè* or even the French *café* but the word appears to have entered English through the Dutch *koffie*, borrowed from the Turkish *kahve* which, in turn, was borrowed from the Arabic *qahwa*). Borrowings are not always easily identifiable as such to speakers of a language. One would have to think carefully about such words as *vest*, *jacket*, *overcoat*, *shoes*, since they are everyday items with nothing seemingly exotic or imported about them (*Overcoat* and *shoes* are native English words; *vest* and *jacket* are not).

Cognates are different from borrowings in that they refer to words that exist in one language, are attested in another and are clearly related in some way. Here, borrowing is not the reason for the existence of similarity. The reason is that the languages in question both possess the word, having inherited it from their ancestral form. Sanskrit contains many words that are cognate with words in other Indo-European languages – and not just those spoken in India. Cognates in English and the Indic languages precede any direct contact or cultural influence between speakers of English and speakers of Indic languages. To use Sir William Jones's words, this indicates that the words in question must have *"sprung from some common source, which, perhaps, no longer exists"*. Jones had roots of verbs and forms of grammar in mind, but the same argument applies to nouns: English *mother* is the Sanskrit **mātṛ**; *brother* is **bhrātṛ**; *name* is **nāma**; *tooth* is **danta** (Consider the words *dentist*, *dental plan*, etc.). Cognates with English and Sanskrit often differ considerably in pronunciation and, very often, the Sanskrit cognate is with an English word that entered the language through borrowing, as is the case with *dentist* and *dental*, from the French *dent* (meaning *tooth*).

Although there are a number of exceptions, languages do not generally borrow their counting systems from other languages, simply because they do not need to. The following table presents the numbers one to ten from English, Sanskrit, Greek, Latin and Lithuanian to illustrate cognate forms.

Cognates

English	*Sanskrit*	*Greek (Ancient)*	*Latin*	*Lithuanian*
one	**eka**	*hen* *	*ūnum* *	*vienas*
two	**dva**	*düo*	*duo* *	*du*
three	**tri**	*tria* *	*tria* *	*trys*
four	**catur**	*tettara* *	*quattuor*	*keturi*
five	**pañca**	*pente*	*quīnque*	*penki*
six	**ṣaṣ**	*heks*	*sex*	*šeši*
seven	**sapta**	*hepta*	*septem*	*septyni*
eight	**aṣṭa**	*oktō*	*octō*	*aštuoni*
nine	**nava**	*ennea*	*novem*	*devyni*
ten	**daśa**	*deka*	*decem*	*dešimt*

Notes

The Sanskrit forms are stem forms, meaning that they do not indicate any grammatical endings.

The neuter nominative forms have been selected for Greek and Latin, where an asterisk appears after the word in question.

For Lithuanian, the forms are masculine.

If the following three sounds changes are considered, the data presented start to take on a remarkable similarity across all four languages:

(i) Where Sanskrit has **c** (pronounced like the *ch* in *chip*), Latin and Lithuanian have a *k*-sound, although Latin has the added feature of an accompanying *w* (k^w). Greek, by contrast, has *t*.
(ii) The Sanskrit **ś** (signifying a *sh*-sound), is a *k*-sound in both Latin and Greek, but Lithuanian aligns with Sanskrit in having a *sh*-sound.
(iii) The Sanskrit **ṣ** (another *sh*-sound), is *k* or *ks* in Greek and Latin, except for when it is at the start of a word. Lithuanian, again, resembles Sanskrit in having *sh*.

1.4 The origin of Sanskrit

What was the 'common source' to which Sir William Jones had referred, in the talk he gave to the Asiatick Society? Linguistics as a discipline did not exist at the time Jones addressed the Society, although philology (the study of language in historical contexts and from historical sources) was certainly an object of interest amongst those educated in the classical languages of Europe. Philology, in Jones's time, was very much the pastime of people who were well-read in Greek and Latin, for there lay the focus: the exploration of the languages of ancient Greece and Rome, and how these had influenced the modern languages of Europe. Language change was – and still is – at the heart of philology, and that was where Jones placed the emphasis.

If one suggests that languages change over the centuries and that they diverge in the process, this accords not only with common sense but acknowledges the data available from, for example, Latin and its descendants, or Old English, Middle English and modern English. What is important is that an assertion as to language change is capable of being proved; that there are data to support such an assertion. With Sanskrit, as Jones was aware, there was ample language information available – it was all around him, in Calcutta, in the mouths of Brahmins and the general population, as they recited scriptures and prayers. What was missing was the information regarding the earliest phase of the language. Certainly, there was Vedic Sanskrit, and that was undoubtedly archaic, but what of the language preceding Vedic Sanskrit? Here, as Jones concluded, was the unknown territory in which one might explore ancient connections between Sanskrit and the classical languages of Europe.

Positing an ancestor for Sanskrit, which would also have had a connection with the oldest-known languages of Europe, was a tricky affair. Much territory lay between India and Europe: the Russian steppes, the Black Sea, the Caucasus (the Russian Empire's 'mountain of languages'), Persia, Afghanistan and the Hindu Kush. If the ancestor of Sanskrit were indeed the same remote ancestor of the classical languages of Europe, it stood to reason that it must have had a point of dispersal – a point from which it spread out, over untold centuries, accounting for the majority of the languages of Europe and northern India. What followed was a hypothesis which has been the basis of an extraordinary amount of heated disagreement and one that has persisted to the present day.

The 'discovery' of Sanskrit by European scholars, properly speaking, was the identification of data which strongly indicated a genetic connection between Sanskrit and the languages of Europe. It coincided with the expansion of the British Empire, particularly in Africa and Asia, and the scholars who expressed an interest in Sanskrit, if not British, came from polities which either had similar expansionist aspirations (France and Russia) or were in the process of working their way to the creation of a nation state (Germany). The 'discovery' in question was, therefore, timely in that it served to advance the case that civilization had come early to Europe and that the Asian territories in which European powers were consolidating their influence, including India, were the heirs of an ancient linguistic heritage that was European in origin.

German scholars adduced data from languages for which they had access to literary sources (Greek and Latin, naturally, but also Gothic and Old Prussian – both extinct – and Lithuanian, related to Old Prussian and still fully alive). Since the data from Gothic, Old Prussian and Lithuanian showed many stark similarities with Sanskrit, it was perhaps natural for German scholarship to conclude that the roots of the ancestral language lay in Nordic or German territory, an area roughly demarcated as lying between southern Sweden and the Baltic coast. The available data permitted such an analysis. In so doing, such scholarship laid the basis for what would, in due course, become a poisonous ideology which conflated language with ethnic identity, culminating in the myth of Aryan supremacy – a concept fully exploited and promoted by the Third Reich with murderous consequences.

British scholarship, by contrast, was more equitable, although the consequences of its findings served to promote cultural (if not indeed outrightly racial) superiority all the same. In the two centuries following Jones's talk to the Asiatick Society, scholarship has tended to support the idea that the ancestor of Sanskrit and the languages of Europe, except for the non-Indo-European Basque, Finnish, Estonian, Hungarian and Maltese, originated from an ill-defined area spanning Anatolia, the Russian steppes and central Asia. There is still no consensus as to precisely where within this vast area the original ancestral language, known as PIE (Proto-Indo-European), had originated. There has been broad consensus as to one thing, however: that PIE did not originate in South Asia. For many Indian researchers, such a thing is unacceptable in that it divorces Sanskrit, the language of Hindu scriptures deemed primordial, from India.

The quest to find the origin of PIE has become, for many, the battle for the ownership of Sanskrit – a battle which has intensified since Indian independence and has attained new heights under the BJP, the ruling party of India at the time the present work is being written. For many millions of Indians, Sanskrit has served from time immemorial as the language of religion and of high culture. It is in every sense the hallmark of a Hindu Indian identity. The extent to which Sanskrit is of significance to the substantial Muslim, Sikh, Buddhist, Jain, Parsee and Christian population of India is something which is difficult to gauge. Sanskrit is not much in evidence in Urdu, where the vocabulary of the language favours words of Persian or Arabic provenance in the higher registers. Urdu is nevertheless an Indic language and, as such, belongs to the same branch of Indo-European as Hindi, Gujarati, Panjabi, etc. The other languages of India (and not simply those which are Indic) are flooded with words from Sanskrit. Sanskrit thus represents, if not a language associated with religious identity, an important element in the make-up of the mother tongue of over a thousand million Indians. If language is identity, then it follows that speakers of Indian languages (Indic and non-Indic alike) have a vested interest in the ownership of Sanskrit.

From a non-Indian perspective, Sanskrit represents a language that is not an intrinsic element in the everyday life of the speaker. If it is important, that is because it is the language of a civilization which has excelled in philosophy and literature and has produced a rich material culture along with a complex musical tradition. For non-Indians, the positing of an Indo-European homeland outside of South Asia is not something likely to provoke an impassioned response. Whether the speakers of PIE migrated to India from an area south of the Black Sea, through Iran, during a prehistoric agricultural revolution (the 'Anatolian Hypothesis') or whether the migration was from the Russian steppes, across what are now the independent states of Kazakhstan, Turkmenistan and Uzbekistan, then down through Afghanistan, is not a matter of much significance. From an Indian perspective, however, the matter is key to cultural identity. The notion of a migration into India, from an area which has yet to be agreed upon, constitutes the 'Aryan Migration Theory' (AMT) on which an enormous amount has been published, largely by researchers working in archaeology and linguistics (The concept of an 'Aryan Invasion Theory' has been superseded but is still evoked by Indian authors). The response to this is the 'Out of India Theory' (OIT), in which the Indus Valley Civilization plays a key role.

1.5 Indus Valley connections

The Indus Valley Civilization arose on the banks of the Indus and was as intimately tied to the Indus River system and dependent on it as the Egyptians were on the Nile. The civilization was an ancient one, as became quickly evident to the first archaeologists to discover sites in the early 1920s. Subsequent archaeological work has hinted at dates around 3500 BCE, meaning that the early stages of the civilization (often called Harappan, after one of the chief sites located at Harappa, in the Indian state of Panjab) predates the building of the pyramids in Egypt by around a thousand years. The Indus Valley Civilization was extensive, with sites discovered in places as far afield as Shortugal, close to the Afghanistan-Tajikistan border, to Sutkagen Dor, near the Pakistan-Iran border. The greater part of the sites are, however, located within the Pakistani provinces of Panjab, Sindh and Balochistan and, across the border, in the Indian states of Panjab, Haryana, Rajasthan and Gujarat (Panjab was divided between Pakistan and India during Partition).

Political factors have not been conducive to the excavation and cataloguing of Indus Valley Civilization sites, with the result that many sites are in a poor state of preservation. This was a civilization built on the alluvial mud of the Indus, baked hard into bricks which, once excavated, are left open to the elements. The artifacts which have come to light are tantalizing. They hint at a sophisticated, urban culture possessing standard weights and measures (strongly indicative of the importance of trade) and settlements were planned with great knowledge concerning the management of water for irrigation and sanitation purposes. Here was the first civilization on Indian soil, hence the importance accorded to it by modern India in its attempt to reclaim and rewrite its ancient history rather than accepting a narrative dating back to colonial times.

The Indus Valley Civilization is, at one and the same time, ancient and relevant to modern India. It is within this context that one must assess the claims made, largely by Indian scholars and researchers, that the Aryans were not an invading force from outside India nor was there any migration of Aryans into India speaking an early form of Sanskrit. The assertion, previously stated as the 'Out of India Theory' (OIT), is that the roots of Sanskrit are Indian and that the Indus Valley Civilization, as old as that of the Sumerians and Egyptians (and considerably older than both Greece and Rome), was the civilization responsible for creating Sanskrit.

There are many problems in attempting to equate the Indus Valley Civilization with the culture associated with Sanskrit. The following points address four such problems:

(i) The language of the Indus Valley Civilization has been preserved in a large number of inscriptions of the cylinder seal variety. These are short inscriptions and there is no evidence of another, better known language to help in the process of decipherment. Claims as to successful decipherment, which periodically surface, have not met with scholarly approval.

(ii) The OIT relies overwhelmingly on evidence from the **Ṛgveda**, the oldest-known text in Sanskrit; but the Ṛgveda was not written in remote antiquity. It was composed and transmitted orally, as continues to be the case amongst Brahmin communities. There is no way of gauging if the original composition has remained unchanged or if there has been later interpolation, when the Ṛgveda was codified. In any event, the Ṛgveda is mute on the subject of Aryan origins.

(iii) Much is made by the OIT of the mention in the Ṛgveda of the **Sarasvatī** river, on whose shores the Ṛgveda was composed. Yet the identification and location of the Sarasvatī is problematic. Sources from Avestan, a sister language of Sanskrit and remarkably close to it in terms of its structure, mentions the river *Harax*^{v}*atī* (Old Persian *Harauvati*), and there is little doubt that this is the *Harut*, in southwest Afghanistan.

(iv) The Indus Valley Civilization went into terminal decline after around 1800 BCE and urban centres such as Harappa were abandoned by about 1300 BCE, according to archaeological findings. There is no evidence of an Aryan Invasion having taken place but ample evidence for shifts in the Indus River system, with rivers changing course or drying up. Whilst this lends the OIT a certain appeal, the fact remains that this would not account for a migration of the Indus Valley population to central Asia or the Iranian plateau. A sedentary society is more likely to have relocated, over the course of several centuries, to an adjacent territory (The Indian Panjab is a prime contender). This means that Sanskrit would not have travelled out of India but, rather, further into India from a territory which was, to the west, bordered by speakers of Iranian languages who may well have been part of this gradual migration.

1.6 Myths and realities

The origin of Sanskrit is obscure, with the prevailing schools of thought inclining towards either the migration of an Indo-European-speaking population to South Asia or a hypothesis that the language was that of the Indus Valley Civilization, from whence Indo-European speech originated. It is not surprising, therefore, that many assertions are made regarding Sanskrit. This leads to the perpetuation of language myths of which four are frequently encountered.

(i) *'Sanskrit is the oldest language'*. This is easily dismissed on the basis that assessing the age of a language is not possible in the absence of documents attesting to its early stages (There is ample evidence, for example, for the development of Afrikaans as distinct from Dutch but none that allows us to speculate as to when ancient Egyptian began to be spoken in the Nile Valley). As regards written evidence for Sanskrit, this is far later than is the case with a number of other Indo-European languages. Both Hittite and Greek are older than Sanskrit, if the determining criterion is written evidence. Until archaeology sheds further light on the writing of Sanskrit, the earliest documentation of it comes from the early centuries of the Common Era. It is not in question that Sanskrit is the oldest language of the Indo-Iranian branch of Indo-European, based on its conservative structure. Whilst the claim that it is the oldest language cannot be supported, it is the oldest-known language within its branch, with only Avestan, on the Iranian side, as a contender with respect to antiquity.

(ii) *'Sanskrit is a perfect language'*. From a purely linguistic perspective, this is easily disproved. Sanskrit contains verbs which are irregular in the way they are formed when conjugated and there are many exceptions to general rules (The reader will be in a better position to evaluate the claim after having read the present work). The notion of a 'perfect' language is highly subjective, appealing to the emotions, and is a consequence of the prestige accorded to the language in question within a specific cultural context. Without a doubt, Sanskrit was the subject of extensive polishing throughout its development, as its very name suggests: it is **Saṃskṛta** (*refined; composed*). It is only from a sociocultural point of view, however, that a claim relating to its perfection has any real credence.

(iii) *'Sanskrit is the mother of all languages'*. Whilst the first two myths contain an element of truth, as discussed, this claim is outrightly false. Sanskrit may, with some justification, be hailed as an older relative of the Indic languages, such as Panjabi, Gujarati, Hindi and Bengali but, even with India, it is not the mother of all the other languages. The four literary languages of the south (Tamil, Telugu, Kannada and Malayalam) have been heavily influenced by Sanskrit, yet they are not descended from it. These languages belong to the Dravidian language family. 'Indic' does not connote 'Indian', for the simple reason that the former is a linguistic term, whilst the latter is geographical/political. Even as regards Sanskrit being the mother of the Indic languages, this obscures the fact that the modern languages are derived from earlier forms of spoken language (the Prakrits) via an intermediate phase (Apabhraṃśa). Sanskrit is not so much the mother of the modern Indic languages as a great aunt. Languages such as Arabic and Hebrew are not related to Sanskrit, since they belong to the Semitic language family. There is nothing in the vocabularies of Arabic or Hebrew to indicate a connection with Sanskrit, nor do the forms of nouns or verbs bear any resemblance to Sanskrit declension or conjugation.

(iv) *'Sanskrit comes from India'*. Notwithstanding the debate regarding the origin of Sanskrit (1.4. and 1.5), it is not in doubt that Sanskrit was cultivated on Indian soil. If one focuses on Sanskrit as the language of Hinduism and of high culture, as opposed to concentrating on the fact that it descended from an earlier form of Indo-European speech, then Sanskrit in its refined form does indeed come from India. An analogy can be made with English, in that English was formed in the British Isles (There is ample documentary evidence regarding its development from Old English through to Middle English and finally to Modern English). It is irrelevant that the roots of English lie in Continental Europe. The language in its earliest, distinct form is a product of the British Isles. By that reasoning, Sanskrit can genuinely be claimed as the product of Indian society, whatever its roots. The claim that Sanskrit descended from earlier speech which was indigenous to India is not supported by the archaeological, historical or linguistic record. Ultimately, such a claim relies on Vedic Sanskrit having been the primordial language, with no antecedents. That is more in the nature of philosophy or belief than provable fact.

2

THE INTERNATIONAL ALPHABET OF SANSKRIT TRANSLITERATION

2.1 Preliminaries

The International Alphabet of Sanskrit Transliteration (henceforth IAST) has a venerable pedigree, owing its inception to the collaboration of Sanskrit scholars in the nineteenth century. It aims to provide an accurate way of transliterating Sanskrit into the Roman alphabet, making Sanskrit more accessible to those unfamiliar with one or more of the numerous Indian writing systems which have, for two thousand years, been used to record Sanskrit and the related Prakrits. It is a stringent system of transliteration, allowing the reader to work with confidence on Sanskrit, knowing that the IAST reflects spelling in the Devanāgarī with complete accuracy. Its usefulness cannot be overstated. Suffice it to say that, with the IAST, one can start studying Sanskrit before one has full functional use of the Devanāgarī. The IAST assists the learner in the process of investigating the language in terms of its structure and its distinctiveness whilst simultaneously working on the Devanāgarī. One does not have to acquire the Devanāgarī prior to taking the first steps into the language. The IAST is the most widely used system of transliteration in scholarly publications relating not only to Sanskrit but to the Prakrits.

Whilst non-Indian scholars of Sanskrit are invariably familiar with the IAST, it is regrettably the case that it continues to elude a considerable number of those with an interest in the language. The Internet bristles with

DOI: 10.4324/9780429325434-3

websites dedicated to yoga and to other matters pertaining to several millennia of Indian thought and cultural practice, yet by no means the majority of such websites – Indian and non-Indian alike – can ensure that Sanskrit is accurately represented in the Roman alphabet. Sometimes, the attempts at transliteration are partial; often, they are merely cursory attempts, undisciplined in their nature, to approximate the sounds of Sanskrit. Yet Sanskrit is precise. Very precise. When a vowel is long, it must be pronounced as long (and indicated as such). Also, there are two distinct sounds for what we would in English write as *sh* and two sets of consonants that, in English, are transliterated using *t*, *d* or *n*, thereby making no distinction between the two. The differences between Sanskrit and English (or, indeed, any other language) must be capable of being reflected by a transliteration system. Casual transliteration fails to do this.

Using English spelling for Sanskrit is not an option for the serious learner. In English, for example, a consonant can be used to indicate a sound which, elsewhere, is usually represented by another letter. Consider the sound which the letter *g* has in the word *exaggerate*. It could be argued that the letter *g* has a sound more customarily associated with the letter *j* and, additionally, that the first *g* has the sound of a *d*. Yet the word is not spelled **exadjerate* (Note, also, the fact that each *e* has a separate pronunciation, with the final one being silent). In Sanskrit, this is not possible. Each letter of the Devanāgarī has its own distinct sound and cannot represent another sound. Furthermore, there are no silent letters in the Devanāgarī. If something is spelled, it is pronounced. The IAST is the transliteration system par excellence for Sanskrit, in that it identifies specific sounds within the language and does not leave room for ambiguity as to the corresponding spelling in the Devanāgarī. Non-IAST transliteration is unsystematic. It does not assist the learner in the least and should be avoided from the outset of one's study of Sanskrit.

2.2 Analysis of a word in the IAST

In the IAST, there are as many letters as are needed to represent, with complete fidelity, the sounds of Sanskrit and the letters of the Devanāgarī writing system. No fewer, no more. There is nothing arbitrary or redundant in the IAST. What is visible in the IAST is audible in Sanskrit and capable, thereby, of being transposed mechanically into the Devanāgarī. The following example shows the extent to which the IAST represents the sounds of

Sanskrit faithfully where other, less principled attempts to represent Sanskrit fall flat:

Non-IAST transliteration:	*Krishna*
IAST transliteration:	**Kr̥ṣṇa**

There are five letters in the IAST in the spelling of the word in question, as opposed to the seven employed in the non-IAST example. First comes the letter **k**, then the short vowel **r̥** (see 3.1.2) followed by one of two *sh*-sounds in Sanskrit (**ṣ**), then a nasal (**ṇ**) and the inherent vowel (**a**) – which the Devanāgarī does not represent, if it occurs in the middle or at the end of a word but which is pronounced all the same (see 3.5.3). Why does the non-IAST spelling use two additional letters?

In the IAST, **r̥** signifies not a consonant but a sound referred to by Sanskritists as the 'vocalic r'. That is to say, it is a vowel. The non-IAST transliteration does not reflect this fact and substitutes the 'vocalic r' with what, in English, is a consonant. Since a vowel is missing in the non-IAST, resulting in the impossible cluster *krshn-*, English spelling requires a vowel to be added in order that the word may be pronounced. The vowel in question is *i*. This is followed by a *sh*-sound which is usually represented in English by the letters *s* and *h* in combination (There are some exceptions, such as the use of *-ss-* in the words *passion*, *Russian*, etc., or the single *s* in names of Celtic origin – *Sean, Sinead*, etc. – and in words such as *sugar* and *sure*). Yet there are two distinct *sh*-sounds in Sanskrit, differentiated according to the position of the tongue during pronunciation. Non-IAST transliteration is unable to distinguish between the two, so attempting to convert the word into Devanāgarī immediately raises the question as to which Sanskrit *sh* is involved. Similarly, there are two *n*-sounds in Sanskrit, again differentiated according to the position of the tongue. Non-IAST transliteration is understandable, given that it is common practice to use the everyday writing system and its conventions when representing words from other languages. Users of English write the Hungarian word *gulyás* as *goulash*, since it is the closest indication of the pronunciation, according to English ears.

The word **Kr̥ṣṇa** contains no ambiguity in the IAST. The letter **k** identifies one – and only one – sound in Sanskrit, for which the Devanāgarī has only one letter. The letter **r̥** likewise indicates only one sound in Sanskrit which, being a vowel, neither needs nor permits the use of a vowel immediately after it (Putting two vowel sounds together in the same word is prohibited according to the rules of Sanskrit phonology, unless dealing with a diphthong). The ambiguity of the two *sh*-sounds of Sanskrit is resolved by the IAST with the use of a dot under the *s* to signify that the *sh*-sound in question is produced by touching the tip of the tongue against the hard palate, situated quite high in the mouth (ṣ). The other *sh*-sound is not formed in this way and does not, as a result, have the same spelling (ś). The IAST also resolves the ambiguity of the nasal (ṇ) by indicating, as with ṣ, that the *n*-sound in question is produced by raising the tip of the tongue and bringing it into contact with the hard palate.

With respect to *Krishna*/**Kr̥ṣṇa**, the only sound which the English pronunciation of the word has in common with the Sanskrit is *k*. The English *ri* does not equate with the Sanskrit **r̥** any more than the English *sh* results in the pronunciation of the Sanskrit **ṣ** or the English *n* equates to the Sanskrit **ṇ**. Neither **ṣ** nor **ṇ** are sounds that a native speaker of English is likely to produce, in that the tip of the tongue is further back in the mouth than is the case for the English *sh* and *n*. The *sh*-sound of Sanskrit closer to the English *sh* is transliterated in the IAST as **ś**. This is the *sh* of **Śiva**. As for the Sanskrit *n*-sound which most closely resembles the English *n*, in words such as *night*, this appears in the IAST as **n** (Note the absence of the dot underneath). Care should be taken, however, in the pronunciation of **n**, since there is a requirement with respect to the position of the tongue in its articulation, as shall be made clear in 3.2. Little mention has been made of the final sound in **Kr̥ṣṇa**, but this will be rectified in due course (3.1).

2.3 Additional remarks

When one sees the letter **ā**, the line above it (the macron) indicates that this is a long vowel. Non-scholarly transliteration often makes use of double letters (e.g. **aa**) to signify that a vowel is long – when an attempt is being made to distinguish vowel length at all, which is not always the case. In slipshod, non-IAST transliteration, the name **Rāma** can appear as either *Raama* or *Rama*. Worse still, the name is sometimes spelled *Raam* or *Ram*, reflecting its pronunciation in the modern languages of India (The removal of the final **a** when reading or reciting Sanskrit is a persistent mispronunciation associated with speakers of modern Indian languages).

There are a number of transliteration systems which sidestep the use of double letters to indicate long vowels by using a capital letter (i.e. *A* for **ā**). An example of one such system is the scholarly Harvard-Kyoto Convention, of which more will be said at the end of the current chapter.

The reason is that the IAST is not keyboard friendly: it contains a macron above the long vowels, a dot below many letters, a dot above a letter (**ṅ**), a tilde (**ñ**) and a slash (**ś**). In most textbooks using the IAST, the vocalic **r̥** and **l̥** are dotted, rather than given a subscript circle. This is a pure software limitation and one that has the disadvantage of occasionally confusing learners into assuming that a cerebral sound is being indicated, as is the case with **ṭ**, **ṭh**, **ḍ**, **ḍh** and **ṇ** (Cerebral sounds are described and explained in 3.2.2.3). Unlike the Harvard-Kyoto Convention, the IAST does not use uppercase letters to indicate vowel length. Uppercase letters are distinctly optional.

Since the IAST is not sensitive to the distinction between uppercase and lowercase letters, it is possible to use uppercase letters for proper nouns, the titles of literary works and philosophical terms. It goes without saying that the use of uppercase letters after a full stop is permissible. About the full stop, this is the only punctuation mark which is necessary when using the IAST. Punctuation is Sanskrit is cursory: there are no signs or symbols equating to the comma, the semicolon, the hyphen, speech marks, the exclamation mark or the question mark. Whether or not a text employing the IAST is enhanced using any of the foregoing is a moot point and must be left up to the discretion of the user. The fact remains that the Devanāgarī writing system recognizes only a single vertical stroke (**daṇḍa**) and a double vertical stroke (**dvadaṇḍa**) to indicate the end of a sentence, and the end of a paragraph, text (or a stanza in poetry), respectively:

daṇḍa	।
dvadaṇḍa	॥

The IAST predates the invention of the modern keyboard and uses diacritical marks whereas the Harvard-Kyoto Convention is keyboard-friendly. As with the IAST, every phoneme of Sanskrit can be represented without any ambiguity by the Harvard-Kyoto Convention. When the learner reaches the point where access to an online Sanskrit dictionary is required, the Harvard-Kyoto Convention becomes indispensable. Adjustment from the IAST to the Harvard-Kyoto Convention is not difficult. Vowels indicated with a macron in the IAST are uppercase letters in the Harvard-Kyoto Convention, as are letters with a dot (or circle) underneath them in the IAST.

There are only a handful of additional differences to keep in mind. The Harvard-Kyoto Convention is case-sensitive, as the following examples demonstrate:

IAST:	**Kṛṣṇa/kṛṣṇa**
Harvard-Kyoto Convention:	kRSNa
IAST:	**Śiva/śiva**
Harvard-Kyoto Convention:	ziva
IAST:	**Rāma/rāma**
Harvard-Kyoto Convention:	rAma

3

THE SOUND SYSTEM

3.1 Vowels and diphthongs

3.1.1 Preliminaries

There are fourteen vocalic sounds in Sanskrit, arranged as follows:

Primary (or simple) vowels:	**a ā i ī u ū r̥ r̥̄ l̥ l̥̄**
Secondary (or complex) vowels:	**e o**
Diphthongs:	**ai au**

To begin with, it is important to distinguish between the primary (or simple) and the secondary (or complex) vowels. Sanskrit considers the primary vowels to be in some sense 'pure' or 'basic', whereas the secondary vowels are deemed to be composed of a fusion of primary vowels. The primary vowels of Sanskrit are equally divided between short and long. Five of them are short and five of them are long. A short vowel is half the length of a long vowel in terms of the time it takes to pronounce it. In this respect, Sanskrit is more scrupulous than English, since the short and long vowels in English do not always differ from each other in length but also in quality. If one listens carefully to the pronunciation of *pull* and *pool*, or *look* and *Luke*, one hears a difference in the vowel which is not just a question of length: the lips are more rounded with the long vowels and, although maybe less perceptible, the tongue is in a different position. This difference does

DOI: 10.4324/9780429325434-4

not occur in Sanskrit. The lips have the same shape for both short and long vowels and the tongue is in the same position.

In Sanskrit, the only distinction between short and long vowels is their duration. This is not always the case as regards **a** and **ā**, as will be noted when investigating pronunciation. The IAST indicates the difference between short and long primary vowels in Sanskrit by placing a macron above the vowel if it is long. This is, however, not the case with **e** and **o** which, being secondary (or complex), are deemed to be long. There is no short **e** or **o** in Sanskrit. Both **e** and **o** possess a strong relationship with the two diphthongs of Sanskrit, **ai** and **au**, respectively. The diphthongs are classified as individual sounds within the vowel system (the vocalic inventory) of Sanskrit.

3.1.2 Pronunciation

When exploring the sound system of Sanskrit, it is appropriate to start with the vowels, as these are the first phonemes identified in the Indic tradition as regards the phonemic inventory of the language. In so doing, the running order of Monier-Williams's *Sanskrit-English Dictionary* will be adhered to, with the exception of the secondary vowels and the diphthongs. Monier-Williams lists **e**, **ai**, **o** and **au**, in that order, whereas it seems appropriate to investigate **e** and **o** first, then **ai** and **au**, given that the latter two are classified as diphthongs (i.e. a vocalic phoneme which contains two audibly distinct vowels, such as we hear in the English pronunciation of the words *ice* and *ounce*).

With the first pair of primary vowels, **a** and **ā**, a word of caution is required. Short **a** is often described as having the sound of the letter *u* in English words such as *cut*, *sum* and *up*, but there is often variation in the pronunciation of **a** amongst Sanskritists. Sanskrit short **a** is realized, by some, as precisely the vowel in English *cut*, *sum*, *up*, etc. For others, it is closer to the American *o* in the word *copper*. There is one piece of information which suggests strongly that the latter pronunciation is to be favoured. Short **a**, if pronounced like the English *u* in *cup*, etc., is not the short equivalent of **ā**. The tongue is in a different position in the mouth, which ought not to be the case. There is greater uniformity in the pronunciation of long **ā**: it is the English *a* in *farmer*, *father*, *calm*, etc. The short equivalent is obtained by reducing the length of time taken to pronounce the *a* in *farmer*, etc. That is like the *o* in the American pronunciation of *Boston*. Another way to produce this sound is to aim for a sound intermediate between English *cut* and *cot*, where it is unclear which of the two words is being pronounced. That is the short **a** in Sanskrit. It is not pronounced like the *a* in *cat*.

With **i** and **ī**, the situation is more straightforward. One has but to bear in mind that the tongue must not move and thereby produce a vowel which is qualitatively different between the short and the long forms. Just as was the case with **a** and **ā**, it is easier to articulate the long vowel and then to shorten it. Long **ī** is the vowel sound one hears in the English *feel*, *peak*, *seat*, etc. The short equivalent has, therefore, the same quality but only half of the duration. With short **u** and long **ū**, one may begin with the short vowel, attested in the English words *book*, *look*, etc., and generate the long vowel by simply lengthening it.

As regards the simple vowels **r̥**, **r̥̄**, **l̥** and **l̥̄**, these are a source of confusion for learners. This is no doubt because speakers of most languages are apt to see the letters *r* and *l* as capable only of being consonants, with the result that the idea they could represent vowels appears outlandish. Nothing could be further from the truth, but one has to bear in mind the following crucial fact about vowels. <u>They do not involve any contact between articulators within the oral tract</u> (lips, teeth, gum, tongue). In fact, such contact is expressly prohibited. When that simple fact is borne in mind, it becomes clear that to pronounce the vowel **r̥** as if it were **ri** or **ru** is to misunderstand the nature of a vowel. Not only is **r** – without the circle beneath it – a different phoneme in Sanskrit, but both ***r̥i** and ***r̥u** represent a diphthong (i.e. a sound made up of two audibly distinct vowel sounds) whereas Sanskrit only recognizes the diphthongs **ai** and **au**. The vowel **r̥** is not composed of the semivowel **r** plus **i** or **u** any more than it is a diphthong comprising **r̥** plus **i** or **u.** The pronunciation of **r̥** as either **ri** or **ru** is widespread but is to be avoided. Such a pronunciation involves a touching of articulators (here, tongue and gum), which is strictly forbidden in the production of vowels. Additionally, the vowel in the syllable **ri** is **i**, not **r̥**.

The actual pronunciation of the vowels **r̥** and **r̥̄** is subject to disagreement between Sanskritists. Under the circumstances, it might be suggested that one aims for a sound simulating a purring cat, without letting the tongue touch the roof of the mouth. The consonant **p** can then be substituted with **k**, to produce the Sanskrit root **kr̥**, meaning *to do, make, fashion* (The vowel **r̥** is by no means rare in Sanskrit, unlike its long equivalent **r̥̄**, which occurs far less frequently). Two Sanskrit words containing **r̥** are likely to be familiar to intending students of Sanskrit. These are **Kr̥ṣṇa** and **Ṛgveda** (Note that **Ṛ** should ideally have a circle below it rather than a dot. This is a font limitation). The pronunciation of both **Kr̥ṣṇa** and **Ṛgveda** with an audible **i** is widespread. This is to be avoided, if at all possible, because it reflects a practice in which the vocal nature of **r̥** is not acknowledged.

With respect to **l̥** and **l̥̄**, very little needs to be said, largely because the former is rare in Sanskrit – rare to the point that a learner can easily complete the first year of study without encountering it – and the latter is not attested in Sanskrit, with the exception of two entries given by Monier-Williams (The first of these is simply the listing of the sound as the tenth vowel of the sound system and the second is a noun which can refer either to the deity **Śiva** or to 'the mother of the cow of plenty'). In terms of its pronunciation, **l̥** requires, as with all vowels, the absence of touching between any of the articulators in the oral tract. It cannot, therefore, be pronounced the same way as the phoneme **l**, which Sanskrit classifies as a semivowel. The sound is, in fact, produced by English speakers in the word *walk*, where the tongue fails to touch the gum behind the top teeth, but is in the right position to do so. In effect, it is the Sanskrit **l** (as semivowel) with no touching taking place. The result is a sound indistinguishable to the Southern English pronunciation of the word *awe*, without the rounding of the lips.

The Sanskrit **e** and **o** are often mispronounced by beginners, amongst whom the tendency exists to pronounce them as if they were the short vowels in the English *forget-me-not*. In fact, the Sanskrit vowels **e** and **o** are closer to *four gate me note*. The caveat here is that neither **e** nor **o** are diphthongs in Sanskrit, meaning that they do not contain secondary vowel sounds. Sanskrit possesses only two diphthongs, **ai** and **au**. Like **e** and **o**, the diphthongs are long only. There are no short equivalents. Whereas they are grouped together, being identifiable as diphthongs, **ai** and **au** can equally be paired up with **e** and **o**, respectively.

The relationship between **e** and **ai** on the one hand, and **o** and **au** on the other, is strong. It is reflected in the Devanāgarī writing system, in that the letter for **e** is the basis of the letter for **ai**, when these are in initial position (i.e. when they are the first letter of a word). Similarly, the initial form of **o** is the basis of the initial form of **au**:

e = ए **ai** = ऐ

o = ओ **au** = औ

The pronunciation of the diphthongs is not problematic: **ai** rhymes with *high*; **au** rhymes with *how*. Hindi speakers often pronounce **ai** as if it were a shortened **e,** and **au** as if it were a short form of **o**. Care must be taken not to conflate **ai** with **e**, or **au** with **o**. They are distinct phonemes. Sanskrit does not contain triphthongs (three vowels sounds together). A word such as the Greek *gaia* would not be permissible in Sanskrit, although Sanskrit can – and does – generate the word **gaya** (*acquisition*), formed as follows: consonant (**g**) + vowel (**a**) + semivowel (**y**) + vowel (**a**).

3.1.3 Overview

Sanskrit identifies twelve vowels, although two of these (ḷ and ḹ) are exceptionally scarce in the language, with the latter attested in only two dictionary entries. The vowels are classified according to whether they are primary or secondary. There are additionally two diphthongs (**ai**) and (**au**) which can, to all extents and purposes, be grouped with the secondary vowels. The primary vowels have short and long forms, whereas the secondary vowels (including the diphthongs) are all long. There are no short secondary vowels. Vowel length is a crucial distinction in Sanskrit, and the learner is urged to pay great attention to it from the outset.

It is common practice for learners to conflate the vowels **a** and **ā**, **i** and **ī**, **u** and **ū**, and care must be taken not to do so. Where a vowel is long, it is said to take two beats to pronounce. Otherwise said, a long vowel ought to be held for twice the length of its short equivalent. Unlike English, the short and long vowels do not differ in quality but in duration. The English words *cut*/*cart*, etc., on closer investigation, involve differences in the position of the tongue. The movement of the tongue is responsible for producing a vowel that has a different quality. One may say, therefore, that the differences between *cut* and *cart* are as much to do with the quality of the vowel as to the fact that they are short and long, respectively. In Sanskrit, short vowels and their long equivalents differ only as regards the amount of time taken to produce them.

Of all the vowels in Sanskrit, simple or complex, **ṛ** and **ṝ** present the speaker of English with the greatest difficulties. These are often referred to as the 'vocalic r', a wholly accurate description and one which asserts the fact that the phoneme is a vowel. It is a primary vowel, hence the presence of both a short and a long form. Given that it is a primary vowel, care must be taken not to permit the inclusion of any other vowel sound in its pronunciation. To pronounce **ṛ** as **ri* or **ru* is, in effect, either to assert that it is some kind of diphthong, a phoneme in which two audibly distinct vocalic sounds may be heard, or that it is nothing other than the syllable **ri**, which is composed of the semivowel **r** and the short vowel **i**. Both of those assertions are inaccurate. The vowel **ṛ** must contain only one sound, its long equivalent likewise. Another common mistake amongst beginners is to persevere with the pronunciation of the complex vowels **e** and **o** as if they were the vowels in the English word *eggnog*. Since they are secondary vowels in Sanskrit, they are automatically long.

3.2 Consonants

3.2.1 Preliminaries

There are thirty-three consonants in Sanskrit arranged in five categories according to how they are pronounced. This number can be increased to thirty-five, if two further sounds are included: **anusvāra** and **visarga** (These are investigated separately, since they merit separate discussion). The five categories correspond to five distinct places of articulation, as follows, with the place of articulation stated in the first column and the adjectives used to describe the sounds in question in the second column:

Throat	Velar (or guttural)	e.g. *core*
Roof of the mouth	Palatal sounds	e.g. *chore*
Hard Palate	Cerebral (or retroflex)	Not attested in English
Teeth	Dental sounds	e.g. *tore; thaw*
Lips	Labial sounds	e.g. *pore*

For ease of exposition, and for the sake of clarity, the present work will first focus on twenty-five consonants equally distributed across the five places of articulation and demonstrating the same pattern in the way in which they are identified (This pattern is not in evidence with the other eight consonants, anusvāra or visarga). The consonants in question are the following:

Velar	**k**	**kh**	**g**	**gh**	**ṅ**
Palatal	**c**	**ch**	**j**	**jh**	**ñ**
Cerebral	**ṭ**	**ṭh**	**ḍ**	**ḍh**	**ṇ**
Dental	**t**	**th**	**d**	**dh**	**n**
Labial	**p**	**ph**	**b**	**bh**	**m**

Note that whereas the IAST requires two letters to identify the consonants **kh**, **gh**, **ch**, **jh**, etc., these are single phonemes in Sanskrit. Otherwise said, Sanskrit does not consider them to be the product of two separate phonemes.

The eight remaining consonants are discussed separately, under the heading of semivowels (3.3) and sibilants (3.4), with anusvāra (3.5.1) and visarga (3.5.2) covered in the chapter dealing with additional sounds. In Sanskrit, the sound of any consonant is stable and predictable in all cases. The English consonant *s* can have a *s*-sound (*sit*), a *sh*-sound (*sugar*), a *z*-sound (*wise*), a *zh*-sound (*leisure*) or, indeed, no sound at all (*island*). In this respect, although the English alphabet contains fewer consonants than the Devanāgarī, letters of the English alphabet do not always represent a single sound. Once this is considered, it soon becomes evident that English can represent a greater number of sounds than are present in Sanskrit, albeit by using a smaller number of letters. Such variation within the realization of phonemes is not possible in the Devanāgarī, where a letter has one (and only one) sound and, conversely, a given sound is represented by one (and only one) letter.

It is important to point out that the notion of what a consonant represents differs between English and Sanskrit. The English alphabet is not the product of a systematic and careful analysis of the sound system of the language. English spelling is a haphazard affair when compared to Sanskrit. A word may contain a vowel sound and yet be spelled using only letters identified as consonants in the English alphabet (*by*, *hymn*, *my*, *rhythm*, *why*, etc.). In addition to being used to indicate a vowel sound, a consonant in English may also have no sound at all (*knight*, *ballet*, etc.). To complicate matters further still, a single consonantal sound in English may be represented by more than one letter: *knight* (the *gh* being, additionally, silent), *rhythm*, etc. Conversely, multiple consonantal sounds may be represented by a single letter, as in the word *taxi*. In Sanskrit, a single consonantal sound is always represented by a single letter in the Devanāgarī, and each consonant letter within the Devanāgarī represents a single, specific consonant, unvarying in its pronunciation.

Given the one-to-one correspondence of a phoneme and its visual representation in the Devanāgarī, no less than the fact that phonemes do not exhibit variation in the way in which they are pronounced, Sanskrit presents the learner with a highly consistent and predictable sound system and associated writing system. Phonemes are classified as logically as possible, and the writing system aims at representing the sound system as accurately as possible. The only legitimate concern that a student of Sanskrit might have is that the phonemic inventory of consonants in Sanskrit contains sounds not attested in English.

3.2.2 Pronunciation

3.2.2.1 Velars

Consonants in Sanskrit are classified according to two criteria: (i) place of articulation and (ii) manner of articulation. The first of these relates to the position of the mouth and the use of the articulators of speech (the soft palate, the hard palate, the teeth, the lips, the tongue); the second relates to how the sound is released, once the articulators are in a particular position. This distinction may easily be grasped by looking at the first set of consonants: the velars (These are also referred to as 'gutturals'). It is useful to include a vowel, so that the consonant can be articulated fully. For this purpose, a short **a** is added to the consonant:

ka **kha** **ga** **gha** **ṅa**

The place of articulation for these consonants is identified as 'velar', which is to say that sounds are produced by the back of the tongue making contact with the soft palate (the velum). The place of articulation remains constant for all five phonemes. At no point must the shape of the mouth or the position of the articulators change. The fact that these phonemes belong to the same place of articulation means they share the common feature of being pronounced from the same place in the oral tract. The first two phonemes in the sequence of velars are **ka** and **kha**: two phonemes distinguished in the IAST by the absence or presence of the letter *h*. The first of these does not have a puff of air, whereas a puff or air is distinctly audible with the second phoneme. This puff of air is referred to as the aspirate. Now consider the following sentence:

That's really thick curtain material.

The first *k*-sound (in the word *thick*) contains no puff of air. Any such puff of air is cut short by the onset of the following word. In the pronunciation of *curtain*, however, the puff of air is present. In Sanskrit, the puff of air should be clearly audible. It is important to remember that, whilst English makes nothing of the difference between the pronunciation of the letters *ck* in *thick* and the *c* in *curtain*, such a distinction in Sanskrit is phonemic. That is to say, the **k** without the puff of air and the **kh** with the puff of air are deemed to be two separate phonemes within the language. A simple test to see if aspiration is being produced is to place one's palm in front of one's mouth and to ensure that a puff of air can be felt.

To grasp the distinction between the **k**, which has no puff of air (i.e. which is unaspirated), and the **kh**, which does (i.e. which is aspirated), a pronunciation out loud of the following phrases ought to suffice. The first of these contains the unaspirated **k**; the second contains the aspirated **kh**:

'Clock out!'
Clock House

Once one can hear (and produce) the difference between the **k** in *Clock out!* and the **kh** in *Clock House*, one will effectively have grasped the distinction between the first two consonantal phonemes in Sanskrit. It is important to stress the fact that **kh** is represented by two letters in the IAST but is one phoneme in Sanskrit. Just as there is a distinction between **k** and **kh** according to the absence or presence of the aspirate, so too this distinction comes into play as regards the following two consonants in the velar series: **g** and **gh**. The same test as to the absence or presence of the aspirate can be applied, using the following sentences:

'Log out!'
Log House

This now accounts for the first four phonemes of the velar series (**k**, **kh**, **g**, **gh**), leaving the fifth (**ṅ**) to discuss. Before doing so, one needs to know **k** and **kh**, as a pair, may be distinguished from **g** and **gh** in a way which is of primary importance. Both **k** and **kh** are voiceless (or unvoiced) whereas both **g** and **gh** are voiced. Alternatively, one may say that the voiced equivalent of **k** is **g**, and the voiced equivalent of **kh** is **gh**. Learners tend to struggle with the concept of voice since, unlike the notion of unaspirated and aspirated, there seems to be no easy test to determine which is which.

A linguist would have no hesitation in explaining that a phoneme is voiced when the vocal cords vibrate and that, conversely, a phoneme is voiceless (or unvoiced) when the vocal cords are at rest. Whilst true, that does not necessarily facilitate matters for the learner of Sanskrit. An easy test is, however, quite literally at hand. If a hand is placed on the throat so that the palm covers snugly the front of the throat and the top row of fingers is held in place by the chin, one ought to feel a difference between **k** and **g** with the following: *'It's c- c- cold!'* and *'It's a goal, goal, goal!'* By repeating *c . . . c . . . c . . .* followed by *g . . . g . . . g . . .*, a buzzing or a resonating in the neck should be discernible with *goal* that is absent with *cold*. This is an example of the vocal cords in action. They resonate with **g**, which is a voiced phoneme, and are at rest with **k**, which is voiceless. Voice is a separate matter to aspiration. Aspiration is always marked by the letter *h* in the IAST. An aspirated phoneme can be voiceless in Sanskrit, as is the case with **kh**, or voiced, as with **gh**.

The fifth phoneme in the velar series of consonants is **ṅ**. As evidenced by the IAST, this phoneme is not subject to aspiration. Indeed, there is no aspirated nasal phoneme in Sanskrit. Nasals, irrespective of the place of articulation, are always voiced. If the nasal **ṅ** is reminiscent of any of the preceding phonemes in the series, it is the unaspirated and voiced phoneme of the series in question. In the case of **ṅ**, that is **g** (Pronouncing **ṅ** with a following vowel is difficult for speakers of English, so it is worth attempting it with a preceding vowel: *long*, *song*, etc.). The nasal is distinct from the other four phonemes of the series in that the air flow is different. In the case of **k**, **kh**, **g** and **gh**, the air flow is through the mouth. One pronounces the first four phonemes of the series by releasing the air from the mouth. If one were to pinch one's nostrils shut, they would sound precisely the same. This is not the case with the nasals, where the air flow is through the nose and the mouth simultaneously. It is not possible to pronounce a nasal if one's nostrils are blocked. A simple test is to pronounce the word *ringer* whilst pinching one's nostrils shut. If the air flow through the nose is completely obstructed, one ought to hear the word *rigger* instead.

The following table identifies the consonants of the velar series according to whether they are unaspirated or aspirated. It will be noted that these terms do not apply to the nasal phoneme, where the term 'nasal' is sufficient to distinguish the distinctiveness of the phoneme within the series. 'Velar nasal' is a full and adequate description of the phoneme **ṅ**. The evidence of air flow through the nose as well as through the mouth is obtained by pinching one's nostrils shut during the pronunciation of *Long House*, resulting in the pronunciation *Log House*.

Consonants: velars				
Voiceless		Voiced		Voiced
Unaspirated	Aspirated	Unaspirated	Aspirated	Nasal
k	**kh**	**g**	**gh**	**ṅ**
'Clock out!'	*Clock House*	*'Log out!'*	*Log House*	*Long House*

3.2.2.2 Palatals

With the palatal consonants, the articulator responsible for producing the phonemes within the series is the body of the tongue (as opposed to the back of the tongue, as is the case with the velars). The tongue is raised, restricting the air channel to a narrow space between the tongue and the roof of the mouth. In forming the mouth to pronounce consonants belonging to this series, one should feel the sides of the tongue being pressed and held in place by the top teeth. The front part of the tongue then brushes against the top of the mouth and traps the air as it attempts to hiss out. Try pronouncing the word *chocolate*, but slowly and hesitantly, as if stammering over the word:

ch . . . ch . . . chocolate?

Think carefully about the position of the tongue during the pronunciation of *ch . . . ch . . .* , since that is the position of the tongue for the pronunciation of all the phonemes of the palatal series of consonants.

As with the velar series, aspiration is found in the palatals. The *ch* of chocolate (assuming that there is not too much breathiness in the pronunciation) is the first consonant of the palatal series, which appears as **c** in the IAST. Note that there is a tendency amongst learners to pronounce the IAST **c** as if it were pronounced *k*, no doubt as a habit formed by familiarity with English spelling. The IAST, is not, however, based on English orthographic conventions or indeed on English pronunciation. The IAST represents the sounds of Sanskrit, not English. A simple way to remember that the IAST **c** is not pronounced like **k** is to bear in mind that the IAST does not have two letters for the same sound.

To obtain the unaspirated and aspirated phonemes which represent the unvoiced palatals **c** and **ch**, one must remember that the first of these lacks an audible puff of air. The same distinction arises between the third and fourth phonemes of the series (**j** and **jh**), expect that these are voiced. In the following table, the phonemes are identified in the same manner as the velar series, with examples from English on the bottom row to help reflect the differences between them. Again, it needs to be stressed that the articulators must remain in the same position for all successive phonemes within the series. To move the tongue to a different position for the palatal nasal (**ñ**) is to disregard completely the basis on which the consonantal inventory is classified in Sanskrit.

Consonants: palatals				
Voiceless		Voiced		Voiced
Unaspirated	Aspirated	Unaspirated	Aspirated	Nasal
c	**ch**	**j**	**jh**	**ñ**
Churchill	*Church Hall*	*Judging*	*'Judge him!'*	*Munchkin*

The palatal nasal **ñ** is often described, in Sanskrit grammars and general descriptions on the sound system of the language, as being pronounced like the first *n* in *onion*; and so it is, but care must be taken not to let the *y*-sound towards the end become too prominent. The phoneme is, after all, a single sound, not the product of a nasal plus **y**, which is a separate phoneme (see 3.3). Think of where the tongue is positioned when it reaches upwards in the mouth to prepare for the articulation of the first *n* in *onion*. It is in the same place as it would be for the *n* in *lunch* or *munchkin*. The tongue is in that position because the phoneme which follows the *n*, in both words, is the palatal sound *ch* – which the IAST spells as **c**. Whilst English orthography is oblivious as to differences in the pronunciation of *n*, Sanskrit is extremely attentive to this. The position of the tongue for the *n* in *onion*, *lunch* and *munchkin* is different to its position in the following instruction:

Ban the bomb!

When *n* comes before a dental sound, it is in contact with the top teeth.

3.2.2.3 Cerebrals

The cerebral series of sounds in Sanskrit are not phonemes typically found in Indo-European languages and suggest a long period of contact between Sanskrit, in its evolution in South Asia, and the languages of the south of India belonging to the Dravidian language family. In Dravidian languages, cerebral sounds occur widely. In Sanskrit, by contrast, the voiced sounds **ḍ** and **ḍh** are infrequent, lending support to the suggestion that they found their way into the language through early contact with Dravidian (It should be pointed out that **ṭ** and **ṭh**, although more frequent in Sanskrit than **ḍ** and **ḍh**, occur far less often than their dental equivalents, **t** and **th**).

The cerebrals are problematic to speakers of English in that they represent sounds which are pronounced with the tip of the tongue striking a point on the hard palate much further back than is the case with the English *t*, *d* or *n*. To English ears, the sounds are distinctly South Asian. Forming them is not difficult. One has only to remember that the tongue needs to touch the part of the mouth behind the teeth, not the gum directly behind the top teeth (which is too far forward) and certainly not the teeth themselves. The cerebrals are often referred to as retroflex sounds. This is a good description, since, in forming these sounds, the tongue tip turns upwards and backwards in the mouth.

There is no equivalent in English for the cerebral phonemes of Sanskrit, so no examples from English can be given. It suffices, however, to remember that the position of the tongue is further back than would be the case for the pronunciation of the English *tuck*, *duck*, etc. Just as with the velars and palatals, the phonemes of the cerebral series are distinguished according to aspiration and voice (**ṭ**, **ṭh**, **ḍ**, **ḍh**) and includes the nasal **ṇ**, pronounced by allowing air to pass through the nasal cavity and through the oral cavity simultaneously.

Consonants: cerebrals				
Voiceless		Voiced		Voiced
Unaspirated	Aspirated	Unaspirated	Aspirated	Nasal
ṭ	**ṭh**	**ḍ**	**ḍh**	**ṇ**
(These sounds are not attested in English.)				

3.2.2.4 Dentals

The dental series of phonemes in Sanskrit do not present the speaker of English with any problems, although it must be stated from the outset that their classification as dentals must be borne in mind. That is to say, they are produced by the tongue being in contact with the top teeth. It is a common error, frequent amongst learners who do not know any Indic languages, to identify these as English dentals, thereby producing sounds not attested in Sanskrit. The phonemes **th** and **dh** are not pronounced like the *th* in the English *thin* and *that*, respectively.

With dental sounds in English, the tip of the tongue is below the top teeth and extends beyond the teeth. In Sanskrit, by contrast, dentals are pronounced with the tip of the tongue against the back of the top teeth. The tongue does not poke out from underneath the teeth. Pronounced this way, the dental sounds are audibly different to the cerebrals, where the tongue tip is a considerable distance away from the teeth. Learners are occasionally confused as to why Sanskrit contains two sets of *t* and *d*. That is to see English as a sort of default model for the consonant systems of other languages, a mindset which results in not grasping the essential point that Sanskrit makes a phonemic distinction between two sets of *t* and *d* according to how – or more specifically where – they are produced.

A shift in the place of articulation, in English, can be grasped by the pronunciation of the word *butter*. This can differ widely according to whether the speaker is English or American. The latter is likely to pronounce the word *butter* almost as if it were spelled *budder* – that is to say, with the tongue in a different part of the mouth. The place of articulation may not be something to which an English speaker pays much attention but, in Sanskrit, it is a crucial factor.

A dental sound in Sanskrit, irrespective of aspiration or voice, involves the tongue in contact with the top teeth and that is true, also, with the nasal phoneme **n**. Consider the pronunciation of *n* in the word *nun*. Does the tip of the tongue touch the teeth? If so, this is the Sanskrit dental **n**. If not, the tongue is likely to be striking the gum behind the teeth (This is known as the alveolar ridge). If the tongue is on the alveolar ridge, all one must do is slide it even further back (and upwards) in the mouth to produce the Sanskrit cerebral **ṇ**. Dental and cerebral phonemes are quite distinct in Sanskrit. With the caveat that the tongue must be in contact with the back of the top teeth, the pronunciation of the dental series is straightforward, as indicated by the English words or phrases in the following table:

Consonants: dentals				
Voiceless		Voiced		Voiced
Unaspirated	Aspirated	Unaspirated	Aspirated	Nasal
t	**th**	**d**	**dh**	**n**
Shorter	*Short hop*	*Rounders*	*Roundhouse*	*Panther*

3.2.2.5 Labials

Along with the velars, the labials are the easiest phonemes for speakers of English to grasp, since their pronunciation is not distinguishable from English to any extent that the ear must be trained to hear a difference. The same requirements nevertheless exist with respect to the way in which this series of sounds is produced. The aspirate must be clearly audible in the case of **ph** and **bh**, as identified in the English words contained in the following table.

Consonants: labials				
Voiceless		Voiced		Voiced
Unaspirated	Aspirated	Unaspirated	Aspirated	Nasal
p	**ph**	**b**	**bh**	**m**
Appalled	*Uphold*	*Abandon*	*Dab hand*	*Glimmer*

3.2.3 Overview

As regards the twenty-five consonants investigated so far, there is a consistent pattern. They are distributed within five series, indicating the place of articulation, and all five series have the same pattern: the first two phonemes are voiceless (or unvoiced), which is to say that the vocal cords do not vibrate. The first of these, furthermore, does not have an aspirate whereas the second one does. The third and fourth phonemes are both voiced and follow the same distribution as the first and the second of the series (i.e. unaspirated followed by aspirated). The fifth phoneme of the series is the nasal appropriate to the series. Here, the air is channeled through the nose as well as the mouth. All nasals are voiced.

With the velar series, the back of the tongue is in contact with the soft palate. With the palatal series, the front of the tongue moves upwards in the mouth, touching the hard palate and leaving only a narrow channel between itself and the hard palate through which air can pass. The cerebral series again involves the tongue but, on this occasion, the tip is quickly touched against the hard palate and released. With the dental series, the tip of the tongue is in contact with the top teeth. Only with the labial series is the tongue not involved in the production of sounds. Here, it is the complete closure of the lips which produces the sound.

3.3 Semivowels

3.3.1 Preliminaries

Semivowels are indicated in Sanskrit grammars as sharing the same place of articulation as the consonants already identified, as follows:

y = palatal
r = cerebral
l = dental
v = labial

Whilst useful, this analysis of the semivowels is based on an approximation of where the tongue is in the mouth during the pronunciation of the phonemes in question. There is no doubt, for example, that the tongue is in a position with **y** that is not discernibly different to where it would be for the pronunciation of **c** or **j**. Here, however, the tongue does not touch the top of the mouth. Instead, the sides of the tongue are in contact with the top teeth – hence there is touching, although it does not involve the front part of the tongue, as would be the case with **c** and **j**. The **y** of Sanskrit is the *y* of English in words such as *yacht*, *yes* and *young*.

3.3.2 Pronunciation

With the semivowel **r**, the tongue is momentarily in touch with the palate. The tongue must be in the position it would occupy in anticipation of pronouncing the English word *rabbit*, ensuring that the tongue tip extends to touch the part of the mouth closest to it. The tongue tip should not touch the top teeth, nor should it be too high up in the mouth. The alveolar ridge, located between the teeth and the roof of the mouth, is the target location. It is important not to trill the **r** in Sanskrit, as in Italian or Spanish, or produce the 'rolling r' of French. The learner, if a speaker of English, should not struggle unduly with the Sanskrit **r**, since it is sufficiently close to the English pronunciation of *r*, albeit with contact between the tongue and the palate.

With **l**, the tip of the tongue is in contact with the back of the top teeth, as is the case for the other dentals (**t**, **th**, **d**, **dh**, **n**). It is not uncommon for **l** to be pronounced with the tongue touching the gum immediately behind the top teeth rather than the teeth themselves. Every language permits slight variation in the pronunciation of its phonemes and Sanskrit is no exception.

The best advice that can be given is for beginners to pronounce **l** as they would in English, making sure that the tip of the tongue is in contact with either the back of the teeth or the gum behind them.

Variation in pronunciation is particularly marked with the fourth and final semivowel, **v**. When Indians pronounce Sanskrit, this phoneme invariably has the sound of the English *w*, hence the pronunciation of **veda** as something which, to English ears, sounds like *wader*. Whilst **v** is identified as a labial sound (the place of articulation being an approximation in the case of semivowels, as noted), the other labial phonemes of Sanskrit all involve contact between both lips (**p**, **ph**, **b**, **bh**, **m**). There is no such meeting of the lips in the articulation of **v**. There must, in fact, be an absence of touching, or else the sound produced is indistinguishable from **b**.

With non-Indian learners of Sanskrit, the semivowel **v** is more often than not pronounced as if it were the English *v* of *vixen*, *voice*, etc. This practice ought to be avoided, since the English pronunciation of *v* involves something which does not happen in Sanskrit: the meeting of the top teeth with the bottom lip. The use of the letter *v* in the IAST is arguably misleading, since it tricks the eye into assuming an English pronunciation for the semivowel **v**. It might have been better for the letter *w* to have been used instead, although that would not have been ideal, either. Despite the Indian pronunciation of **v** as the English *w*, the phoneme does not involve the rounding of the lips as with **u** and **ū**. The lips are kept unrounded for the pronunciation of **v**. Alternatively stated, the phoneme is pronounced like the English *v*, with the crucial distinction that the teeth must not touch the lip.

3.3.3 Overview

Three of the semivowels (**y**, **r** and **l**) are not problematic to the speaker of English, with only **v** calling for particular attention. The semivowel **r** is close to its English counterpart but requires the tip of the tongue to be in contact with the gum behind the upper teeth. There should be no trilling or rolling with **r**. A simple, quick touch is all that is involved. The semivowel **v** is more of a challenge because care must be taken not to use the teeth in the pronunciation of this phoneme. For those who are familiar with Spanish, the letter *b* in the word *beber* comes close in terms of pronunciation to the Sanskrit **v**. All semivowels are voiced.

3.4 Sibilants

3.4.1 Preliminaries

Strictly speaking, the sibilants in Sanskrit are three in number: **ś**, **ṣ** and **s**. Whilst the phoneme **h** is not strictly a sibilant ('whistling sound') but an aspirate, it will be included alongside the sibilants pure and simple. In Sanskrit, in any event, all four phonemes are grouped together under the term **ūṣman** (*the heating ones*; *the ones producing vapour*). The term **ūṣman** is particularly fitting when one considers that all four phonemes in the category of that name (i.e. the three sibilants and the aspirate) involve an airflow which can be sustained for many seconds. These are the sounds capable of producing a visible cloud in cold weather. The sibilants are voiceless. Sanskrit does not, for example, have a voiced equivalent for **ś**, heard in the word *Asia*, nor does it have a voiced equivalent for **s**, which is the English *z*.

3.4.2 Pronunciation

The phoneme **ś** is straightforward for speakers of English, since it is indistinguishable to the pronunciation of *sh* in words such as *short* and *shy*. The tongue is in the same position in the mouth as it is for **ch**, **j** and **jh**. For that reason, it is classified in Sanskrit as the palatal sibilant. Consider how one might pronounce *cat chew*. It is not much different to how one would pronounce *cat shoe*, were the pronunciation not to be accompanied by a short pause between syllables in the case of the former.

The pronunciation of **s** is as unproblematic as **ś**. It is the same *s* as in *sort* and *sigh*. The only sibilant with which English speakers struggle is the cerebral **ṣ**. Here, the thing to remember is that the dot below the letter in the IAST acts as a prompt. It is the same subscript dot which one finds with the cerebral (or retroflex) consonants **ṭ**, **ṭh**, **ḍ**, **ḍh** and **ṇ**. The tongue tip touches a part of the mouth which is higher than is the case for **ś**. The comments made regarding the place of articulation of the cerebral consonants apply (see 3.2.2.3).

Finally, as regards the phoneme **h**, this is technically an aspirate rather than a sibilant – which is to say it is the same sound associated with the aspirated consonants (**kh**, **gh**, **ch**, **jh**, **ṭh**, **ḍh**, **th**, **dh**, **ph**, **bh**). Quite simply, **h** is the sharp breathing out heard in the expletive: *'ha!'*

3.4.3 Overview

Unlike the sibilants, the consonantal phonemes investigated in 3.2 cannot be pronounced with sustained breath. They are produced by the build-up of air at some point in the oral tract and released in one go. The phonemes in the fifth column (the nasals) are different, in that they can be produced with a sustained airflow, by virtue of the fact that there is airflow through the nose as well as through the mouth. The sibilants share the feature of a sustained airflow with the semivowels and the vowels but, crucially, the sibilants are not voiced. An easy way to remember this is the fact that the expletive used in trying to get people to be silent is: *'shhh!'*. As with the semivowels, the sibilants are allocated a place of articulation which is approximate, as follows:

ś = palatal
ṣ = cerebral
s = dental

Unlike the semivowels, there is no labial sibilant. That would involve an impossible situation, ruled out by articulatory constraints, in which the breath would need to be released whilst the lips were in contact.

3.5 Additional sounds

Along with vowels and consonants, Sanskrit possesses two sounds and two orthographic conventions which play an essential role in the pronunciation of the language. The present work proposes that the sounds in question should not be identified as consonantal phonemes. This view is supported by the fact that they do not function as consonants within the Devanāgarī. The first of these (**anusvāra**) relates to nasality and therefore involves the nasals (**ṅ, ñ, ṇ, n, m**). The second (**visarga**) is conventionally pronounced as the aspirate **h** – but is not identical to it, since there is an additional feature involved in its pronunciation. As for orthographic conventions (the inherent vowel and **virāma**), these have a relationship to each other which may be expressed as complementary, in that they both relate to the phoneme **a**. Whilst virāma has a symbol, the inherent vowel has no symbol at all. In brief, the inherent vowel and virāma are every bit as important to the pronunciation of Sanskrit as the phonemes investigated in the previous pages.

3.5.1 Anusvāra

When a word ends with the phoneme **m**, it is not always the case that the letter *m* is marked in the Devanāgarī. Often, what one sees is a dot in its place. This is indicated in the IAST by the letter **ṃ**. It is important to note that, whilst the IAST places the dot underneath the letter *m*, anusvāra is written at the top in the Devanāgarī (Some authors employ a variant form of the IAST which mimics the Devanāgarī practice, hence **ṁ**).

Consider the following examples in the Devanāgarī, both using the letter **ka**:

Without anusvāra:	क **ka**
With anusvāra:	कं **kaṃ**

The letter/syllable **ka**, with the anusvāra, is transliterated by the IAST as **kaṃ**, although it is worth bearing in mind that the transliteration **kaṁ** is occasionally found (This is a rare example of variation within the IAST, the other being the infrequent representation of the diphthongs as **āi** and **āu**).

The following sentences clarify the use of anusvāra:

Rāmaḥ nagaraṃ gacchati
Rāma goes to (the) town.

Rāmaḥ nagaram agacchat
Rāma went to (the) town.

The final word in both sentences is the verb. In the first sentence, the verb form (**gacchati**) begins with the consonant **g**. This is preceded by the phoneme **m**, which takes anusvāra. In the second sentence, the verb form (**agacchat**) begins with a vowel. It is preceded by **m**, which does <u>not</u> take anusvāra. In the first sentence, **nagaraṃ** (*town*) uses anusvāra, whilst this is not the case with respect to the second sentence. The explanation of anusvāra is that it occurs when the phoneme which follows is a consonant. Where a word-final **m** is followed by a word beginning with a vowel, there is no place for anusvāra. Alternatively said, anusvāra is dependent on a word-final **m** being followed by consonant.

It is worth remarking that, if a sentence ends with a word-final **m**, there can be no anusvāra, since the conditions of its use are not met. Furthermore, a word-final consonant at the end of a sentence requires a special sign to indicate that it is not followed by the inherent vowel **a**. The sign in question is virāma, investigated in 3.5.4.

There is one complicating issue as regards the pronunciation of anusvāra, and this is connected to the place of articulation of the following phoneme. An adjustment in pronunciation is preferred amongst those who chant or recite Sanskrit. Effectively, anusvāra takes on the identity of the nasal belonging to the same place of articulation as the following phoneme. The spelling of anusvāra does not normally change, irrespective of whether or not one makes the adjustment in pronunciation from **m** to the class nasal of the following phoneme. That said, there are traditions relating to the writing of Sanskrit in which the spelling is indeed amended to reflect pronunciation changes. In such traditions, anusvāra is replaced by the relevant nasal in the Devanāgarī:

Rāmaḥ nagaraṅ gacchati (etc.)

Anusvāra can (and frequently does) occur in the middle of a word. The circumstances under which that happens are identical to those where it is attested at the end of a word; that is to say, when **m** is followed by a consonant, semivowel or sibilant. As with the adjustment which occurs with word-final anusvāra, its pronunciation is that of the class nasal of the following phoneme. Note the following examples:

śaṃkara (*offering a blessing; epithet for* **śiva**)	Pronounced **śaṅkara**
saṃcaya (*an accumulation*)	Pronounced **sañcaya**
saṃḍīna (*flying together*)	Pronounced **saṇḍīna**
saṃtoṣa (*contentment; joy*)	Pronounced **santoṣa**
saṃpūrṇa (*filled*)	Pronounced **sampūrṇa**

3.5.2 Visarga

Along with anusvāra, the Devanāgarī possesses a sign that has an impact on pronunciation, albeit that it is not classified as a letter within the writing system. This sign is visarga, whose name means *a sending forth* – in the context of pronunciation, an emission of breath. Its pronunciation is conventionally not distinguishable from the aspirate **h**, but it differs from the aspirate in one crucial respect. Visarga stipulates for a glide vowel or echo vowel. Take, for example, the two-word phrase **sukha duḥkha** (*pleasure misery; the ups and downs of existence*). Here, visarga is present in the second word, indicated in the IAST as a dotted *h*. The aspirate is also present, not by itself but as a feature within the unvoiced velar consonant, **kh**. Whilst most users of Sanskrit might not distinguish between visarga (**ḥ**) and the aspirate (**h**), there is nevertheless a technical distinction between the two. Visarga specifies for the repetition of the vowel immediately preceding it. With this is mind, one ought really to hear something resembling **sukha duḥ^{u}kha**. The **u** in the first syllable of both words has the same quality and length, but the *u*-sound following the visarga is a mere whisper and not subject to any stress.

Students often struggle with visarga and there is a marked persistence in producing a short **a** after it, irrespective of the vowel preceding it. This is a bad habit and one that the learner is strongly advised not to acquire. It is extremely rare for visarga to appear within a word, making **sukha duḥkha** something of an anomaly, but it is frequently encountered at the end of words. So pervasive is visarga that it is subject to a comprehensive set of rules relating to modifications in its pronunciation (This set of rules is **visarga sandhi**, the bane of the learner of Sanskrit in his or her first year of study, if not beyond). It is not a bad mistake to pronounce visarga as if it were none other than the aspirate **h**; certainly, this is more acceptable than producing the wrong echo vowel after visarga. It is desirable, all the same, that an effort be made to disambiguate between the two. Visarga gives a certain cadence to the language which is unique. Consider the closing utterance of mantras: **śāntiḥ śāntiḥ śāntiḥ**. (*peace, peace, peace*). The final phoneme of each word is the visarga. This means that the vowel **i** is heard twice in each word: once before the visarga and again after it, as an echo vowel: **śāntiḥ^{i} śāntiḥ^{i} śāntiḥ^{i}** (There is a convention, when reciting a mantra, to draw out the last sound until the breath is exhausted, making the final echo vowel a long one. This is in stark contradiction to the articulation of the echo vowel elsewhere).

Since visarga is flanked by a vowel – the same vowel, invariably – this has led to speculation amongst linguists that it may originally have differed from the aspirate in being a voiced sound. There has similarly been speculation that visarga differed, in antiquity, from the aspirate in that it had a different quality, namely that of being a scraping or hissing sound as is heard in the Scottish word *loch* (Speakers of German might recognize this sound in the pronunciation of words such as *ich* and *milch*, although there is admittedly variation in the way that German speakers produce the sound in question). This is the stuff of linguistic speculation. All that need concern the student of Sanskrit is that visarga produces an echo vowel whereas the aspirate does not. What if visarga is preceded by a diphthong rather than a vowel (either simple or complex)? The answer is an obvious one: it is the second element of the diphthong which surfaces as the echo vowel. The word **aśvaiḥ** (*by/with horses*) results in the pronunciation

aśvaiḥ^{i}, not ***aśvaiḥ**^{a}. The echo vowel should be kept short, even if the vowel preceding visarga is long. Remember that the echo vowel does not take stress – nor should it be given any, since it does not produce an extra syllable in the word.

3.5.3 The inherent vowel

Before looking at the final symbol recognized in the Devanāgarī, something needs to be said about the notion of the inherent vowel, since the final symbol is virāma (*cessation*), which indicates the removal of the inherent vowel. So what is the inherent vowel? It is none other than the phoneme **a**. When the Devanāgarī represents a consonant, semivowel or sibilant, the phoneme in question is automatically accompanied by a short **a**. In effect, the Devanāgarī is not an alphabet but a writing system designed to indicate syllables; and every syllable requires a vowel. The first consonant identified in Sanskrit is **k** – yet the Devanāgarī does not represent the letter *k*. It represents the syllable **ka**:

क
ka

The principle is not dissimilar to the English alphabet. One pronounces *b*, *c* and *d* as *'bee'*, *'see'* and *'dee'*. For *f*, a vowel sound precedes the consonant: *'eff'*; and so on and so forth. Where Sanskrit and English are markedly different is that, if one wants to write the phoneme **k** rather than the syllable **ka**, one must add a sign to achieve this.

When the sound *k* is articulated, it is followed by something which sounds distinctly vowel-like but indeterminate in quality. The indeterminate vowel is, in fact, the most common vowel sound in English, in that it accounts for most *a* and *e* sounds which do not receive stress. For example, one hears the indeterminate vowel in the initial *a* of *about*, *around*, *assume*, etc., and in the second *e* of *emerald*, *pepper*, *telephone* (The word *emerald* contains the indeterminate vowel twice: *emerald*).

Sanskrit does not recognize an indeterminate vowel. The closest thing that the language possesses to this is the short vowel **a**. It is unsurprising, therefore, that this is this sound which the Devanāgarī writing system chooses in lieu of the inherent vowel: the vowel that accompanies all non-vocalic sounds unless indicated to the contrary. It is important for learners to avoid producing the indeterminate vowel in Sanskrit. The following word, which means *gold* in Sanskrit, contains three instances of the short vowel **a** – and the short vowel must be audible and identical in all cases:

कनक
kanaka

Vowels in Sanskrit do <u>not</u> undergo a change in pronunciation according to where they occur in a word. Their quality and length remain constant. It is also essential to avoid the pronunciation heard amongst speakers of modern Indian languages, where the final **a** in a word is omitted altogether (**kanak*). Whilst this might be a pronunciation feature of the modern Indian languages, it is not one associated with Sanskrit.

3.5.4 Virāma

The principle of the Devanāgarī is that individual letters represent syllables. The implication is that, whereas vowel letters indicate individual vowels with no other phonemic material present, the letters for the consonants automatically include the inherent vowel. In describing the sound system of Sanskrit, the present work uses the IAST which, unlike the Devanāgarī, allows one to identify <u>individual</u> phonemes rather than having recourse to a writing system in which the syllable is the basic sound unit. The principle adopted by the Devanāgarī has certain consequences and it is fitting, in the concluding parts of a chapter dealing with the sound system of Sanskrit, to investigate precisely what these consequences are.

As shown in 3.5.3, the Devanāgarī letter for the first consonant, in terms of the traditional running order of the consonants, involves the phoneme **k**. However, the sound *k* does not by itself constitute a syllable, since it lacks a vowel, and the Devanāgarī, as noted, is a writing system aimed at representing syllables. This is where virāma comes into play. Virāma is a diagonal slash placed at the base of a letter. It instructs the reader to remove the inherent vowel implied by the Devanāgarī:

Without virāma:	क **ka**
With virāma:	क् **k**

The use of virāma is restricted to the end of a sentence and is not available, in authentic Sanskrit, anywhere else within the sentence. This leads to the inevitable question: how, then, can the inherent vowel be removed when two (or more) consonants occur in a cluster, without intervening vowels? The solution adopted by the Devanāgarī is to create a conjunct form, merging the consonants to produce a shape which indicates that the inherent vowel is not present. Usually, conjunct forms are instantly recognizable; sometimes, however, they are not. An investigation of the strategies of conjunct formation requires familiarity with the basic forms of the Devanāgarī, to which 4.2 is dedicated.

Virāma is not used if a consonant is followed by a vowel other than **a**. In this event, the vowel in question replaces the inherent vowel, thereby creating a syllable, in adherence to the principles of the Devanāgarī (This is explored in greater detail in 4.2.2).

k + a	**k + ā**	**k + i**	**k + ī**	**k + u**	**k + ū**
क	का	कि	की	कु	कू

k + e	**k + ai**	**k + o**	**k + au**
के	कै	को	कौ

3.6 Exercise: true or false?

The following exercise contains twelve questions aimed at allowing the reader to test himself or herself on the information presented so far. The questions are based on misunderstandings frequent amongst learners, so one ought to make a note of which questions are answered incorrectly and reread the relevant chapter to resolve the misunderstanding. The answers are given on the same page, for convenience's sake.

Questions

(i) The IAST indicates all long vowels with a macron.
(ii) There are only two diphthongs: **ia** and **ua**.
(iii) Diphthongs are classified as two phonemes joined together.
(iv) All semivowels are voiced, and all sibilants are voiceless.
(v) The phonemes r̥ and l̥ are semivowels.
(vi) The aspirate (**h**) is voiceless, therefore all aspirated phonemes must also be voiceless.
(vii) All nasals are voiced.
(viii) The symbols **ṇ** and **ṅ** are interchangeable.
(ix) The symbols **ṃ** and **ṁ** are interchangeable.
(x) The echo vowel after visarga is always the same as the vowel before visarga.
(xi) Capital letters are not permitted in the IAST.
(xii) The only punctuation marks are । and ॥.

Answers

(i) **False.** Both **e** and **o** are long, even though they are not marked with a macron.
(ii) **False.** The only two diphthongs in Sanskrit are **ai** and **au**.
(iii) **False.** Diphthongs are classified as individual phonemes.
(iv) **True.**
(v) **False.** They are vowels.
(vi) **False.** There are as many voiced aspirated consonants (**gh**, **jh**, **ḍh**, **dh**, **bh**) as there are voiceless aspirated consonants (**kh**, **ch**, **ṭh**, **th**, **ph**).
(vii) **True.**
(viii) **False.** The first of these is the palatal nasal; the second is the velar nasal.
(ix) **True.** That said, a text ought to use one or the other, not both.
(x) **True.**
(xi) **False.** The IAST does not require capital letters, but many authors use them in the spelling of proper nouns (etc.) and at the start of sentences. Capital letters are used by the Harvard-Kyoto Convention to identify specific phonemes.
(xii) **True.**

4

THE WRITING SYSTEM

4.1 Origin of the Devanāgarī

The **Brāhmī** writing system is the ancestor of all the scripts of India, irrespective of whether they are Indic languages (and therefore Indo-European) or members of another family, such as Dravidian. Urdu is the exception, since it uses a modified form of the Perso-Arabic script. It is worth noting that Panjabi, Sindhi and Kashmiri can also appear in the Perso-Arabic script, although they possess Brāhmī-based writing systems (The choice of script tends to depend on whether literacy practices are being undertaken by a Muslim or a Hindu speaker of the language in question – or a Sikh, in the case of Panjabi).

The Brāhmī is the oldest-known writing system for the Indic languages, with inscriptions dating to around 250 BCE still visible on pillars erected by the Emperor **Aśoka**, a convert to Buddhism. Aśoka's edicts were carved in the vernacular – the Prakrit – and were aimed at allowing anyone who was literate and able to read the Buddhist content of the text. Attempts to connect the Brāhmī with the Indus Valley script have not been persuasive, since the forms of the Brāhmī do not resemble those of the Indus Valley script, with the exception of a few symbols which would appear to be the result of nothing more than coincidence. In any event, the Indus Valley writing system used hundreds of symbols

DOI: 10.4324/9780429325434-5

not attested in the Brāhmī, and there is more than a millennium separating the collapse of the Indus Valley Civilization and the monumental edicts of Aśoka.

The suggestion that the Brāhmī arose from contact with Greek (more in the nature of stimulus diffusion than the actual borrowing of Greek letters) seems ill-founded. Greek expansion into western and central Asia, made possible by the destruction of the Persian Empire in 331 BCE, reached its height less than a century before the Aśokan inscriptions in Brāhmī. This period is too short to account for the development of the Brāhmī into a mature writing system, using quite distinct principles from the alphabetic Greek. Whatever its place of origin and however ancient the Brāhmī may prove to be, no evidence has yet come to light of it being used to record Sanskrit. That said, the abugida principles of the Brāhmī confirm it, beyond doubt, to be the ancestor of the Devanāgarī – the writing system with which Sanskrit is primarily associated.

4.2 The Devanāgarī investigated

4.2.1 Preliminaries

The Devanāgarī is one of the principal writing systems of South Asia, descended from the Brāhmī script and written from left to right. Although the Devanāgarī is frequently referred to as an alphabet, it is technically an abugida. The difference between an alphabet and an abugida is that, whereas the alphabet treats vowels and consonants as having equal value in terms of their representation, the abugida places an emphasis on the representation of the syllable, where the consonant takes pride of place and the vowel is indicated as a secondary feature. The combination consonant + vowel is less complex in terms of composition than the combination vowel + consonant, as the following example demonstrates:

क **ka**

अक् **ak**

With **ak**, the Devanāgarī uses the initial form of the vowel **a**, followed by the body shape of the consonant **k**. Virāma is then applied to remove the inherent vowel which would otherwise produce the syllable **ka**. Omitting the virāma would result in the disyllabic **aka**.

In Sanskrit, a word cannot contain two vowels together. The diphthongs **ai** and **au** are not exceptions to this rule since they are individual phonemes. Sanskrit does, however, allow for a semivowel to occur before or after a vowel representing what in other languages may be indicated by a diphthong. For example, the diphthongs *ia* and *ua* are absent in Sanskrit but note the following:

यव

yava (*barley*)

The word **yava** contains two syllables, **ya** and **va**. The first phoneme in the word is indicated by **y**, which is then followed by the inherent vowel **a**, not visually represented when in non-initial position in the word; the second syllable contains **v**, similarly followed by the inherent vowel **a**. At this juncture, it is desirable to see the Devanāgarī in its entirety. To this end, the abugida is set out on the following page. The running order of the letters, as presented, is found in Sanskrit dictionaries. The Devanāgarī starts with the vowel **a** and ends with the aspirate **h**, as indicated.

Vowels

Primary	**a**	**ā**	**i**	**ī**	**u**	**ū**	**ṛ**	**ṝ**	**ḷ**	**ḹ**
Secondary (+ diphthongs)	**e**	**ai**	**o**	**au**						

Consonants

Velar	**k**	**kh**	**g**	**gh**	**ṅ**
Palatal	**c**	**ch**	**j**	**jh**	**ñ**
Cerebral	**ṭ**	**ṭh**	**ḍ**	**ḍh**	**ṇ**
Dental	**t**	**th**	**d**	**dh**	**n**
Labial	**p**	**ph**	**b**	**bh**	**m**
Semivowels	**y**	**r**	**l**	**v**	
Sibilants	**ś**	**ṣ**	**s**		
Aspirate	**h**				

Vowels

Primary	अ आ इ ई उ ऊ ऋ ॠ ऌ ॡ
Secondary (+ diphthongs)	ए ऐ ओ औ

Consonants

Velar	क	ख	ग	घ	ङ
Palatal	च	छ	ज	झ	ञ
Cerebral	ट	ठ	ड	ढ	ण
Dental	त	थ	द	ध	न
Labial	प	फ	ब	भ	म
Semivowels	य	र	ल	व	
Sibilants	श	ष	स		
Aspirate	ह				

4.2.2 Vowels

The Devanāgarī differs from an alphabet in another respect: it possesses two sets of signs for vowels according to where in the word the vowel occurs. If the vowel is word-initial, the Devanāgarī uses a full form. This is also the form in which a vowel would appear if it were to be written by itself. The difference between the forms is not one of uppercase as opposed to lowercase letters. The Devanāgarī does not make such a distinction. Initial forms are more complex in terms of their shape than their medial (non-initial) equivalents. It is worth remembering that the inherent vowel has no form at all when it is not initial. Fortunately, it is the only vowel to lack a form in medial position. Were it the case the other vowels followed suit, the Devanāgarī would be a vowel-defective writing system, as is the case with the old Semitic alphabet – that is to say, the original alphabet – and some of its living descendants, such as Hebrew and Arabic (and alphabets adapted from Arabic, like Persian and Urdu).

The initial forms of the vowels display a strategy which, whilst not entirely consistent, greatly assists the learner. Since Sanskrit recognizes the relationship between short vowels and their long equivalents, that relationship is visually reflected in the Devanāgarī. Effectively, the form of the initial short vowel provides a template for the long vowel, which is distinguished from the short vowel by the addition of an element. The element in question is either a vertical stroke or a hook. The following table shows the initial forms of the simple vowels in more detail:

Short vowel		*Long vowel*		*Strategy*
अ	**a**	आ	**ā**	The long vowel adds a vertical stroke to the right of the short form
इ	**i**	ई	**ī**	The long vowel adds a hook above the short form
उ	**u**	ऊ	**ū**	The long vowel adds a hook to the right of the short form
ऋ	**ṛ**	ॠ	**ṝ**	The long vowel adds a hook to the bottom right of the short form
ऌ	**ḷ**	ॡ	**ḹ**	The long vowel adds a hook to the bottom right of the short form

As regards the complex vowels and the diphthongs, they too display a strategy, but one that is different to the simple vowels. The distinction is not one of length, since the complex vowels and the diphthongs are long. There are no short equivalents. Here, the distinction is between long vowel and diphthong, and it is appropriate that the strategy used to distinguish between the phonemes is not the same strategy employed with the simple vowels. With the complex vowels and diphthongs, the strategy involves the addition of a diagonal slash above the body shape of the diphthong, even if a diagonal slash is already present.

Complex vowel		*Diphthong*		*Strategy*
ए	**e**	ऐ	**ai**	The diphthong adds a diagonal slash above the body shape for **e**
ओ	**o**	औ	**au**	The diphthong adds a further diagonal slash to the body shape for **o**

It is regrettable that the Devanāgarī recycles the body shape of the letter **a** to produce not only the long equivalent, **ā**, but also the complex vowel **o** and the diphthong **au**. This is not helpful to the learner. A simple way to remember which phoneme is being indicated is to bear in mind that **o** and **au** are both long and, as such, employ the body shape of **ā**. There are two vertical strokes in the formation of the body shape. The diagonal slash – either single or double – is a property of long vowels and diphthongs only. It is not used with short vowels (This theme reoccurs with the medial forms).

अ = a आ = ā ओ = o ऐ = ai औ = au

It seems to be desirable, at this point, to discuss the OM sign which, whilst not a letter of the Devanāgarī, is frequently encountered. There are two ways of representing OM: by using the symbol or by using the letters of the Devanāgarī. This situation is analogous to the choice presented in the use of *&* or *and*. Whilst deemed in Hinduism to be the primordial sound, OM is composed of three elements according to the Devanāgarī: **a** + **u** + **m** (Note that **a** + **u** does not produce the diphthong **au** but, rather, a complete fusion of the simple vowels, resulting in the complex vowel **o**).

ॐ = ओं **oṃ** (with anusvāra) or ओम् **om** (with **m** and a virāma)

The medial forms of the vowels, as noted, are different to the initial forms. These are less complicated in their formation and exemplify the point that the Devanāgarī is an abugida rather than an alphabet. Here, the vowels are written around the consonant. Most vowels, in this form, appear above or below the consonant, but there are two notable exceptions. These exceptions relate to the short vowel **i** and the long equivalent, **ī**. On the following page, a table is given in which both the initial forms are given (above) and the medial forms (below). The medial forms are accompanied by a dotted circle which indicates the location of the consonant vis-à-vis the vowel in its medial form.

As was seen with **a** and **ā**, the short **a** does not possess a medial form, since the concept of the inherent vowel comes into operation. With **ā**, a vertical stroke is added to the right of the consonant, just as there was an additional vertical stroke in the initial form, to distinguish it from its short counterpart. With **i** and **ī**, the strategy is different. Short **i** is indicated, unlike short **a**. It appears as a vertical stroke above which there is a crest – and it appears before the consonant. It is the singular exception to the rule that the Devanāgarī is written from left to right. The medial form of **i** is a source of frustration to anyone who writes Sanskrit, where the tendency exists to write the consonant without leaving space for the short **i**. The medial form of **ī** is much more in keeping with the principles of the Devanāgarī: it occurs after the consonant.

With **u** and **ū**, the strategy is different again. Here, the vowel is indicated below the consonant. With **u**, the medial form resembles the number 6 which has fallen backwards; with **ū**, the number 6 has toppled forwards. The easiest way to remember the distinction is to remember the sequence: *short and long;*

backwards and forwards. As for the remaining simple vowels (**r̥**, **r̥̄**, **l̥** and **l̥̄**), yet another strategy is employed, but a simple one. With **r̥**, a little hook, somewhat resembling the letter *c* in English, is added below the consonant. As for its long counterpart, **r̥̄**, two little hooks are added. The medial form of **l̥** mimics the initial form, without the top line and the neck attaching the top line to the body shape of the letter, and the medial form of **l̥̄** is not found in Sanskrit. If it were, it would resemble its short equivalent, with an extra little hook (For the medial forms of **e**, **ai**, **o** and **au**, see the following notes accompanying the table).

Vowels

Primary vowels
(Initial and medial forms)

अ a n/a	आ ā ◌ा	इ i ि◌	ई ī ◌ी	उ u ◌ु	ऊ ū ◌ू
	ऋ r̥ ◌ृ	ॠ r̥̄ ◌ॄ	ऌ l̥ ◌ॢ	ॡ l̥̄ ◌ॣ	

Secondary vowels (+ diphthongs)
(Initial and medial forms)

ए e ◌े	ऐ ai ◌ै	ओ o ◌ो	औ au ◌ौ

Note on the secondary vowels (+ diphthongs)

The medial forms of **e**, **ai**, **o** and **au** follow a certain logic, although it must be said that they are responsible for the greater part of reading errors amongst learners. With this in mind, the following points ought to assist matters:

(i) All secondary vowels and diphthongs in Sanskrit are long.
(ii) The initial forms of **o** and **au** use the body shape of short **a** – but with an additional vertical stroke (resulting in **ā**) which remains visible in the medial form.
(iii) The diagonal slash, present in all four medial forms, is reserved to **e**, **o** and the diphthongs.

(iv) The key to remembering these medial forms is to focus on **e** and **o**. The first of these uses the diagonal slash only; the second one has the diagonal slash above a vertical stroke. The associated diphthongs, **ai** and **au** respectively, merely add an additional diagonal slash.

4.2.3 Consonants

As discussed in 3.2, the Devanāgarī presents twenty-five consonants out of thirty-three in an order which is much more patterned than is the case with the vowels. These twenty-five consonants are accommodated within a structure in which each component of the structure, based on the place of articulation, adheres to a principled and logical pattern. First comes the phoneme which possesses neither voice nor aspiration (**k**, **c**, **ṭ**, **t**, **p**), followed by the phoneme which, whilst still voiceless, contains aspiration (**kh**, **ch**, **ṭh**, **th**, **ph**). This accounts for all the voiceless consonants of Sanskrit, except for the sibilants. Then follow the phonemes which are the voiced equivalents of the first two, similarly distinguished by the unaspirated phoneme followed by its aspirated equivalent: **g**, **gh**; **j**, **jh**; **ḍ**, **ḍh**; **d**, **dh**; **b**, **bh**. The fifth phoneme in the sequence is the nasal for the place of articulation in question (**ṅ**, **ñ**, **ṇ**, **n**, **m**). All nasals are voiced and unaspirated.

In contrast to the situation with the vowels, the Devanāgarī does not indicate a visual relationship between consonants. Aspirated phonemes and their unaspirated equivalents, for example, have quite distinct letter shapes (except for two pairs of consonants, as discussed in the following paragraph). Whilst marvellously classified and arranged with respect to their sound, the consonants are a lot less 'tidy' in their visual representation. Indeed, learners invariably encounter difficulties in distinguishing between consonants as they are represented by the Devanāgarī – a task not facilitated by the similarities between various letters. Note the similarities in form between the following pairs, as this is where confusion regularly occurs (The inherent vowel is present and therefore indicated in the IAST).

घ **gha** ध **dha**

ङ **ṅa** ड **ḍa**

ज **ja** ञ **ña**

ट **ṭa** द **da**

भ **bha** म **ma**

There are some similarities between consonants which assist the learner. Such similarities are, however, limited to two pairs of consonants:

ट **ṭa** ठ **ṭha**
प **pa** फ **pha**

With **ṭa/ṭha** and **pa/pha**, a strategy takes place which is not dissimilar to one encountered with a number of vowels. With **ṭa**, the tail of the body shape does not complete a circle, unlike **ṭha**. In other words, there is an addition to the body shape of a letter to create a distinction between two phonemes which are in some sense paired (With the vowels, the pairing is the relationship between short and long counterparts). This is also the case with **pa** and **pha**, where we see a strategy hardly to be differentiated from **u** and **ū**. There, a hook is added to the right-hand side of the body shape of **pa** to create **pha**. The pairing of these consonants is not one of length, since Sanskrit does not classify consonants as short or long, but a distinction between unaspirated and aspirated counterparts.

Variation between fonts is relevant when discussing the consonants. This will be explored in more detail (4.4.2). For now, it is opportune to look at the variation which may occur between consonants which are frequently confused for others in the Devanāgarī. The present work uses a font (Sanskrit Text) in which the body shapes of the consonant pairs **gha/dha** and **bha/ma** are disambiguated by the presence of a curl on the top left of **dha** and **bha**. Whilst these curls might be present in most (if not indeed all) contemporary fonts, the Devanāgarī one sees in textbooks from the period before the second half of the twentieth century does not exhibit them. The resulting problems in disambiguation are compounded by the fact that the typeface in older Sanskrit textbooks often has poor legibility. When the curls in both **dha** and **bha** are replaced by a short top line, the similarity in form with **gha** and **ma**, respectively, is increased. The only disambiguating factor is that with **gha** and **ma**, there is a continuous topline but with **dha** and **bha**, the top line is interrupted.

Old typeface	*Sanskrit Text*	*IAST*
ध	ध	**dha**
भ	भ	**bha**

Consonants

Velars				
Voiceless		Voiced		Voiced
Unaspirated	Aspirated	Unaspirated	Aspirated	Nasal
क **ka**	ख **kha**	ग **ga**	घ **gha**	ङ **ṅa**
'Clock out!'	*Clock House*	*'Log out!'*	*Log House*	*Long House*

Palatals				
Voiceless		Voiced		Voiced
Unaspirated	Aspirated	Unaspirated	Aspirated	Nasal
च **ca**	छ **cha**	ज **ja**	झ **jha**	ञ **ña**
Churchill	*Church Hall*	*Judging*	*'Judge him!'*	*Munchkin*

Cerebrals				
Voiceless		Voiced		Voiced
Unaspirated	Aspirated	Unaspirated	Aspirated	Nasal
ट **ṭa**	ठ **ṭha**	ड **ḍa**	ढ **ḍha**	ण **ṇa**
(These sounds are not attested in English.)				

Dentals				
Voiceless		Voiced		Voiced
Unaspirated	Aspirated	Unaspirated	Aspirated	Nasal
त **ta**	थ **tha**	द **da**	ध **dha**	न **na**
Shorter	*Short hop*	*Rounders*	*Roundhouse*	*Panther*

Labials				
Voiceless		Voiced		Voiced
Unaspirated	Aspirated	Unaspirated	Aspirated	Nasal
प **pa**	फ **pha**	ब **ba**	भ **bha**	म **ma**
Appalled	*Uphold*	*Abandon*	*Dab hand*	*Glimmer*

4.2.4 Semivowels and sibilants

The semivowels and sibilants, as with the other consonants (but not the vowels), are accompanied by virāma when the inherent vowel is removed. The examples on the following page do not contain virāma. Accordingly, the IAST accompanying the Devanāgarī includes a short **a**. The Devanāgarī letters for the semivowels and sibilants are unique, in that they are not deemed to be modifications of the letters representing any of the vowels or the consonants. That said, there are similarities in form which need to be addressed. In this respect, the Devanāgarī letters representing the syllables **ra**, **va** and **ṣa** deserve a mention.

The semivowel **ra** has a similar form to the initial stroke of the body shape for the letter **kha**. In fact, the letter **kha**, in many fonts (such as Nirmala), is disconcertingly close to the Devanāgarī spelling of **rava**.

Nirmala	*Sanskrit Text*	*IAST*
र	र	**ra**
ख	ख	**kha**
रव	रव	**rava**

With **kha**, the initial (left-hand) stroke of the body shape should curl over to the right at the base. It is not necessary for this stroke to touch the body shape to the right of it but, as is the case in many fonts (including Sanskrit Text), that is precisely what it does. This is good practice to adopt in handwriting, given that the touching of the two elements comprising the body shape of **kha** serves to disambiguate **kha** from **rava**.

As regards **va** and **ṣa**, these are only distinguished from **ba** and **pa**, respectively, by the absence or presence of a diagonal slash within the body shape of the letter.

व **va** ब **ba**
ष **ṣa** प **pa**

Semivowels and sibilants

Velars	
Semivowel (voiced)	Aspirate (voiceless)
n/a	ह
	ha
	Hear

Palatals	
Semivowel (voiced)	Sibilant (voiceless)
य	श
ya	**śa**
Yoghurt	*Fish*

Cerebrals	
Semivowel (voiced)	Sibilant (voiceless)
र	ष
ra	**ṣa**
Rare	*Hushed*

Dentals	
Semivowel (voiced)	Sibilant (voiceless)
ल	स
la	**sa**
Follow	*Snake*

Labials	
Semivowel (voiced)	Sibilant (voiceless)
व	n/a
va	
(See 3.3.2.)	

4.3 Conjuncts and conjunct formation

4.3.1 Preliminaries

Conjuncts are often referred to as 'conjunct consonants' or 'compound consonants'. This indicates that the phenomenon in question is one which involves consonants only. A conjunct is the outcome, in the Devanāgarī, of representing two or more non-vowel sounds together, without an intervening vowel. Sanskrit, as explained, has thirty-three consonants, composed of the twenty-five investigated in 3.2 (distributed across five places of articulation and distinguished according to whether they are voiceless/voiced, unaspirated/aspirated), four semivowels, three sibilants and the aspirate. All consonants are involved in conjunct formation, vowels are not. Anusvāra and visarga do not form conjuncts.

Conjuncts can be straightforward to read, in cases where the Devanāgarī letters suddenly undergo a transformation from their basic forms but remain legible all the same. That said, conjuncts can take on a form in which the individual elements involved are not discernible. At that point, no amount of peering at a page illustrating the basic forms of the Devanāgarī, attempting to investigate possible contenders, is likely to shed any light. Conjuncts of this type (see 4.3.5) are, fortunately, in the minority. They must be learnt as unique forms, such as the following:

क् **k** + ष **ṣa** = क्ष **kṣa** e.g. मोक्ष **mokṣa** (*liberation*)

Why do conjuncts exist? Quite simply, because the Devanāgarī assumes the presence of the inherent vowel **a** in the pronunciation of any letter indicating a consonant, unless the inherent vowel is removed (The removal is achieved with virāma, as seen in 3.5.4). All well and good, but this does beg the question as to why, if the removal of the inherent vowel is easily undertaken by the insertions of virāma, there should be any need for the compounding of letters. There is no obvious answer to this question. The answer is quite likely to be connected to philosophical perspectives on the primordial nature of the syllable. Certainly, virāma is used by the Devanāgarī, illustrating the point that a consonant, vowel or semivowel without the following inherent vowel is easily represented by the writing system. The Devanāgarī does not, however, technically allow for the use of virāma unless the letter to which it is attached is the final letter of the sentence.

All of the writing systems descended from the Brāhmī use conjunct forms, with the notable exception (amongst the Indic languages) of the

Gurmukhī script devised for Panjabi. The Gurmukhī effectively limits conjunct formation to two phonemes, **r** and **v**, reducing these to subscript letters whose forms are immediately legible. Further south, the Dravidian languages have adopted the principle of conjunct forms. Here too, there is a singular exception, with Tamil showing innovation in the creation of a sign (a dot above the letter as opposed to a slash below the letter, like virāma) to remove the inherent vowel. Conjuncts are, therefore, a feature in the writing systems of most of the languages of India. They are by no means restricted to the Devanāgarī.

Attempting to enumerate the conjunct forms is a pointless exercise, and it suffices to say that the number of conjuncts attested in the Devanāgarī runs into the high hundreds. It is certainly not the case that one has but to calculate the sum of 33 x 33 (33 representing the total number of letters for the consonants). Such a thing ignores two crucial points: (i) a given consonant does not automatically generate a conjunct form with all other consonants, and (ii) conjuncts are not limited to two elements, but may contain three, four or even five. Despite the high number of conjunct forms, there are strategies which make the recognition of conjuncts considerably less arduous than might otherwise be the case. These strategies will now be explored.

4.3.2 Removal of the vertical stroke

A cursory glance at the Devanāgarī reveals that most of the letters representing consonants are typified by having a vertical stroke on the right-hand side of the body shape of the letter (where 'body shape' indicates the form of the letter without the horizontal top line). This vertical stroke provides the means for the first and most extensively used strategy in the formation of conjuncts. Quite simply, if the first element in a conjunct contains a vertical right-hand stroke, this is removed and the remaining strokes of the body shape of the letter are merged with the following element. Occasionally, when the following consonant also contains a vertical stroke, the vertical stroke of that letter is adopted by the body shape of the previous element. This results in the second element within the resulting conjunct being in some way displaced. Consider the following examples:

न् **n** + त **ta** = न्त **nta** e.g वेदान्त **vedānta** (*end of the Vedas*)

ख् **kh** + य **ya** = ख्य **khya** e.g. ख्यात **khyāta** (*named*)

(All examples of conjuncts will include the inherent vowel **a** at the end, so that the conjunct can be articulated. Removing the inherent vowel would require the final element of the conjunct to be marked with a virāma.)

With **nta** and **khya**, there is no displacement of the second element (**-t** and **-y**, respectively), which keeps its shape intact. Note, however, the following conjunct, where the second element (**-n**) is displaced and, in the process, the horizontal stroke in the body shape of the letter dips by 45°:

ग् **g** + न **na** = ग्न **gna** (Often confused with ग्र **gr**)

From the outset of investigating conjunct forms, it is important to note that variation exists according to the Devanāgarī font selected by an author. In fairness, this is not a modern phenomenon, given the great variation in conjuncts in the Sanskrit manuscript tradition. It seems quite fitting that computer fonts should mimic the situation as it has always been with respect to the writing of Sanskrit (see 4.4.2 for more on font variation). The conjunct **gna** appears in the Mangal font as the following:

ग्न **gna**

With the Mangal font, it is evident that the strategy is much more in keeping with the examples for **nta** and **khya**, where the first element merely forfeits its right-hand vertical stroke. By contrast, it could said that the other font (Sanskrit Text) generates a conjunct in which elements are subject to a stacking strategy. Such a strategy certainly exists and it is to this that the discussion now turns.

4.3.3 Stacking

The removal of the vertical stroke in letters containing a vertical stroke is the main strategy in conjunct formation. This is to be expected, given that twenty-two out of the thirty-three eligible letters are accommodated, where they constitute the first element of a conjunct. There are eleven letters, as follows, where such a strategy is not available:

Velar:	**k, ṅ, h**
Palatal:	**ch**
Cerebral:	**ṭ, ṭh, ḍ, ḍh, r**
Dental:	**d**
Labial:	**ph**

(Note that the aspirate **h** and the semivowel **r** are given in terms of their place of articulation and that there are no sibilants involved.)

Where one of these eleven letters constitutes the first element of a conjunct, the strategy adopted by the Devanāgarī is to stack them on top of the following element within the conjunct. Although not invariably the case, such a strategy results in the second element losing part of the shape it possesses when written separately. The loss can involve the top line (as in the conjunct **ṅga**) additionally involve a 45° anticlockwise rotation (as with **ddha**) or take the form of the removal of part of the body shape of the second element (**hma**).

ङ् **ṅ** + ग **ga** = ङ्ग **ṅga** e.g. गङ्गा **gaṅgā** (*the Ganges*)
द् **d** + ध **dha** = द्ध **ddha** e.g. बुद्ध **buddha** (*the Buddha*)
ह् **h** + म **ma** = ह्म **hma** e.g. ब्राह्मण **brāhmaṇa** (*a Brahman*)

From the foregoing examples, it can be noted that the first and second elements do not allow for a space to be left between them. This a point worth noting. Despite what certain fonts might indicate, conjuncts require the shapes of the letters involved to be in contact with each other. Otherwise said, the elements must touch.

Conjuncts can be very subtle in their representation. With **ṅga**, one sees the base of the letter **ṅa**, albeit not flat, standing in place of the top line which would be a feature of the letter **ga**. With **ddha**, the letter **da** lends its tail to **dha**, which then treats it as if it were its vertical right-hand stroke, rotated. The conjunct **hma** involves neither of these things but, instead, sees the loop of the body shape for **ha** acting like a tendril and attaching itself to the square body shape of the letter **ma**, which loses the left-hand vertical stroke in the process. The word **brāhmaṇa** contains two conjuncts: **hma**, as already seen, and **bra**. Conjuncts involving the semivowel **r** have unique forms that are both simple and regular.

4.3.4 Conjuncts involving r

As with the other consonants, the Devanāgarī letter **ra** represents a syllable (i.e. **r** plus the inherent vowel **a**) unless virāma is added to it, removing the inherent vowel and reducing the syllable down to the bare phoneme, **r**. This phoneme is extremely prevalent in conjunct formation and possesses its own strategy. Effectively, it takes one of two signs, according to whether it is the first element in a conjunct (**r-**) or the second or subsequent element (**-r**).

When **r** is the first element in a conjunct, it takes the form of a semicircular loop above the top line of the letter of the second element. Remember that conjuncts are read from top to bottom when they are stacked, so the placing of the loop in this fashion is completely consistent with this principle. It is important to note that, where the letter following **r** has a right-hand vertical stroke, the loop is positioned directly above this.

र् **r** + ग **ga** = र्ग **rga**

There is one complicating factor in this process, and it is one which causes difficulties to the majority of learners as regards learning to read with confidence. The loop will occupy a vertical line that stands on its own in preference to one which forms the body shape of a letter. In other words, it will more readily attach to the medial form of the long vowel **ā**, if such an option presents itself. The loop can be displaced quite far to the right of the word, causing the reader to fail to pronounce **r** at the proper time.

मार्गाः **mārgāḥ** (*roads*)

(This is not pronounced ***māgrāḥ**, since that would involve a conjunct in which **-r** were the second element, for which the loop is not used.)

The displacement of the loop to the right can be considerable, such is the fondness which **r-** displays for occupying a vertical stroke.

कार्त्स्न्य **kārtsnya** (*entirety*)

When there is no vertical stroke following **r-**, the loop has no choice but to settle over the letter it precedes.

मर्द **marda** (*friction*)

By contrast with the strategy employed by **r-**, **-r** (where **r** constitutes the second element in a conjunct) is much more straightforward. In this instance, **-r** takes the form of a diagonal line added to the first element, at its base. Where the body shape of the preceding letter has a vertical stroke, the diagonal line attaches itself to it.

ग् **g** + र **ra** = ग्र **gra**

क् **k** + र **ra** = क्र **kra**

In cases where the letter preceding **-r** does not contain a vertical stroke, a pseudo-vertical stroke is provided, but rotated through 45°. This results in what resembles an upside-down ‘v’ at the base of the preceding letter.

ट् **ṭ** + र **ra** = ट्र **ṭra**

छ् **ch** + र **ra** = छ्र **chra**

द् **d** + र **ra** = द्र **dra**

(The letter **da** has a tail which may appear either as a curl or as a straight line, depending on handwriting or the choice of font. In either event, it is straightened to accommodate the conjunct sign for **-r**.)

There are two conjuncts involving **-r**, namely **hra** and **śra**, that are worth a separate mention. Although the letter **ha** does not possess a vertical stroke, it attracts the same conjunct sign for **-r** as if it did. Also, the conjunct **śra**, despite possessing a vertical stroke, does not simply add the conjunct sign for **-r** to the body shape of the letter **śa**.

ह् **h** + र **ra** = ह्र **hra**

श् **ś** + र **ra** = श्र **śra**

With **śra**, the body shape of the letter **ś** undergoes a radical change, where the left-hand stroke (and the top line above it) is reduced to what resembles a ribbon. This is a reminder that, like **ra**, other letter shapes can also become modified in forming conjuncts, to the extent that they become distinct in form.

4.3.5 Unique forms

In 4.3.2 and 4.3.3, the main conjunct strategies were explored. In 4.3.4, it was demonstrated that the letter **ra** undergoes a transformation according to whether the phoneme **r** is the first element within a conjunct or the second (or subsequent) element. Further, 4.3.4 identified the letter **śa** as having a distinctive form when it was the first element in the conjunct **śra**. The reader will be pleased to know that the major conjunct strategies described, together with those used by **r**, account for the overwhelming number of conjuncts encountered in the Devanāgarī. The conjunct **śra** may have appeared to add an unwelcome complication to matters, but it should be noted that **śa**, unlike **ra**, reserves its transformation to when it is the first element of a conjunct – and even then, the transformation in question does not always occur. Where it is the second element of a conjunct (which is rare), it retains its body shape.

श् **ś** + र **ra** = श्र **śra** (with transformation)

श् **ś** + व **va** = श्व **śva** (with transformation)

श् **ś** + म **ma** = श्म **śma** (without transformation)

श् **ś** + य **ya** = श्य **śya** (without transformation)

ञ् **ñ** + श **śa** = ञ्श **ñśa** (with **ś** as second element)

There are a number of conjunct forms which are unique and have simply to be learnt as they are encountered. These unique forms may not account for more than about one in twenty of all conjuncts, but some are extremely frequent. Great care should, therefore, be taken from the outset of one's study of Sanskrit to learn them as they appear in a text. Whilst most textbooks aimed at the learner use virāma to simplify the process of reading the Devanāgarī, which is useful and serves a purpose, the unique forms cannot be derived through an application of the strategies discussed. They do not follow any identifiable strategy. On the following page, some of the most common unique conjuncts are given. It is, however, merely an introduction to unique conjunct forms, the recognition of which must form part of ongoing study.

It is not uncommon, when starting to read Sanskrit, to come across conjunct forms which appear to differ from those printed in a textbook with which one may have become familiar. The difference is a consequence of font selection and the learner needs to be aware of this (see 4.4.2). There is no 'right or wrong' conjunct form, where legitimate differences (i.e. variant forms) exist, as the following examples illustrate:

क् **k** + त **ta** = क्त **kta** e.g. भक्ति **bhakti** (*devotion*)

क् **k** + त **ta** = क्‍त **kta** e.g. भक्‍ति **bhakti**

As regards the two ways of representing the conjunct **kta** in **bhakti**, it is important to note that the first example contains a unique form, which is to say that it is not the product of the removal of the vertical stroke or of a stacking strategy. For that matter, the second example neither removes a vertical stroke (**ka** does not have a right-hand vertical stroke to remove), nor does it adopt a stacking strategy, yet the body shapes of **ka** and **ta** remain clearly discernible. Both examples are licit. The same is not, however, true with the conjunct **kṣa**, for which there is only one licit form.

क् **k** + ष **ṣa** = क्ष **kṣa** e.g. मोक्ष **mokṣa** (*liberation*)

Here, the option does not exist to clip the right-hand stroke of **ka** and to attach the modified body shape to the left of the following letter.

There are four further unique forms which the learner is strongly advised to memorize alongside the basic forms of the Devanāgarī, given that they are not subject to an analysis according to the strategies investigated. These conjunct forms have a high frequency:

ज् **j** + ञ **ña** = ज्ञ **jña** e.g. ज्ञान **jñāna** (*knowledge; thinking*)

द् **d** + य **ya** = द्य **dya** e.g. विद्या **vidyā** (*knowledge; learning*)

त् **t** + त **ta** = त्त **tta** e.g. चित्त **citta** (*noticed*)

(Contrast this with क्त **kta**, with which it is easily confused)

त् **t** + र **ra** = त्र **tra** e.g. कुत्र **kutra** (*where?)*

(Contrast this with न्न **nna**, with which it is easily confused)

4.3.6 Multiple conjuncts

Conjuncts are not restricted to two elements but may contain three or four. Words containing three conjunct elements are by no means rare, although four-element conjuncts are substantially less common. The maximum number of conjunct elements in a word is five – but such a thing is extremely rare. The forms which these conjuncts take are not any more complex than those present in the two-element conjuncts. Quite simply, a multiple conjunct works in precisely the same way as a two-element conjunct as regards the strategies employed in its formation.

With three-element conjuncts, the first and second elements generate the same form as the two-element conjunct. The second element, in turn, joins with the third in precisely the same manner as one would expect with a two-element conjunct.

त् **t** + स् **s** = त्स् **ts** + न **na** = त्स्न **tsna**

With **tsna**, the process of creating the conjunct is straightforward. The letter **ta** possesses a right-hand vertical stroke which is removed, with the remaining body shape merging with that of the letter **sa**. The letter **sa** also possesses a right-hand vertical stroke, and this is similarly removed when it conjoins with **na**. In the example given, the horizontal stroke of the body shape of **na** rotates anticlockwise by 45°. Such a phenomenon has already been encountered. The conjunct exhibits minimal difference with font variation (The font in the example which follows is Mangal).

त् **t** + स् **s** = त्स् **ts** + न **na** = त्स्न **tsna**

Conjunct forms which adopt the strategy of stacking continue to do so in multiple conjuncts, as is evident in the following example (Note the rotation of the **va** by 45°, using the tail of **da** as a pseudo-vertical stroke).

द् **d** + ध् **dh** = द्ध् **ddh** + व **va** = द्ध्व **ddhva**

Not all fonts are currently capable of generating three-element conjuncts. In such cases, virāma is deployed (The font is Nirmala).

द् **d** + ध् **dh** = द्ध् **ddh** + व **va** = द्‌ध्व **ddhva**

As regards unique conjunct forms, these too are represented in multiple conjuncts in precisely the same way as with two-element conjuncts, as the following example illustrates:

क् **k** + त् **t** = क्त् **kt** + व **va** = क्त्व **ktva**

As explained in 4.3.5, where a variant exists for a two-element conjunct, that is the form which will be represented in a multiple conjunct (The font is Nirmala).

क् **k** + त् **t** = क्त् **kt** + व **va** = क्त्व **ktva**

Four-element conjuncts act no differently to three-element conjuncts in terms of the procedure followed. The first element joins with the second, producing the relevant conjunct; the second element then joins with the third, and so forth. The only difficulty likely to be encountered by the learner is when a unique form occurs between the second and third elements, or between the third and fourth. The approach here is to bear in mind that unique forms will be produced wherever the letters that generate them occur in the relevant sequence. In the following example, the first and second elements (**ṅ** + **k**) create a conjunct form which then undergoes subsequent transformation, since the second and third elements (**k** + **ṣ**) generate a unique form:

ङ् **ṅ** + क् **k** = ङ्क् **ṅk** + ष् **ṣ** = ङ्क्ष् **ṅkṣ** + व **va** = ङ्क्ष्व **ṅkṣva**

Finally, we come to a five-element conjunct which, whilst alarming as a concept, is remarkably straightforward in design. It is unsurprising that the conjunct in question contains a semivowel (two, in fact), since that is something which one may regularly expect with conjuncts at the point where more than three elements are involved. Sanskrit does not favour complex clusters any more than English does. In the word **kārtsnya** (*totality; entirety*), there is a cluster comprising three elements (**-tsn-**) surrounded by two semivowels (**r-**; **-y**).

र् **r** + त् **t** + स् **s** + न् **n** + य **ya** = र्त्स्न्य **rtsnya**

All the consonants contain right-hand vertical strokes and accord with the strategy in 4.3.2. As for the phoneme **r-**, it is the first element in the conjunct and has the form as discussed in 4.3.4, over a vertical stroke.

4.4 Variant forms

4.4.1 Orthographic variants

Before returning to the issue of variation within the Devanāgarī, according to the font used, it is worth looking at letter shapes frequently encountered in Sanskrit texts. These letter shapes are occasionally referred to as 'older forms' and, certainly, they are the forms which appear in Sanskrit manuscripts. Some textbooks use the forms in question, although those which do are increasingly in the minority. These forms are worth learning from the outset, to be saved a surprise when coming across them at a subsequent point in one's study of Sanskrit.

The short **a** has a more intricate shape in the older form (OF) than the one employed by the Sanskrit Text font (ST). In essence, it rather resembles the letter **pa**, with three strokes attached to the left-hand side of the body shape. If a text uses this form of the letter **a**, it follows that the initial forms for **ā**, **o** and **au** also contain the form in question. In addition to initial **a**, **ā**, **o** and **au**, there are also two consonants, **jha** and **ṇa**, possessing older forms. It is a moot point as to whether **ṛ** and **ṝ** have older forms or whether the differences, as they appear in certain texts, are merely an example of font variation. In any event, being able to recognize the Devanāgarī letters for those vowels in the font used in the present work allows the reader to identify the variant forms for **ṛ** and **ṝ**. On that basis, the orthographic variants for **ṛ** and **ṝ** are not illustrated.

OF	ST	IAST
अ	अ	**a**

OF	ST	IAST
झ	झ	**jha**

OF	ST	IAST
ण	ण	**ṇa**

4.4.2 Font variation

There are many fonts available for the Devanāgarī. Two of these (Mangal and Nirmala) appeared in 4.3.6. In principle, a good grasp of the Devanāgarī gained in one font ought to suffice with respect to helping the eye adjust to reading other fonts. Those who learn English, whose first language does not use the Roman alphabet, are faced with a considerable number of variant forms, as the following indicates with just two letters (The names of the fonts are given in brackets).

a (Viner Hand) *a (Script MS)* a (Calibri)

g (Viner Hand) *g (Script MS)* g (Calibri)

It is unsurprising, given the examples from the Roman alphabet, that there is variation between fonts available for the Devanāgarī. The variation is considerably reduced when one considers that the Devanāgarī does not have the distinction, unlike the Roman alphabet, of uppercase and lowercase letters (It is worth noting that Latin did not originally possess such a distinction – as was the case with ancient Greek also). That said, font variation in the Devanāgarī can become slightly problematic where conjuncts are concerned. As can be seen with the following examples, conjunct formation strategies can vary according to the font used. Note how both Mangal and Aparajita opt for the removal of the vertical stroke of the first conjunct element whilst Sanskrit Text uses the stacking strategy:

Mangal	Sanskrit Text	IAST
न्न	न्न	**nna**

Aparajita	Sanskrit Text	IAST
ष्ठ	ष्ठ	**ṣṭha**

Given that the learner of Sanskrit is increasingly more likely to want to type Sanskrit than to write it, helped by the existence of the requisite software, it pays to think carefully about font selection. Nirmala appears to be popular and it is certainly less ornate than some other fonts, although it represents conjuncts as they appear in Hindi rather than Sanskrit: the stacking strategy is avoided in favour of one which places the conjunct elements side by side, even where the body shape of the letter for the first element does not have a final right-hand vertical stroke or where a unique form is attested in the Devanāgarī.

Nirmala	Sanskrit Text	IAST
क्क	क्क	**kka**

Nirmala	Sanskrit Text	IAST
क्त	क्त	**kta**

The choice of font is entirely up to the student, who is free to choose whichever font represents the easiest way to distinguish the basic letter shapes of the Devanāgarī. In 4.4.3, various fonts are demonstrated. This ought to be sufficient to allow the learner to decide which font is the most suitable. Fonts such as Aparajita are ornate and move away from anything resembling Devanāgarī in its written form. For that point alone, the learner is advised to refrain from making Aparajita the font of choice.

In selecting a font, it is important to consider that much of the printed material for Sanskrit texts, especially if it comes from India, is highly unlikely to use a font resembling Aparajita or Mangal. Both are indicative of fonts used for Hindi in newspapers, advertisements, shop signs and banners. Most of the Sanskrit literature printed by India's most prominent provider of such, Motilal Banarsidass, uses not only the older forms illustrated in 4.4.1 but a font which closely resembles Sanskrit Text. From that perspective, making Sanskrit Text one's 'go to' font has considerable merit.

4.4.3 Sample text in various fonts

The learner is encouraged to accustom the eye to differences that exist between some of the more frequently used Devanāgarī fonts and to put into practice the ability to identify the Devanāgarī letters, including conjunct forms. The IAST version accompanies a text in various fonts, allowing the learner to match the Devanāgarī to its transliteration.

The Sanskrit text is the opening verse of the Bhagavadgītā, in which Dhṛtarāṣṭra, head of the Kaurava clan, addresses his minister, Saṃjaya. Dhṛtarāṣṭra asks Saṃjaya to describe the field of combat on which the armies of the Kauravas and the Pāṇḍavas are assembling on the eve of war. This is the great war which forms the basis of the Indian epic, the Mahābhārata (A translation of the verse is given in 9.3.1).

Sanskrit Text

धर्मक्षेत्रे कुरुक्षेत्रे समवेता युयुत्सवः ।
मामकाः पाण्डवाश्चैव किमकुर्वत संजय ॥

Nirmala

धर्मक्षेत्रे कुरुक्षेत्रे समवेता युयुत्सवः ।
मामकाः पाण्डवाश्चैव किमकुर्वत संजय ॥

Mangal

धर्मक्षेत्रे कुरुक्षेत्रे समवेता युयुत्सवः ।
मामकाः पाण्डवाश्चैव किमकुर्वत संजय ॥

Aparajita

धर्मक्षेत्रे कुरुक्षेत्रे समवेता युयुत्सवः ।
मामकाः पाण्डवाश्चैव किमकुर्वत संजय ॥

IAST

dharmakṣetre kurukṣetre samavetā yuyutsavaḥ
māmakāḥ pāṇḍavāś|caiva[1] kim|akurvata[2] saṃjaya

Notes

1 What appears to be one word in the Devanāgarī is actually a combination of three: **pāṇḍavāḥ** + **ca** + **eva**. The visarga (**ḥ**), when followed by **c**, transforms to **ś**. This is a part of a regular process known as visarga sandhi, which will be investigated in 8.2. Since **ś** and **c** are then in contact, with no intervening vowel, a conjunct is produced. The conjunct causes **pāṇḍavāś** + **ca** to be written together (Remember that virāma can only legitimately be deployed right at the end of a sentence). Further, the words **ca** + **eva** cannot be placed together, since ***ae** is not a diphthong recognized in Sanskrit. Here, vowel sandhi is applied, replacing the impermissible ***ae** with a diphthong that is permitted: **ai** (see 8.4).

2 Bearing in mind that the Devanāgarī does not permit the use of virāma unless at the end of a sentence, the upshot is that a word which ends with **m** will be subject to one or other of the following: (i) if followed by a consonant, it will become anusvāra (see 3.5.1); (ii) if followed by a vowel, the vowel in question will take the medial form and the two words will then be written together (see 4.2.2). The latter situation occurs with **kim** + **akurvata**. Remember that short **a** does not have a medial form.

There is agreement, in all four Devanāgarī fonts, as to the unique conjunct form for **kṣa**. In addition, the strategies for conjuncts involving **r-** (**dharmakṣetre**; **akurvata**) and **-r** (**dharmakṣetre**; **kurukṣetre**) are also consistent across fonts. Furthermore, the conjuncts **ts** (**yuyutsavaḥ**) and **ṇḍ** (**pāṇḍavāś**) show no differences in terms of strategy, although the elements **t-** and **-s** are not in actual contact with each other in Mangal and Aparajita. Look carefully, however, at the conjunct **śc** (**pāṇḍavāśca**). Here, Sanskrit Text, Nirmala and Aparajita adopt the stacking strategy, whilst Mangal places the letter **ś** to the left of **ca** rather than above it. In Mangal, the **ś** does not have the special, ribbon-like form it often has when it is the initial element of a conjunct. The right-hand vertical stroke of **ś** has been removed, pure and simple. This strategy is perfectly licit, in that other conjunct forms allow for the removal of the right-hand vertical stroke of **ś**, as seen with **śma** and **śya** in 4.3.5.

4.4.4 Other writing systems

There are many writing systems in India – many more than is the case in Europe, where the overwhelming majority of languages are written in the Roman alphabet. Diacritical marks are easily added to the letters of the Roman alphabet to indicate sounds specific to a given language and for which a basic letter shape is not deemed sufficient. French, for example, regularly employs three diacritical marks over the letter 'e' (**è**, **é**, **ê**) and possesses a much rarer fourth (**ë**, as in *Citroën*). For certain languages of Eastern Europe, the Cyrillic script is (or has been) used. This is the script generally associated with Russian. There is only one language that uses neither the Roman alphabet nor Cyrillic: Greek.

The proliferation of different scripts in India is notably different to the situation in Europe. This is in no small part because the printing press came late to South Asia. It was established by the British in the 1780s, in Calcutta, and intended for English. One has, however, to consider the other forces at work which delayed widespread literacy and its associated practices. Sanskrit occupied a position of cultural preeminence amongst the Hindu population, and the language tradition was heavily identified with Brahmins amongst whom oral transmission was the norm. Also, the dominant power in South Asia, until the British challenged it, was the Moghul Empire. For Moghul rulers, literacy practices tended strongly to favour Persian, where manuscript traditions prevailed.

Notwithstanding the dominance of Sanskrit, Persian and English during the early modern period, there nevertheless existed a literacy tradition amongst the vernacular languages of India (The Tamil tradition, in the south of India, is one such example and an ancient one). In the north of India, the Bhakti movement had provided a strong incentive for the writing of vernacular languages, in sharp distinction to the oracy practices of Sanskrit, on the one hand, and the high culture which found expression in manuscripts written in a non-Indian language, on the other. Vernacular languages were not in any meaningful sense subject to the type of prescriptivism associated with language planning. These languages were left to develop organically, and a diversity in both language and script was the natural outcome. In the following, a small sample is given of five phonemes as they appear in the chief writing systems of contemporary North India. A comparison with the Devanāgarī is useful, since it sheds light on how Devanāgarī letters can be formed.

Other writing systems

Devanāgarī	Panjabi	Gujarati	Oriya	Bengali
ग	ਗ	ગ	ଗ	গ
ga				

Devanāgarī	Panjabi	Gujarati	Oriya	Bengali
थ	ਥ	થ	ଥ	থ
tha				

Devanāgarī	Panjabi	Gujarati	Oriya	Bengali
न	ਨ	ન	ନ	ন
na				

Devanāgarī	Panjabi	Gujarati	Oriya	Bengali
य	ਯ	ય	ଯ	য
ya				

Devanāgarī	Panjabi	Gujarati	Oriya	Bengali
ल	ਲ	લ	ଲ	ল
la				

Note

The Devanāgarī writing system is one amongst many in India. The other major writing systems of northern India are those associated with Panjabi, Gujarati, Oriya, Bengali, Assamese and Urdu – all official languages, as per the Indian Constitution. Bengali and Assamese share the same writing system. Urdu is distinct in that it is not descended from Brāhmī but uses the Perso-Arabic script.

4.5 Writing the Devanāgarī

Most textbooks on Sanskrit begin by introducing the Devanāgarī from the first chapter or lesson, having dedicated a few pages in the preliminary chapters to letter formation. Whilst this has the virtue of obliging the learner to work on Sanskrit in the Devanāgarī, it can take learners a number of months to adjust fully to the writing system. The result is that lessons can, for many, be extremely challenging, in that the learner is faced with a grammatically complex language presented in a script which has yet to fall into place. Conjuncts frustrate matters, leaving some learners with the overriding sensation that Sanskrit is simply beyond them, at which point they disengage with their study of the language.

Letter formation is important for those who intend to write Sanskrit manually, although it is increasingly the case that learners seek out the requisite software which allows them to generate the Devanāgarī electronically. On the basis that it is useful to be able to practise the Devanāgarī by hand, a few pages will be devoted to illustrating how the letters are formed. As with the writing of any script, it is important not to be overly prescriptive. There are only a couple of principles to remember, when writing the Devanāgarī. Once these have been accepted, whatever strategy the learner employs to form the letters is acceptable. The key point is to make the letters distinct, where similarities exist, so that ambiguity does not arise.

Some of the other major writing systems for the Indic languages, particularly Gujarati, offer insights into letter formation. Gujarati script differs from the Devanāgarī in one crucial aspect: it does not possess the horizontal top line, the **mātrā** (*measure*), which is a hallmark of the Devanāgarī. In essence, the Gujarati script is derived from the writing practices of merchants who devised a script which could be written hastily. A glance at the Devanāgarī and Gujarati letters for **ga** shows that the Devanāgarī has two vertical strokes hanging down from the mātrā, whereas Gujarati has two strokes and no mātrā. In the Gujarati letter, the left-hand shape, resembling a semicircle, is written first. One goes from top to bottom, clockwise. Having formed the first element, the right-hand element is then added. This is precisely the case with the Devanāgarī, which then completes the letter by adding the mātrā, from left to right. These are the guiding principles in writing the Devanāgarī: top to bottom, left to right, with the mātrā written as the final stroke.

The principles of letter formation can be explored very easily by looking at the letters for consonants in the first two series (velar and palatal). These contain all the information necessary to write the other consonants, semivowels, sibilants and vowels. The principles apply in all cases. The first letter in the velar series represents the syllable **ka**, which requires four strokes (With the exception of initial **ā**, **ṛ**, **ṝ** and **o**, all the Devanāgarī letters are formed by three, four or five strokes). The letter **ka** is a good model with which to explore the principles in question.

The letter **ka** is formed by the following four strokes, in sequence: (i) the leftmost element of the body shape of the letter, formed anticlockwise; (ii) the middle element of the body shape, from top to bottom; (iii) the right-hand element of the body shape, from left to right (where the pen does not have to be lifted after the second stroke but can travel upwards to the middle of the letter and across to the right); (iv) the mātrā, written from left to right.

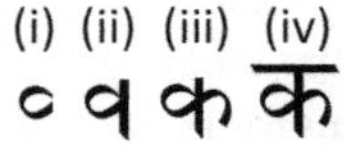

If we look at the first series of consonants (the velars), bearing in mind the principles applied with the formation of **ka**, letter formation becomes straightforward (The formation is given from top to bottom rather than, as with the example of **ka**, left to right, almost by way of reinforcing the principles underlying letter formation).

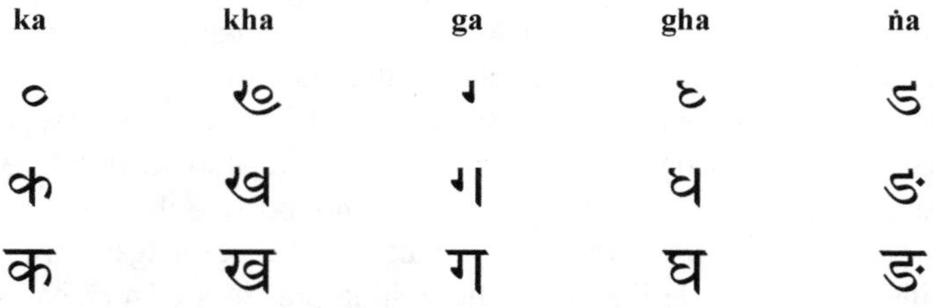

As noted earlier, the letter **ga** is formed with three strokes, as opposed to the four needed for **ka** (and indeed **gha** and **ṅa**). That said, the formation of the velars can be shown in three phases: the initial stroke or strokes – proceeding always from left to right – terminating with the mātrā, similarly written from left to right. Note that, with **kha**, there is a sickle shape to the left of the circle which one finds in **ka**. Since that is the leftmost element, it is written first. As for **ṅa**, there is a dot to the right of the body shape of the letter. This is written <u>after</u> the body shape and <u>before</u> the mātrā.

The same principles of letter formation are applied to consonants from the second series (the palatals). The leftmost element is written first, followed by the vertical stroke – preceded, in the case of **jha** and **ña**, by a connecting stroke. The mātrā is written last. The only letter which merits special attention is **cha**, where there is no vertical stroke in the letter but, instead, a short neck above the loop of the body shape. This is added <u>after</u> the body shape and <u>before</u> the mātrā.

ca	**cha**	**ja**	**jha**	**ña**

If the learner can keep in mind the principles demonstrated, there is no letter for which formation remains unclear. The dentals **ta** and **na** occasionally elicit questions, in that the leftmost element in the body shapes of these letters requires a stroke which travels upwards. This is true but one may, with both **ta** and **na**, give priority to the principle of proceeding from top to bottom (with the exception, naturally, of the mātrā, which must remain the final stroke). If that is the strategy preferred by the learner, the starting point in letter formation is the centre of the body shape, going from right to left to form the 'leg' of the **ta** or the notched horizontal line of the **na**, and proceeding from top to bottom in the process. Practice makes perfect and the point is perhaps best iterated that a prescriptive approach to the formation of the letters of the Devanāgarī serves no purpose at all.

4.6 Exercises

4.6.1 Identify the consonant

The reader may now consolidate the current chapter by attempting two exercises. The first exercise relates to the consonants identified in 3.2, since the knowledge of the first twenty-five consonants involves, aside from the ability to pronounce them, an awareness of whether they are voiced or voiceless, aspirated or unaspirated (This is relevant to Chapter 8, where sound changes are explored). The answers are given on the same page, for convenience's sake.

Questions

Identify the following consonants according to their description.

Labial – V, +A	Velar – V, -A	Dental +V, +A	Palatal Nasal	Cerebral +V, +A
Labial Nasal	Cerebral – V, -A	Dental Nasal	Palatal – V, +A	Velar Nasal
Labial +V, -A	Palatal – V, -A	Labial +V, +A	Cerebral – V, +A	Velar +V, +A
Velar – V, +A	Palatal +V, +A	Dental – V, -A	Labial – V, -A	Cerebral +V, -A
Velar +V, -A	Dental +V, -A	Cerebral Nasal	Palatal +V, -A	Dental – V, +A

Answers

Labial – V, +A फ **pha**	Velar – V, -A क **ka**	Dental +V, +A ध **dha**	Palatal Nasal ञ **ña**	Cerebral +V, +A ढ **ḍha**
Labial Nasal म **ma**	Cerebral – V, -A ट **ṭa**	Dental Nasal न **na**	Palatal – V, +A छ **cha**	Velar Nasal ङ **ṅa**
Labial +V, -A ब **ba**	Palatal – V, -A च **ca**	Labial +V, +A भ **bha**	Cerebral – V, +A ठ **ṭha**	Velar +V, +A घ **gha**
Velar – V, +A ख **kha**	Palatal +V, +A झ **jha**	Dental – V, -A त **ta**	Labial – V, -A प **pa**	Cerebral +V, -A ड **ḍa**
Velar +V, -A ग **ga**	Dental +V, -A द **da**	Cerebral Nasal ण **ṇa**	Palatal +V, -A ज **ja**	Dental – V, +A थ **tha**

4.6.2 Transliteration

A second exercise asks the reader to attempt transliteration from the Devanāgarī to the IAST. The ability to read both systems accurately is important, given that a good knowledge of the IAST indicates a good grasp of the sound system of Sanskrit. Until the time when one is fully able to read the Devanāgarī (and thereby dispense with the IAST), the IAST represents the best means of accessing information about the language. The answers are given on the following page.

Questions

Give the IAST for the following words:

(i) Words without conjuncts.

कनक
देव
नृप
मानुष
रामायण
ऋषि

(ii) Words with conjuncts.

वेदान्त
अश्व
ग्राम
मार्ग
मोक्ष
संस्कृत

Answers

(i) Words without conjuncts.

कनक	**kanaka** (*gold*)
देव	**deva** (*god*)
नृप	**nṛpa** (*king*)
मानुष	**mānuṣa** (*man*)
रामायण	**rāmāyaṇa** (*the Rāmāyaṇa*)
ऋषि	**ṛṣi** (*a sage; rishi*)

(i) Words with conjuncts.

वेदान्त	**vedānta** (*end of the Vedas*)
अश्व	**aśva** (*horse*)
ग्राम	**grāma** (*village*)
मार्ग	**mārga** (*road*)
मोक्ष	**mokṣa** (*liberation*)
संस्कृत	**saṃskṛta** (*Sanskrit*)

This exercise allows the reader to identify any revision requirements. See 4.2.2 if the revision involves the representation of the vowels and 4.3 if a reminder is needed as to conjunct formation. Note that the words **rāmāyaṇa**, **vedānta** and **saṃskṛta** have not been spelled with an initial capital letter. This accords with the more orthodox use of the IAST, in which capital letters are unnecessary and therefore avoided. It is a minor point, in that the capital letters do not affect the IAST one way or another.

Only once the reader is confident with the material covered up to this point is progression to Chapter 5 advised.

5

THE SANSKRIT WORD

5.1 Preliminaries

In this chapter, the aim is to assist the learner to migrate from the investigation of individual sounds and syllables to the exploration of complete words in Sanskrit. Although a few words were introduced in the previous chapters, this was by way of consolidating the ability to read them. The tactic is now to subject a short list of words to a greater analysis, looking at how they are formed as well as what they mean. The intention is to multitask by doing three things at once: building up a number of words that are likely to be encountered early in the study of Sanskrit (thereby beginning the process of acquiring vocabulary); exploring the primordial nature of the verbal root, which lies at the heart of the Sanskrit word; and teasing out information from the verbal root to see what may be deduced about the literal meaning of the words in question.

A Sanskrit text can often be subject to a baffling number of translations which appear to differ, one from the other, to the point where the reader begins to wonder which translation (if indeed any of them) comes close to capturing the original meaning. Sanskrit is subtle. It can embed layers of meaning into a single word which, to any translator, represents a challenge. It should always be borne in mind that Sanskrit is the product of an ancient culture. There are all too often multiple choices in rendering a Sanskrit word into English – but with each word failing to catch entirely the concept which the word embodies. The Italian expression *traduttore, traditore* comes to

DOI: 10.4324/9780429325434-6

mind: *translator, traitor*. In essence, translation from Sanskrit aims at an approximation in meaning but, if concepts in Sanskrit do not directly map onto these which may be expressed in the target language, something is invariably lost.

In the following pages, twelve words are investigated. Each of these are theoretically derived from a verbal root, of which more will be said in Chapter 7, which looks at the Sanskrit verb and at conjugation. The verbal root is indicated by an appropriate symbol (√). Each word is a noun and is given according to its citation form – the form in which it appears in a Sanskrit dictionary before any grammatical information has been added. The Sanskrit noun and its declension are dealt with in the following chapter. For now, it suffices to see how much information may be extracted from the Sanskrit word before grammar is even considered.

5.2 Analysis of words

(i) देव **deva** (√ **div**)

The word **deva** (god) is an easy one to read. It contains an initial consonant (**d**) above which the vowel **e** appears. This is nevertheless noteworthy in that it shows the assertion to be false that, when reading the Devanāgarī, one reads from the top to the bottom of a syllable. Doing so would result in the reading of the first syllable as ***ed**. The Devanāgarī syllable is correctly identified by reading the body shape of the letter and by looking to see if anything is added above the topline, below the body shape or to the right of it. The only exception to this is the short medial **i**, which is written before the consonant, semivowel or sibilant. **Deva** is derived from the verbal root **div** (*to shine; be bright*) and is cognate with the Latin *deus*, Italian *dio* and French *dieu*. English, borrowing heavily from Latin (often via French), has words such as *divine* and *divinity*, both of which can be connected with the word **deva**. Whereas the word for the singular God (or one of many gods, in a non-monotheistic belief system) may not bring to mind a shining or resplendent entity in other languages, it does so overtly in Sanskrit. A **deva** is a resplendent being.

Philologists have reconstructed the possible form and meaning of the word **deva** as it may have been uttered in the ancestor of the Indo-European languages (Sir William Jones's 'common source'). This reconstructed form, named 'Proto-Indo-European' (PIE), contains the root **dyew* (*sky; heaven*), suggesting that the concept of a shining, supernatural being was connected to the luminescence of the sky or to daylight. Latin sheds some light on this – no pun intended – in the word *diēs* (*day*). It is worth mentioning that the Latin *Iuppiter* (which appears in English as *Jupiter*), albeit borrowed into Latin from an earlier Italic language in which the dropping of initial *d-* was a feature, allows philologists to hypothesize that the name for the Father of the Gods, in the Roman pantheon, was Father of the Sky: **dyew patēr* (Note that variations in PIE reconstructions are almost as numerous as the researchers engaged in such an activity. Since reconstructed forms are not actually attested, in that PIE predates literary records, all forms are routinely given with a preceding asterisk). What the Sanskrit **deva** shows us is that the English words *divine*, *deity* and *day* are related, as are the Latin and Greek *Iuppiter* and *Zeus*, respectively, and that there is a clarity in Sanskrit with respect to its structure which permits such insights.

(ii) **कमल kamala (√ kam (?))**

The Sanskrit word **kamala** is one of a number of words for the lotus. Its symbolism is pervasive in Indic culture. It is a thing of beauty which grows from the mud and is, therefore, a most suitable symbol for the triumph of human consciousness, transcending both humble origins and the chores of everyday existence. Little wonder, then, that the lotus is a symbol associated strongly with the Buddha and with any number of devas within Hinduism, frequently portrayed as accompanied by the lotus or, indeed, rising from it. The noun **kamala** is neuter but, with the appropriate adjustment to the ending, a feminine noun can be created (see the following page and 6.1 as regards grammatical gender). **Kamalā** is not an uncommon name in India. It is an epithet for the goddess **Lakṣmī**.

It may be that the word **kamala** is derived from the verbal root **kam** (*to love; long for*), a possibility alluded to by Monier-Williams, in listing one of the meanings as *desirous, lustful*. This would be consistent with the reddish pink of the lotus, a colour associated with blushing or desire. If Monier-Williams is correct, it could be argued that **kamala** encodes the concept of worldly desire which the Buddha, being seated on a lotus, has transcended. That said, the exercise of searching for the etymology of a word must be taken with a pinch of salt. Etymology can be – and frequently is – subject to assumptions engrained in popular tradition but for which a linguistic analysis offers only a tentative suggestion. There are no PIE connections to speak of with the word **kamala**, which is but one of many words in Sanskrit for a lotus.

As regards the verbal root **kam**, it is found in several words within Sanskrit and is at the core of the word **kāma** (as in **Kāmasutra**, the ancient Indian treatise on love-making). It is to be noted that the word **kāma** is a noun (*sensuality; desire*) and that the vowel in the verbal root has been mutated in the creation of the noun (**kam → kāma**). This is a common feature in Sanskrit, as can be seen in the word **vāda** (*a saying; speech*) from √ **vad**. In this manner, a considerable number of nouns may be derived from the same verbal root. The mutation of the root vowel is not always obvious, requiring the learner to investigate and to be familiar with a phenomenon referred to as 'vowel mutation', 'vowel gradation', 'vowel strengthening' or **guṇa** and **vṛddhi**. This phenomenon is further explored in Chapter 7, since it is crucial in the derivation of a stem from a verbal root, which is the first step in conjugation.

(iii) **विद्या vidyā** (√ **vid**)

The spelling of the word **vidyā** is considerably more complex than that of **kamala** in three respects: it contains the medial form of the vowel **i** which is exceptional in being written <u>before</u> the phoneme with which it forms a syllable; second, it contains a conjunct (**dya**) which falls into the category of being a unique form (as described in 4.3.5); and third, it contains the long vowel **ā**, where **kamala** only has the short **a**, not indicated by the Devanāgarī unless it is in word-initial position. The word **vidyā** is derived from the verbal root **vid** (*to know*), cognate with the German *wissen* (which has the same meaning) and glimpsed in the English expression *to be out of one's wits*. It is most likely cognate with Latin *vidēre* (*to see*), given that seeing appears to be closely linked with the concept of knowing. Consider, for example, how one may respond, in English, to a statement containing information: *'I see'* (i.e. certain information has been presented to me and I understand its significance). Care must be taken not to conflate **vid** (*to know*) with another verbal root which is spelled the same way and, consequently, is pronounced the same way in Sanskrit. That is the verbal root **vid** (*to be found; exist*). Sanskrit does not have many homophones – far fewer than other languages – but it is still the case that there are words which differ in meaning yet have the same pronunciation and spelling.

The existence of a final, long **ā** in the noun **vidyā** is ample proof that not all noun stems end in a short **a** (A noun stem is the form which a noun has before grammatical endings are applied. This is of prime consideration in the process of declension, investigated in Chapter 6). The words **deva** and **kamala** both end in a short **a**; but **deva** is referred to as a 'masculine short **-a** stem' and **kamala** as a 'neuter short **-a** stem'. Before approaching Chapter 6, it is worth drawing to the reader's attention that Sanskrit possesses grammatical gender. A noun is masculine (**deva**), neuter (**kamala**) or feminine (**vidyā**). Only feminine nouns end in **-ā** and **-ī**, although the situation is not as clear in cases where the stem ending is **-a**. Additionally, not all nouns end in **-a -ā**, or **-ī**. It is important for the Sanskrit student to approach the acquisition of vocabulary with gender in mind. All nouns must be learnt together with their gender. Whilst this is not an issue with **vidyā**, given that the long **-ā** identifies it as a feminine noun, short **-a** can indicate either a masculine or a neuter noun. Nouns are listed in the Index, along with their gender.

(iv) **रात्री** **rātrī** (√ **ram** (?))

The word **rātrī** is one of several Sanskrit words for *night* (Another, which occurs frequently and appears in the current work, is **niśā**). It is clearly not cognate with the English *night*, German *nacht* or Latin *nox* – all of these identifiable with the PIE reconstruction **nókʷts*. As with **kamala**, the verbal root is speculative. Monier-Williams's *Sanskrit-English Dictionary* suggests √ **ram** (*to rest*) as 'probable' rather than certain. Indeed, the learner of Sanskrit is urged to be cautious with respect to assuming that all nouns may be derived from verbal roots. The Sanskrit grammatical tradition demonstrates an exceptional acuity as regards ascribing nouns to verbal roots, but that is not to say that all nouns can be so derived or, indeed, that the Sanskrit grammatical tradition claims this to be the case. Whatever the origin of the word **rātrī**, the important point to note (as with **kamala**) is that Sanskrit has more than one word for a phenomenon where English, or any number of other languages, might simply have one. It comes as no surprise, therefore, that Sanskrit vocabulary is extensive. With **rātrī**, it should be noted that the Devanāgarī contains the medial form of long **ā** (as does **vidyā**) and the medial form of long **ī**, which differs from the short **i** of **vidyā**. There is also a conjunct (**tra**), which is similar in form to the conjunct **nna** (see the final example given in 4.3.5).

(v) **अग्नि** **agni** (√ **ag** (?))

The word **agni** equates with the English *fire* and is cognate with Latin *ignis* (Note the English words *ignite*; *ignition*). Although contested, it is possible that it is derived from √ **ag** (*to move tortuously*) which would mean that the root captures the concept of movement rather than the heating or burning qualities of fire. Such speculation is possible because Sanskrit preserved, as has been noted, a list of the verbal elements from which a large element of the language was deemed to be comprised. This list, the **Dhātupāṭha**, was transmitted orally, along with the structural outline and rules of the language. It formed an integral part of a grammatical tradition of considerable antiquity which culminated in **Pāṇini**, the author of the world's first known systematic grammar. Whilst Pāṇini's dates are subject to much speculation, a suggestion as to the period 500–350 BCE is in order. The precise origin of the Dhātupāṭha has not been established. It is often ascribed to Pāṇini himself, although it seems more plausible that the concept of verbal roots predates Pāṇini, as a result of the assiduous attention paid to the language of Vedic ritual practice.

The word **agni** offers an insight into how there is not always agreement within the Sanskritic tradition as to verbal roots. In antiquity, √ **aj** (*to drive; propel*) was proposed as the verbal root; this is indeed possible but appears less plausible. Such a proposal would certainly suggest a cognate with Latin *agere* (*to drive; act*), yet this would move even further away from describing fire in terms either of its action or its qualities. Another proposal suggests **agri**. As mentioned in Monier-Williams, **agri** was created to explain the etymology of **agni** and is not a serious contender. Whatever the verbal root of **agni**, be it √ **ag** or √ **aj**, it is an important word in the **Ṛgveda**, the oldest literary work of ancient India. There, it is the name of a deity which, along with **Indra** and **Soma**, belongs to the early belief system of the people which history and tradition have termed 'Aryan' (in Sanskrit, **ārya**).

As regards spelling, **agni** contains the initial form of **a** and the medial form of **i**, seen in **vidyā**). It is worth noting that medial **i** is written immediately before the conjunct. It does <u>not</u> split the conjunct by inserting itself between the elements comprising it. It is also worth noting that the conjunct **gna** bears a striking resemblance to the conjunct **gra**. Care must be taken not to conflate the forms.

ग्न **gna** ग्र **gra**

(vi) गुरु **guru** (√ **gṝ**)

The association in meaning between a verbal root and a noun derived from it may not always be evident. This is the case with **guru** (*teacher;*

preceptor). The verbal root is √ **gṝ** (*to make known; teach*), yet the word **guru** defines someone who has substance or a thing which is weighty (In Sanskrit, a long syllable is termed **guru**, for example, and a short syllable is **laghu**: *light*). The notion of weightiness is a far cry from the concept of teaching – unless one assumes that the act of teaching involves the imparting of information which has substance. In that case, it is possible to argue for a semantic connection between weight and learning. The word *gravitas* lends support to the argument that a guru is weighty not because of body fat but, rather, on account of the learning acquired. This is not an outlandish argument, given that such a connection exists in other Indo-European languages. One speaks of a person who has *gravitas*, which comes from the Latin *gravis* (*heavy; serious)*.

The spelling of **guru** in the Devanāgarī is straightforward. It is disyllabic (**gu** + **ru**) and contains no conjuncts. That said, the reader is asked to refer to the second syllable and to pay close attention to the fact that the short medial **u** is not at the base of the body shape for the letter **ra**. Both short **u** and long **ū**, when medial (a term which also includes the representation of vowels when they are word final), have a distinct form when they follow the phoneme **r**:

रु **ru** रू **rū**

(vii) कर्म **karma** (√ **kṛ**)

The Sanskrit word **karma** is widely known by speakers of English who have never studied Sanskrit, since it has entered English in such expressions as: *'That's karma for you'* – an expression which in some sense signifies that an action has met with its appropriate reward. In Sanskrit, however, the word means nothing other than the sum of one's actions, from √ **kṛ** (*to make; fashion; do; create*). There is no sense that justice has been meted out. **Karma** is simply action, devoid of any divine justice. The term has philosophic overtones, all the same. One's actions may be prescribed and proscribed according to what it is one does or is supposed to do. *'Bad karma'*, in this context, represents a course of action which is inappropriate for a person, all circumstances being considered. If there is any judgement pursuant on one's actions, that is **dharma**.

(viii) धर्म dharma (√ dhr̥)

Just as **karma** is one of the most widely known of Sanskrit words amongst non-Sanskritists, **dharma** is a prime contender with respect to being one of the most debated as regards meaning. A great number of words are candidates in the attempt to translate it. The word comes from √ **dhr̥** (*to protect; preserve; restrain*). Notions of **dharma** as a form of judgement do not entirely capture the concept, since the universe is dispassionate; but to translate the word as law – not a human law but one which is dispassionate as, for example, the laws of nature or those of physics – similarly fails to capture the concept. **Dharma** is the force which keeps the universe balanced as regards righteousness. On a more mundane note, the verbal root can be used to signify nothing other than protection or preservation, as with the name of the blind king in the **Mahābhārata, Dhr̥tarāṣṭra**: *the one who protects* (**dhr̥ta**) *the kingdom* (**rāṣṭra**).

(ix) मोक्ष mokṣa (√ muc)

The concept of the liberation of the Self – the **ātman** – is fundamental to Hinduism, where the union of the Self (often couched in Judaeo-Christian terms as the soul) with the universe ensures that one's consciousness becomes part of the infinite. For Hindus, it is a consummation, as expressed by Hamlet, devoutly to be wished. It is the great liberation (**mokṣa**) from the cycle of birth, death and rebirth. The verbal root could not be clearer and is not subject to any disagreement. It is √ **muc** (*to let loose; release*). The reader might wonder at the fact that the verbal root contains the phoneme **c**, which is neither audible nor visible in the word **mokṣa**; or, for that matter, that **mokṣa** contains **o** whereas the root does not. In both cases, Sanskrit phonology provides the answer.

It has already been noted that, when verbal roots are used to generate nouns, vowel mutation often occurs (Chapter 7 explains this in more detail). In a nutshell, vowel mutation (**guṇa**) results in the following changes:

Simple vowel	a or ā	i or ī	u or ū	r̥ or r̥̄	l̥
Mutation	a	e	o	ar	al

Whilst these changes are not attested in √ **vid** → **vidyā**, √ **ram** → **rātrī** and √ **gṝ** → **guru**, they predict √ **div** → **deva**, √ **kam** → **kamala** and √ **ag** → **agni** (Admittedly, mutation does not result in a visible change, where a verbal root contains **a**). Mutation is, however, visible with √ **kṛ** → **karma** and **dhṛ** → **dharma**. It is to be noted that √ **vid** → **veda** does indeed accord with the mutations presented, as does √ **gṝ** → **garīyas** (*heavier*). With the word **buddha** (the next word to be investigated), the verbal root is √ **budh**. The derivation of the noun **buddha** does not accord with the information in the table; but it does so with the word **bodhisattva** (*one who helps others attain* **nirvāṇa**).

Returning to √ **muc**, one may predict that, if the root is subject to any mutation in the derivation of a noun, the mutation would result in ***moc**. Sanskrit phonology, at this stage, then transforms the final **c** to **kṣ**, following a complex sound change, predicated around the fact that a fully formed word cannot end in **-c**. The result is neither ***moca** nor ***mok** but a hybrid of both which preserves the fricative *sh*-sound inherent in the palatal **c**: **mokṣa**.

(x) बुद्ध **buddha** (√ **budh**)

The word **buddha** connects linguistically with the contemporary concept of being 'woke' – a term which, whilst current at the time of writing, has yet to show whether it will stand the test of time. **Buddha** is an epithet for the person born **Siddhārtha Gautama**, whose birthplace is generally accepted to have been Lumbini, in the south of Nepal. There can be no doubt as to the fact that the teachings of the Buddha have endured, having spread out from northern India to what is now Afghanistan and central Asia and, courtesy of the Silk Road, to Tibet, Mongolia, China, Korea and Japan. Buddhism also expanded further south, to Sri Lanka, Burma, Thailand, Laos, Cambodia, Vietnam and Indonesia. Within the vast area in which Buddhist thought became known, Sanskrit and the related Pali were the languages in which such thought found expression.

Whereas to be 'woke' in the twenty-first century is to be aware of social injustice, the Buddha was awoken to the suffering of existence and how such suffering could be ended. His epithet does not call him a saviour or redeemer but comes from the verbal root **budh** (*to awaken*), an everyday word with no overtly spiritual meaning. The difference between √ **budh** and **buddha** is an interesting one and sheds light on the pervasiveness of sound changes in Sanskrit. **Buddha** may be termed a proper noun, since it is a name, albeit an epithet. It is also, technically speaking, a past passive participle, which usually take the form of a suffix **-ta** after the verbal root (More will be said about the past passive participle in 7.7, viii and 9.3.1). **Siddhārtha Gautama** is not, however, referred to as the ***Budhta**, so something has clearly happened to alter the pronunciation. The explanation is twofold.

When elements which constitute a word (i.e. morphemes: units of meaning) come together in Sanskrit, they are often subject to a sound change. As seen with the sound system (Chapter 3), most consonants are classified as voiceless or voiced, unaspirated or aspirated (Nasals and semivowels are voiced; sibilants are unvoiced. Aspiration is not a feature of nasals, semivowels or sibilants). The subject of sound changes within Sanskrit is the source of the greatest frustration for learners of the language in their first few months of study. Fuller investigation of sound changes is the subject of Chapter 8. For now, it suffices to note that, in the bringing together of √ **budh** and the participle **-ta**, the following changes take place:

budh (where **dh** is voiced) + **-ta** (where **t** is voiceless)
First step: **t** changes to its voiced equivalent, **d**.
Result: ***budh+da**

So far, so good, but ***budhda** is still not the final form. The aspirate (**h**) is now trapped, in that it cannot be released without a vowel to assist it.

Second step: displace the aspirate so that it comes before a vowel.
Result: **buddha**

Fortunately, not all Sanskrit words undergo such complex sound changes. The learner should, all the same, be linguistically 'woke' to the fact that sounds changes are an extremely important feature of the language. When morphemes come together, voice (and often aspiration) can trigger a change in sound and spelling.

(xi) निर्वाण **nirvāṇa (nir- + √ vā)**

Nirvāṇa is the final destination of the Self for Buddhists, just as **mokṣa** represents the goal in Hinduism. It is derived from √ **vā** (*to be blown out; extinguished; made calm*). The reader will notice that something comes before **vā**; this is a prefix, as opposed to **-ta**, which is a suffix. Prefixes are common in Sanskrit, but it is well beyond the scope of the present work to discuss them. Prefixes can either modify the concept contained in the verbal root – sometimes a little, often quite considerably – or have no real effect on the root meaning. Only exposure to Sanskrit vocabulary will clarify the extent to which prefixes can modify meaning. For the learner who is new to Sanskrit, the study of prefixes is best put to one side until more basic concepts have been grasped.

The word **nirvāṇa** contains a conjunct in which **r** is the first element (**rv**). Accordingly, **r** takes the form of a crest, written above a vertical stroke. The vertical stroke is not that of the body shape of the letter **va** but, instead, the following vertical stroke which represents the medial form of **ā**. The crest of the **r** prefers not to share a vertical belonging to the body shape of a letter. If a medial **ā** is present, the crest will appear above it.

(xii) उपनिषद् **upaniṣad** (**upa-** + **ni-** + √ **sad**. Note that **sadhu** is not derived from √ **sad** but from √ **sādh**: *to attain a goal*)

The **Upaniṣads** (frequently appearing in the English spelling *Upanishads*) constitute a culturally important body of texts relating to speculative thought in which the nature of the ultimate reality and the Self are the focus. They are post-Vedic works, in that they come after the **Ṛgveda** in terms of their composition. As such, the term **Vedānta** (*end of the Vedas*) is often applied to them. As with the word **Buddha**, the verbal root does not imply anything spiritual. Here, the root means nothing other than *to sit; be seated* (√ **sad**). As with **nirvāṇa**, there is a prefix – two of them, in fact: **upa-** and **ni-**. Between them, the prefixes serve to modify the verbal root by giving some information on the state of sitting, which is defined as being close to (**upa-**) and below (**ni-**) something or someone. This is highly descriptive of the traditional social setting in which the **Upaniṣads** were transmitted in antiquity: the guru would be seated, close enough to his students to be audible to them, and the students would be seated below him, showing the requisite level of respect.

There is a sound change, from **sad** to **ṣad**, but this is not of concern for the moment. It is not a sound change triggered by voice or aspiration. In terms of its spelling, the Devanāgarī is straightforward: no conjuncts and no conventions to consider, such as the fondness of the crested **r** (in conjunct state) for a particular type of vertical stroke.

Attention should be paid to the virāma, at the end of the word, which ensures that the pronunciation is not ***upaniṣada**. There is, however, a small point which is nevertheless worth raising. Just as Sanskrit does not permit **c** in word-final position, as we saw with **mokṣa**, so too **d** is not a permitted final. The term 'permitted final' relates to a number of phonemes with which any given word may end. Vowels are all permitted finals but, as concerns the consonants, semivowels and sibilants, only the following are technically allowed: **k**, **ṭ**, **t**, **p**, **ṅ**, **n**, **m**, **r** (Strictly speaking, therefore, the word **upaniṣad**, if occurring by itself or followed by a word beginning with a voiceless phoneme, is **upaniṣat**). Anusvāra and visarga are also permitted word-finally. On that note, fair notice should be given to the reader that visarga is subject to a systematic number of sound changes. These will be investigated in Chapter 8. The following section will focus on Sanskrit grammar, on which matter a few preliminary comments are highly desirable.

5.3 Approaching Sanskrit grammar

Whatever one's knowledge of complex grammatical systems and however well one may know an Indic language or one such as French (which has grammatical gender) or German (which has both grammatical gender and case), Sanskrit presents the learner with ample challenges. It is, as Sir William Jones aptly remarked, "*more perfect than the Greek, more copious than the Latin*". Examples have been used, in the earlier chapters of the present work, to illustrate cognates with Sanskrit. Often, the example was drawn from Latin. This is not to say that Latin, or indeed any other language, is necessary for the study of Sanskrit. Familiarity with grammar can be acquired from scratch. It does not have to be applied from an existing knowledge, gained by the formal acquisition of another language. For the learner for whom grammatical terminology is a thing of mystery, a glossary of terms is provided by the present work. The reader who feels slightly out of his or her comfort zone is strongly advised to consult the glossary as and when required.

A good grasp of the sound system is crucial to the study of Sanskrit. Words are formed and are subject to change in Sanskrit according to the principles of the sound system. To ignore the differences between voiced and voiceless sounds is to court disaster; but the voiced or voiceless nature of phonemes is just one of many phenomena of which the Sanskrit student should be aware. The key sound changes will be explored (Chapter 8). First, however, must come something which allows one to see what Sanskrit grammar looks like, beginning with the noun (Chapter 6) and moving on to the verb (Chapter 7). The Sanskrit noun is masculine, neuter or feminine, which means that the word for any given thing has to be learnt along with its gender. That is just the starting point. As for the verb, arguably the most complex component of Sanskrit grammar, gender is not an issue, but the Sanskrit verb is composed of ten classes, each class exhibiting a different pattern, either in how the verbal root generates a stem on which the personal endings (*I*, *you*, *he/she/it*, etc.) can be added, or in the way in which the verb is conjugated. The following two chapters of the present work are dedicated to presenting the Sanskrit noun and the Sanskrit verb as simply as possible, giving the reader the confidence to continue with his or her study of what is a challenging but immensely rewarding language. One should not rush into Sanskrit grammar. Time taken to grasp the basic principles is time very well spent.

6

THE SANSKRIT NOUN

Declension

6.1 Preliminaries

In the previous chapter, a dozen words were investigated, allowing for a discussion on various things which they were able to reveal, both about the culture with which Sanskrit is associated and as regards certain purely linguistic matters, including the Devanāgarī writing system. The words in question were all nouns. They related to things or to people, whether tangible (such as **kamala**, **guru**, **buddha**) or abstract (**vidyā**, **karma**, **dharma**). They did not, however, all have the same endings. Whilst several of the words ended in **-a**, there were some for which the final phoneme was another short vowel (**-i**, **-u**), a long vowel (**-ā**, **-ī**) or a consonant (**-d**/ **-t**). These endings are important, since they indicate something about the noun which is central to the process of declension, where a noun takes various endings according to the grammatical information it contains.

In English, one distinguishes a difference between *tree* and *trees*. The former indicates a singular tree; the latter, two or more. The distinction, grammatically speaking, is that *tree* appears in the singular number whilst *trees* indicates the plural number. The term 'number' is as simple as that, in English: it identifies whether something is in the singular or in the plural. The ending *-s* is the phoneme in English which distinguishes *tree* from *trees*. As such, linguists and grammarians refer to it as the 'plural morpheme'. It is a unit of meaning which can be added to a word to contribute to its overall sense. English is not consistent in its application of the plural morpheme.

DOI: 10.4324/9780429325434-6

Whilst a singular *cat* is made plural by its addition (*cats*), as too with *dog* and *dogs*, the plural morpheme is not applied to the end of the word *mouse* (i.e. the plural is *mice*, not **mouses*).

Sanskrit possesses not only the singular and plural numbers but also the dual number, which indicates two (and only two) of something. The dual is an ancient feature in Indo-European languages. Latin did not use it and Greek contained a few examples but had largely abandoned it by the classical period. It is residual in modern English, although its function has been lexicalized, meaning that a separate word is provided to indicate its presence, with the noun itself appearing in the plural: *a pair of cats*; *both mice*, *a brace of pheasants*. In Sanskrit, both nouns and verbs possess dual endings, which are quite distinct from the singular and the plural.

The present work does not investigate the dual number. Whilst it may be a basic feature of Sanskrit, declension presents the learner with sufficient challenges with singular and plural endings. The dual is far less frequent in Sanskrit texts than the singular and the plural, so it makes good sense to keep matters as simple as possible for a learner taking the first steps into the language. Only once a knowledge of basic declension has been firmly grasped with respect to singular and plural forms ought the learner to approach the dual. The presence of cases in Sanskrit (of which more will be said in 6.2) inflates the number of possible forms for the noun to sixteen: eight for the singular; eight for the plurals. Adding the dual would result in twenty-four forms, which makes grasping declension a daunting prospect at the outset of one's study of Sanskrit.

Returning to the words which were investigated in 5.2, it was noted that they display a number of different endings. These endings indicate, in most (but not all) cases, whether a noun is masculine, neuter or feminine. This is not grammatical number but grammatical gender. Many Indo-European languages have maintained the concept of grammatical gender. French has two genders: masculine (e.g. *le chat*: *the cat*) and feminine (*la souris*: *the mouse*). German has three: masculine (*der Hund*: *the dog*); feminine (*die Katze*: *the cat*); neuter (*das Schaf*: *the sheep*). In French and German, it is not possible to determine the gender of a noun from the final sound or letter in the noun. A final *-t* in a French noun, for example, does not indicate the masculine gender any more than a final *-s* indicates feminine gender (*la jument*: *the mare*; *le fils*: *the son*). As with number, Sanskrit exhibits more consistency.

A short, final **-a** in the stem form of a noun (which is the citation or dictionary form, before any grammar has been added) indicates that a noun is either masculine or neuter. It cannot be feminine. The word **deva** is masculine, whilst **kamala** is neuter. That may not be terribly useful with respect to being able to distinguish the gender of a noun ending in **-a**, but it does at least rule out the feminine as a possibility. As for **niśā** and **rātrī**, they are both feminine. The endings **-ā** and **-ī** are reserved for feminine nouns. Things are not always cut and dried in terms of distinguishing the gender of a noun in Sanskrit: short **-i** and **-u** can be masculine, neuter or feminine – although neuter nouns ending in **-i** and **-u** are rather limited. All told, the Sanskrit noun is reasonably explicative in terms of indicating gender. This is as well, given the intricacies of Sanskrit declension.

6.2 Cases and case functions

Grammatical gender is not a matter which is likely to cause the reader any conceptual difficulty – especially if the reader has any exposure, however minimal, to such languages as French, German, Italian or Spanish (which remain the most widely learnt languages for English speakers in Europe and the United States). As for those already familiar with any of the Indic languages, such as Panjabi, Gujarati and Hindi, a knowledge of what grammatical gender represents will already be in place. The same cannot be said with case, which is by no means present in all languages that have grammatical gender. Whilst German has cases, French, Italian and Spanish do not. Case endings were lost in the development of French, Italian and Spanish from Latin, just as modern English lost the cases which Old English possessed, replacing them by prepositions (*of, from, to*, etc.).

Case indicates the various forms which a noun undergoes as it reflects its function within a sentence. Whilst it is true that modern English no longer has case as part of its grammatical system, the vestiges of case are still evident. If we investigate the sentence: *she sees me and I greet her*, the words *she* and *her* are different, although they appear to relate to the same person. This is true, also, of the words *me* and *I*. Speakers of English would have no difficulty in identifying the following sentence as ungrammatical:

**Her sees I and me greets she.*

She/her and *I/me* are personal pronouns and these, in English, are the remnants of case as it existed in Old English. *She* is the one controlling the verb *to see*, but *I* am the one controlling the verb *to greet*. The recipient of the action of seeing is *me*, whilst the recipient of the action of greeting is *her*. The person or thing controlling the verb is the <u>subject</u> of the sentence (*she*; *I*). The one who is the recipient of the verb is the <u>object</u> of the sentence (*me*; *her*). In Sanskrit, case endings applied to the end of a noun allow us to know who or what is the subject of the sentence and who or what is the object (Sanskrit also possesses personal pronouns, which are explored in 6.6). The case which indicates the subject is the nominative case, whilst the object of a sentence is marked in the accusative case – unless the accusative is overridden by another case indicating further information about the object. These are the first two cases (of which there are eight) that the learner should explore.

The following is a complete sentence in Sanskrit which uses both the nominative and the accusative:

रामः अश्वं पश्यति

Rāmaḥ aśvaṃ paśyati

Rāma sees the horse.

Rāma is the subject of the sentence, since he controls the verb of seeing (**paśyati**: *he sees; is seeing*). The recipient of the action of seeing is the horse (**aśva**). **Rāma** is, accordingly, indicated by the nominative case and **aśva** by the accusative. Both words have an ending which signifies the relevant case. With **Rāma**, it is **-ḥ**, with **aśva**, it is **-m**. The reader will note that that ending **-m** appears as a dotted letter in the IAST. This is anusvāra, which indicates that a word-final **-m** is followed by a sound other than a vowel. The word order of the sentence is subject, object, verb. Regrettably for the learner, Sanskrit recognizes a phenomenon called **sandhi**, of which more will be said in Chapter 8. For the time being, indulgence is asked of the reader to accept that the sentence, once sandhi has been applied, reads as follows:

रामोऽश्वं पश्यति

Rāmo 'śvaṃ paśyati

Rāma sees the horse.

Sandhi is momentarily deferred for the sake of exposition, but it cannot be ignored for long. Authentic Sanskrit (as opposed to Sanskrit that has been simplified to ease the learner into the language) is fully sandhified.

Sanskrit word order can be extremely flexible, given that case endings serve to identify the relationship of a noun within the sentence. The following sentence would mean the same as the previous one – and there are no sandhi changes to make:

अश्वं रामः पश्यति

aśvaṃ Rāmaḥ paśyati

Rāma sees the horse.

The extent to which the second sentence might differ in terms of nuance from the first is something which is connected to stylistics rather than grammar. From a grammatical point of view, the subject and object are clearly identifiable, and the interpretation is the same. Stylistically, one could posit that a displacement of the words **Rāmaḥ** and **aśvaṃ**, so that the object appears first, might indicate an emphasis which would be reflected in the English translation: *It is the horse that is being seen by Rāma* (as opposed to some other creature or thing). That might be a suitable translation, according to the context in which the sentence occurs, but it ought to be stressed that such a translation reflects a passive construction, not an active one (i.e. something is seen by someone). Passive constructions in Sanskrit, as with English, have a different structure. To explore these at this juncture would obscure matters rather than clarify them.

Aside from the nominative and accusative cases, Sanskrit possesses six others, which need now to be investigated. It is worth, always, learning Sanskrit according to patterns, as these facilitate the absorption and retention of new information. This is certainly true of the running order of the cases, which the learner is strongly encouraged to learn in the following sequence:

Nominative
Accusative
Instrumental
Dative
Ablative
Genitive
Locative
Vocative

The information which cases provide, aside from the nominative and accusative, is indicated by a number of prepositions in English (As regards the nominative and accusative, reflecting the grammatical subject and object, respectively, English employs word order: *Mary sees James* puts the subject before the verb and the object after it, in an active construction. *Mary* is therefore the subject and *James* is the object). If the learner can keep in mind the functions of the individual cases, together with the prepositions which English uses to represent them, a good start will have been made in grasping Sanskrit declension.

Starting with the instrumental, this is the case which English expresses with the prepositions *by* or *with.* The clue to remembering this is to bear in mind what purpose an instrument serves in English. If it is a musical instrument, one makes music *with* it; if a surgical instrument, a surgical procedure is undertaken *by means of* it. If Rāma goes to town on horseback, Sanskrit determines that he goes (**gacchati**) to town (**nagara**) by means of the horse (i.e. he uses the horse as an instrument of travel). Accordingly, the horse appears in the instrumental case.

रामः अश्वेन नगरं गच्छति

Rāmaḥ aśvena nagaraṃ gacchati
(With sandhi: **Rāmo 'śvena nagaraṃ gacchati**)

Rāma goes to town by horse.

It is important to point out that the sentence contains one subject (Rāma) and two objects (the town and the horse). The town is the direct object, since it is the recipient of the action of going (It is the thing 'being gone to'). As for the horse, it is an indirect object, since it is not directly related, grammatically speaking, to the action of going. Care needs to be taken to avoid something that is the cause of confusion amongst many learners. If Rāma goes *to* town (with or without a horse), he moves *towards* it. The preposition *to* is somewhat ambiguous in English. One sees it in the sentence: *I gave a book to Mark.* In Sanskrit, however, that example of *to* captures the notion of giving or of doing something *for* someone's benefit – and that is not the accusative but the dative case.

The dative case, as noted, is the *case of giving.* This is an exact translation of the Latin *cāsus datīvus*. In Sanskrit, the person or thing which is the recipient of the action of giving is marked with the dative case. If Rāma gives (**yacchati**) food (**anna**) to the horse, the sentence which states this in Sanskrit is as follows:

रामः अश्वाय अन्नं यच्छति

Rāmaḥ aśvāya annaṃ yacchati
(With sandhi: **Rāmo 'śvāyānnaṃ yacchati**)

Rāma gives food to the horse.

It is not the food which is marked as dative, since it is not the recipient of the action of giving. The food takes the accusative case. Rāma remains the subject, marked by the nominative case, because he is the one performing the verb. The recipient of the action of giving is the horse.

Both Rāma and the horse are masculine short **-a** stems, whilst **nagara** and **anna** are neuter short **-a** stems. This does not make any difference as regards the instrumental or dative cases, where the singular endings are **-ena** and **-āya**, respectively, with both the masculine and the neuter short **-a** stems. This is true of the next three cases also (the ablative, genitive and locative). Once one knows the singular case endings for masculine short **-a** stems, one also knows the singular case endings for the neuter short **-a** stems, except for the nominative. This is a pattern to which the learner's attention is drawn. As previously stated, patterns are useful in the learning of Sanskrit.

The ablative case corresponds to the English proposition *from*. It is one of the easiest cases to grasp, conceptually, for a speaker of English. Both the masculine and neuter short **-a** stems take the case ending **-āt** in the singular. The word **nagara** (*town*), as mentioned, is neuter:

रामः अश्वाः च नगरात् आगच्छन्ति

Rāmaḥ aśvāḥ ca nagarāt āgacchanti
(With sandhi: **Rāmo 'śvāś ca nagarād āgacchanti**)

Rāma and the horses come from the town.

Note the word **ca**, in the example given, which is the English *and*. It does not come between the two things which it joins together but after both. *Rāma and the horse* is thus *Rāma horse and* in Sanskrit. The definite article (*the*) does not exist as such in Sanskrit, although Sanskrit possesses a demonstrative pronoun which can express definiteness (The demonstrative pronoun is investigated in 6.5). Note, also that the verb **gacchati** is prefixed with **ā-** which gives the meaning *to come* rather than *to go*. The verb also contains the plural ending **-anti** rather than **-ati**, since there is one Rāma and at least three horses involved in the action of coming from town. Sanskrit makes it clear that there is not a single horse or indeed two, since the case ending for *horse* is the nominative plural, not the nominative singular or the nominative dual.

There is something worth remarking, as concerns the ablative case ending in the plural. This is **-ebhyaḥ**, a form which is shared by the dative case ending for both the masculine and neuter short **-a** stems. Whereas this might seem to the learner to be a bonus, in that fewer forms must be committed to memory, the ideal situation would be one in which all case endings were distinct, one from the other. The sharing of endings results in a grammatical ambiguity where one is reliant on context to determine which case is being represented.

The genitive ending, in the singular of both masculine and neuter short **-a** stems is **-asya**. English, too, has a genitive ending, visible by what linguists and grammarians refer to as the 'genitive apostrophe'. *The pen belonging to Mary* may also be expressed as *Mary's pen.* Although frequently misunderstood, and consequently omitted, in contemporary English – even by the press – the genitive apostrophe is also used in the plural: *the horses' stable* does not refer to a stable for a singular horse (that would be *the horse's stable*) but for two or more horses.

रामस्य सूतः नगरात् आगच्छति

Rāmasya sūtaḥ nagarāt āgacchati
(With sandhi: **Rāmasya sūto nagarād āgacchati**)

Rāma's charioteer comes from the town.

Note that the word **sūta** (*charioteer*) is a masculine short **-a** stem, for which the conjugational endings are the same as **aśva** – and, for that matter, **Rāma** (although a plural form for Rāma is unlikely ever to be encountered in a Sanskrit text). Since the subject is in the singular, the verb form is **āgacchati**. The plural form of the verb (**āgacchanti**), in the previous sentence, reflected the fact that there were two subjects equally controlling the verb; Rāma as the first subject and at least three horses as the second (i.e. a singular subject and a plural subject). Had there been only two horses, the plural form of the verb would still have been appropriate, since there would have been three entities (one human and two equine), but the declensional ending for the horses would have necessitated a dual form. As concerns the dual number, the learner is encouraged to bear in mind its existence from the outset, although it is best to focus on the singular and plural forms. Once the latter are learnt, the dual can then easily be incorporated. At the very beginning of one's study of Sanskrit, clarity is always best.

There are two remaining cases in Sanskrit: the locative and the vocative. The locative locates an action as its name suggests. The English prepositions *in, on, at* or *through* are the ones most likely to be used to translate the Sanskrit locative. Consider the following example, in which the subject of the sentence is not, on this occasion, Rāma but his charioteer. Again, the verbal ending is **-ati**, because the subject is in the singular (This is the present tense, which is investigated in Chapter 7). Here, the verb is *to be* (**bhavati**: *he/she/it is*) rather than *to see, to go* or *to come*. The locative singular ending **-e** relates to the town:

रामस्य सूतः नगरे भवति

Rāmasya sūtaḥ nagare bhavati
(With sandhi: **Rāmasya sūto nagare bhavati**)

Rāma's charioteer is in (the) town.

This brings us to the last of eight cases, which is the vocative. This is the case of calling out – just as one's vocation is one's calling. If Rāma's horse were capable of articulate speech, he might wish to attract Rāma's attention. Since Rāma is a short **-a** masculine stem, the horse would have but to use the vocative case (in the singular, since there is only one Rāma). The vocative singular, for short **-a** stems, has the same appearance as the stem form. The vocative singular (*o Rāma!*) is **Rāma**. Similarly, if Rāma were to call to his horse, he would say **aśva** (*o horse!*).

The existence of eight cases may seem daunting to the learner, but there is some consolation to be had in knowing that Sanskrit is extremely methodical in their application. Declensional patterns are repetitive. Once the learner has grasped a handful of patterns, the others can be learnt by analogy. In other words, one works with what one already knows, noting the differences that occur between a familiar declensional pattern and one that is less familiar. There are more similarities between declensional patterns than there are differences. Bucknell (1994 – see Chapter 10) identifies forty declensional patterns as regular, noting an additional thirty-three that show irregularities. In the following four pages, two declensional patterns (or paradigms) will be discussed for short **-a** stems; one for masculine nouns, one for neuter nouns. These exhibit minimal differences. We will then turn to the declensional patterns for the long **-ā** and long **-ī** stems (feminine), where the differences with the masculine and neuter paradigms are more pronounced.

6.3 Sample paradigms: short -a stems

On the following page, two paradigms are given: one for a short **-a** masculine stem (**deva**) and one for a short **-a** neuter stem (**kamala**). Departing from a practice employed so far, only the endings are bolded, allowing for them to be more legible. Where there is no difference between the endings for the masculine and neuter declensional forms, there is no use of italics. Italics indicate the existence of a difference between the declension of **deva** and **kamala**. These differences occur in the nominative singular and nominative, accusative and vocative plurals.

The reader will note something important about the nominative singular ending for **kamala**. It is the same as the accusative singular form. Unless one knows that a short **-a** stem is neuter, one is likely to assume that **kamalam** indicates the accusative singular only, with the consequence that a sentence containing **kamalam** will be understood as one in which **kamalam** must be the object. The following sentence therefore presents the learner with a conundrum. The lotus (**kamala**) grows (**rohati**) in the garden (**udyāna**). The word **udyāna** is not problematic, in that the ending clearly indicates the presence of the locative singular case ending **-e**, whether the stem is masculine or neuter (It is, in fact, neuter).

kamalam udyāne rohati
A/the lotus grows in the garden.

If one has assumed that **kamala** is masculine, then the case ending **-m** indicates an object. Yet the lotus is the thing controlling the verb of growing, meaning that it must be the subject, which calls for a nominative case ending.

Two other points are worth noting. First, the dative and ablative singular endings are distinct with both the masculine and neuter short **-a** stems but are the same in the plural. Second, the masculine vocative singular does not have a final visarga (**-ḥ**) and the neuter vocative singular does not have a final **-m**. In effect, the vocative singular forms in both genders have the same appearance as the citation form of the noun: **deva** and **kamala**. With both **deva** and **kamala**, the vocative plural endings are the same as the nominative plural endings. This pattern is repeated time and again in Sanskrit declension and explains why the Sanskrit grammatical tradition did not identify the vocative as a separate case.

Sample paradigms: short -a stems

deva (*god*) Masculine		
Case	Singular	Plural
Nominative	dev***aḥ***	dev***āḥ***
Accusative	dev**am**	dev***ān***
Instrumental	dev**ena**	dev**aiḥ**
Dative	dev**āya**	dev**ebhyaḥ**
Ablative	dev**āt**	dev**ebhyaḥ**
Genitive	dev**asya**	dev**ānām**
Locative	dev**e**	dev**eṣu**
Vocative	dev**a**	dev***āḥ***

kamala (*lotus*) Neuter		
Case	Singular	Plural
Nominative	kamal***am***	kamal***āni***
Accusative	kamal**am**	kamal***āni***
Instrumental	kamal**ena**	kamal**aiḥ**
Dative	kamal**āya**	kamal**ebhyaḥ**
Ablative	kamal**āt**	kamal**ebhyaḥ**
Genitive	kamal**asya**	kamal**ānām**
Locative	kamal**e**	kamal**eṣu**
Vocative	kamal**a**	kamal***āni***

6.4 More paradigms: long -ā and long -ī stems

Long **-ā** and long **-ī** stems have declensional endings that are quite distinct from the short **-a** stems. Whilst this might strike the learner as dispiriting, the good news is that long **-ā** and long **-ī** stems exhibit a number of similarities to each other. Knowledge of one assists greatly with the acquisition of the other, albeit that there are a few more differences than exist between the short **-a** masculine and short **-a** neuter stems. Long **-ā** and long **-ī** stems are feminine.

As with the nominative and vocative endings in the short **-a** stems, the nominative and vocative singular endings in the long **-ā** and long **-ī** stems are not the same as each other. Whereas the vocative singular endings in the short **-a** stems are identical to the citation form of the noun, that is not so with the long **-ā** and long **-ī** stems (**niśā** → **niśe**; **rātrī** → **rātri**). The citation form is, instead, seen in the nominative singular of both the long **-ā** and long **-ī** stems. There is pattern with the vocative plural endings that is consistent with the short **-a** stems: the nominative and vocative plural endings are the same (**devāḥ/devāḥ**; **kamalāni/kamalāni**; **niśāḥ/niśāḥ**; **rātryaḥ/rātryaḥ**).

Another pattern which the long **-ā** and long **-ī** stems share with the short **-a** stems is that the declensional forms are the same in the dative and ablative plural (**-ebhyaḥ** in the short **-a** stems, **-bhyaḥ** in the long **-ā** and long **-ī** stems). There is a difference in the sibilant between the locative plural endings **niśāsu** and **rātrīṣu**, and a difference in the nasal between the genitive plural endings **niśānām** and **rātrīṇām**. These relate to internal sandhi rules which are investigated in 8.5.

Note the addition of **y** after the stem (i.e. **niśā**+**y**) where the declensional endings begin with a vowel. This prevents the outcome **a**+**ā**, **ā** +**a** or **ā**+**ā**, which Sanskrit does not permit. A similar violation to Sanskrit phonology is sidestepped in **rātrī**, where the **ī** in the stem is substituted by the semivowel **y**, preventing the impermissible diphthongs ***īa** and **īā**, not to mention the triphthong ***īai**. Note, also, that the **-ā** in the stem form **niśā** is short in the instrumental singular (i.e. **niśayā**, not ***niśāyā**).

If the learner can master the short **-a** stems (masculine and neuter) and the long **-ā** and long **-ī** stems (feminine), a great stride will have been taken into Sanskrit declension. These paradigms merit careful perusal.

More paradigms: long -ā and long -ī stems

niśā (*night*) Feminine		
Case	Singular	Plural
Nominative	niśā	niśā*ḥ*
Accusative	niśā**m**	niśā**ḥ**
Instrumental	niśay**ā**	niśā**bhiḥ**
Dative	niśāy**ai**	niśā**bhyaḥ**
Ablative	niśāy**āḥ**	niśā**bhyaḥ**
Genitive	niśāy**āḥ**	niśā**nām**
Locative	niśāy**ām**	niśā***su***
Vocative	niś*e*	niśā*ḥ*

rātrī (*night*) Feminine		
Case	Singular	Plural
Nominative	rātrī	rātry***aḥ***
Accusative	rātrī**m**	rātrī**ḥ**
Instrumental	rātry**ā**	rātrī**bhiḥ**
Dative	rātry**ai**	rātrī**bhyaḥ**
Ablative	rātry**āḥ**	rātrī**bhyaḥ**
Genitive	rātry**āḥ**	rātrī**ṇām**
Locative	rātry**ām**	rātrī***ṣu***
Vocative	rātr***i***	rātry***aḥ***

6.5 The demonstrative pronoun tat

Sanskrit possesses a number of words to signify *this one*, *that one*, *it*. These are words which refer to someone or something whose identity has been established in the context of an utterance or sentence and, in this respect, they function as such words do in English. For example, if one has been discussing the cost of an item, one might choose not to refer to the item by using its noun form again but, instead, using the appropriate pronoun, as the following example illustrates:

The seafood pasta looks nice, but it is too expensive.

English is sensitive to gender if the entity is a person – less so, if the entity is an animal (Babies tend also to be indeterminate as regards gender).

Mary is upset with James. She doesn't like him to drink too much.
Jim's dog is enormous. He is/It is a real beast.

(*He* makes it ambiguous as to whether it is Jim or his dog being discussed.)

The words *he/she/it*, substituting for nouns, are pronouns. Sanskrit possesses these as well as English. In fact, the Sanskrit demonstrative pronoun **tat** is unlikely to evade the learner for long, so pervasive is it in all manner of texts. It is 'demonstrative' in that it points to someone or something, although it should be noted that it also happens to be the third person pronoun. As such, **tat** can be understood to be *that one*, *this one*, *those*, *these*, *he*, *she*, *it*, *they* (etc.) according to the context. Since Sanskrit has grammatical number and case, it follows that **tat** may have many different forms, according to how many entities are involved and what the case relationship happens to be between the entity or entities in question and the other words within the sentence.

When a **tat**-form is used for a god, already present in the discourse, the **tat**-form in question must be masculine, because the Sanskrit noun is masculine (**deva:** *god*). Just as the masculine short **-a** stem **deva** can take several case endings in the singular (and also the dual and plural), so too can the **tat**-form. The exception is the vocative case, which does not apply with **tat**. The endings of **tat**-forms often resemble those of the nouns to which they refer. There are differences all the same and these must be learnt quite early in the study of Sanskrit.

The demonstrative pronoun: tat **with short -a stems**

tat + **deva** (*god*) Masculine		
Case	Singular	Plural
Nominative	**saḥ** devaḥ [1]	**te** devāḥ
Accusative	**tam** devam [2]	**tān** devān
Instrumental	**tena** devena	**taiḥ** devaiḥ [5]
Dative	**tasmai** devāya	**tebhyaḥ** devebhyaḥ [4]
Ablative	**tasmāt** devāt [3]	**tebhyaḥ** devebhyaḥ [4]
Genitive	**tasya** devasya	**teṣām** devānām [2]
Locative	**tasmin** deve	**teṣu** deveṣu
Vocative	n/a	n/a

tat + **kamala** (*lotus*) Neuter		
Case	Singular	Plural
Nominative	**tat** kamalam	**tāni** kamalāni
Accusative	**tat** kamalam	**tāni** kamalāni
Instrumental	**tena** kamalena	**taiḥ** kamalaiḥ
Dative	**tasmai** kamalāya	**tebhyaḥ** kamalebhyaḥ
Ablative	**tasmāt** kamalāt	**tebhyaḥ** kamalebhyaḥ
Genitive	**tasya** kamalasya	**teṣām** kamalānām [2]
Locative	**tasmin** kamale	**teṣu** kamaleṣu
Vocative	n/a	n/a

Notes

1 The form **saḥ** has a special set of rules. The visarga is dropped in all cases except if **saḥ** comes at the end of a sentence. Also, if followed by short **a**, it changes to **so** and the short **a-** is dropped (e.g. **saḥ aham** → **so 'ham**).

2 If a **tat**-form ends with **-m** and is followed by any consonant, semivowel or sibilant, anusvāra applies (e.g. **taṃ devam**; **tesāṃ kamalānām**, etc.).

3 If a **tat**-form ends with **-t** and is followed by a voiced consonant, the ending changes to **-d** (e.g. **tasmād devāt**). This is a consonant sandhi rule (8.3).

4 If a **tat**-form ends with **-aḥ** and is followed by a voiced consonant, semivowel or **h**, the ending changes to **-o** (e.g. **tebhyo devebhyaḥ**). See 8.2.

5 If a **tat**-form ends with **-aiḥ** and is followed by a voiced consonant, semivowel or **h**, the ending changes to **-air** (e.g. **tair devaiḥ**). See 8.2.

If a **tat**-form is used alongside the noun to which it refers, it lends the noun a degree of definiteness. The noun phrase **saḥ devaḥ** (which becomes **sa devaḥ**, with the dropping of the visarga, as mentioned in the first note on the previous page) can be translated as *that god, this god* or simply *the god*, according to context. **Tat** may function, therefore as the Sanskrit equivalent of the definite article in English. Strictly speaking, **tat** is a neuter form which identifies neuter nouns in both the nominative and accusative singular. Its name is retained irrespective of whether it is being used for masculine and feminine nouns. Many Sanskrit grammars refer to it as **tad**, which is perfectly acceptable. The only difference between **tat** and **tad** is whether it is followed by a phoneme which is voiceless (in which case it is **tat**) or voiced (requiring the form **tad**). With the nominative and accusative singular noun **kamalam**, beginning with the voiceless **k**, it has the form **tat**: **tat kamalam** (*that/this/the lotus*).

The learning of **tat** may seem arduous, but it is worth the perseverance. Not only is **tat** frequently encountered but it also gives the student of Sanskrit further declensional patterns for free. Once learnt, **tat**-forms provide the basis for the declension of another demonstrative pronoun, **etat/etad**, which is deemed to refer to an entity closer to the speaker than **tat** (*This one here* rather than *that one there*) and is identical to **tat**, with the addition of **e-** at the beginning (There are two minor differences, relating to the change in the sibilant in the nominative singular masculine and feminine forms. The predicted ***esaḥ** and ***esā**, respectively, are not attested and appear instead as **eṣaḥ** and **eṣā**). Importantly, **tat**-forms have the same endings as **yat/yad**: the relative pronoun, indicating *who(m)*, *whose*, *which*, etc. The use of the relative pronoun is best seen in context. It appears in the last of four readings from the Bhagavadgītā (9.3.4).

In terms of <u>when</u> the learner might wish to consider committing **tat**-forms to memory, the answer is 'as soon as practicable'. First, however, the learner must be secure as regards his or her grasp of the declension of short **-a** stems (both masculine and neuter) and at least the long **-ā** feminine stem. Most **tat**-forms have the same endings as the stems in question. The dual forms of **tat**, as with the declensional paradigms presented, have not been included. These are less frequent than the singular and plural forms and, on that basis, may profitably be deferred until the singular and plural forms have become familiar. In the study of Sanskrit, rushing to learn everything at once is never advisable.

The demonstrative pronoun: tat with long -ā/-ī stems

tat + **niśā** (*night*) Feminine		
Case	Singular	Plural
Nominative	**sā** niśā [1]	**tāḥ** niśāḥ [3]
Accusative	**tām** niśām [2]	**tāḥ** niśāḥ [3]
Instrumental	**tayā** niśayā	**tābhiḥ** niśābhiḥ [5]
Dative	**tasyai** niśāyai	**tābhyaḥ** niśābhyaḥ [4]
Ablative	**tasyāḥ** niśāyāḥ [3]	**tābhyaḥ** niśābhyaḥ [4]
Genitive	**tasyāḥ** niśāyāḥ [3]	**tāsām** niśānām [2]
Locative	**tasyām** niśāyām [2]	**tāsu** niśāsu
Vocative	n/a	n/a

tat + **rātrī** (*night*) Feminine		
Case	Singular	Plural
Nominative	**sā** rātrī	**tāḥ** rātryaḥ [3]
Accusative	**tām** rātrīm [2]	**tāḥ** rātrīḥ [3]
Instrumental	**tayā** rātryā	**tābhiḥ** rātrībhiḥ [5]
Dative	**tasyai** rātryai	**tābhyaḥ** rātrībhyaḥ [4]
Ablative	**tasyāḥ** rātryāḥ [3]	**tābhyaḥ** rātrībhyaḥ [4]
Genitive	**tasyāḥ** rātryāḥ [3]	**tāsām** rātrīṇām [2]
Locative	**tasyām** rātryām [2]	**tāsu** rātrīṣu
Vocative	n/a	n/a

Notes

1 The form **sā** stays unchanged. There is no final visarga.

2 If a **tat**-form ends with **-m** and is followed by any consonant, semivowel or sibilant, anusvāra applies (e.g. **tām niśām**; **tām rātrīm**, etc.).

3 If a **tat**-form ends with **-āḥ** and is followed by a voiced consonant or semivowel, the visarga is simply dropped (e.g. **tā niśāḥ**, etc.). See 8.2.

4 If a **tat**-form ends with **-aḥ** and is followed by a voiced consonant or semivowel, the ending changes to **-o** (e.g. **tābhyo niśābhyaḥ**). See 8.2.

5 It a **tat**-form ends with **-iḥ** and is followed by a voiced consonant, semivowel or **h**, the ending changes to **-ir** (e.g. **tābhir niśābhiḥ**). There is one exception: if the following phoneme is **r**, the visarga is dropped and the preceding vowel is lengthened (e.g. **tābhī rātrībhiḥ**). See 8.2.

6.6 Personal pronouns

As with **tat**, the personal pronouns indicate a noun, but they do so without stating the noun. In English, there are only a few forms for the personal pronouns, because there are few case functions in English. As demonstrated in

6.2, whilst English may not formally recognize grammatical case, it is nevertheless sensitive to the fact that a noun or its pronoun may be the subject of a sentence, the object or a possessor. These are, of course, the nominative, accusative and genitive cases, respectively, of Sanskrit. The following tables match the personal pronouns of the first and second person to their Sanskrit equivalents. In having eight cases (seven of which have person pronoun forms), not to mention a dual number, the number of forms is much greater in Sanskrit:

First Person	Singular	Plural	Singular	Plural
Nominative	*I*	*we*	**aham**	**vayam**
Accusative	*me*	*us*	**mām**	**asmān**
Genitive	*my/mine*	*our(s)*	**mama**	**asmākam**

Second Person	Singular	Plural	Singular	Plural
Nominative	*you*	*you*	**tvam**	**yūyam**
Accusative	*you*	*you*	**tvām**	**yuṣmān**
Genitive	*your(s)*	*your(s)*	**tava**	**yuṣmākam**

It is relevant to mention that the singular forms of the second person in English are identical to the plural ones. Modern English started to abandon the singular forms (*thou, thee, thy/thine*) in favour of the plurals. Although attested in writing of the Tudor and Jacobean periods and occasionally still heard in dialect English, use of the older forms of the singular decreased during the seventeenth century. Had they been retained, the similarities between English and Sanskrit would have been much more evident. The older English second person singular forms began with *th-*, the Sanskrit ones have **t** as the initial phoneme, as do the French forms (*toi/tu*, *te*, *tien*). Be that as it may, ample similarities remain between English personal pronoun forms and Sanskrit ones. Note how the first person singular shows a predominance of forms beginning with *m* in both languages and the English plural forms have *w/u/ou-/* in contrast to the **v/a** of Sanskrit (The second person plural forms show an even greater similarity between English and Sanskrit).

Personal pronouns

First Person		
Case	Singular	Plural
Nominative	**aham**	**vayam**
Accusative	**mām (mā)**	**asmān (naḥ)**
Instrumental	**mayā**	**asmābhiḥ**
Dative	**mahyam (me)**	**asmabhyam (naḥ)**
Ablative	**mat**	**asmat**
Genitive	**mama (me)**	**asmākam (naḥ)**
Locative	**mayi**	**asmāsu**
Vocative	n/a	n/a

Second Person		
Case	Singular	Plural
Nominative	**tvam**	**yūyam**
Accusative	**tvām (tvā)**	**yuṣmān (vaḥ)**
Instrumental	**tvayā**	**yuṣmābhiḥ**
Dative	**tubhyam (te)**	**yuṣmabhyam (vaḥ)**
Ablative	**tvat**	**yuṣmat**
Genitive	**tava (te)**	**yuṣmākam (vaḥ)**
Locative	**tvayi**	**yuṣmāsu**
Vocative	n/a	n/a

Notes

1 Some grammars of Sanskrit cite the first person singular and plural ablative forms as **mad** and **asmad**, respectively, and the second person singular and plural ablative forms as **tvad** and **yuṣmad**, respectively. Such grammars are likely, also, to cite **tat** as **tad**, **etat** as **etad**. This is perfectly in order.

2 The dual forms are not shown. The first person dual equates, in concept, *to the two of us*; the second person dual to *the two of you*. The dual forms may be ignored until the learner encounters them in a reading passage. They do not occur in the present work.

If a personal pronoun qualifies a noun, as with **tat**, it precedes the noun in question (**Tat** is, after all, the personal pronoun for the third person as well as a demonstrative pronoun). There are, however, shortened forms of various pronouns that are placed after the noun which they qualify. These are known as 'enclitic' forms, in that they cannot come before the noun in question. The reader has already encountered an enclitic. That was the conjunction **ca** (*and*), placed after the words that it joins together (see 6.2, with reference to the comments made relating to the ablative case). In the table on the previous page, these enclitic forms are indicated in brackets. They do not have unique forms and can, as a result, cause ambiguity to arise. Context is needed, with the enclitic forms of the personal pronouns, to figure out the case that is being represented.

With the non-enclitic form:

मम पुत्रः जीवति

mama putraḥ jīvati

(With sandhi: **mama putro jīvati**)

My son (**putra**) *lives* (**jīvati**).

With the enclitic form:

पुत्रः मे जीवति

putraḥ me jīvati

(With sandhi: **putro me jīvati**)

My son lives.

Enclitic forms are by no means rare. The greeting exchanged daily between millions of Hindus is **namaste**. That is not a single word but two: **namas** (*salutation; homage*) and the enclitic form of the second person singular dative (**te**: *to you*). The non-enclitic form, whilst grammatically correct is not used as variant form of the greeting (***tubhyaṃ namas**). As for the other common greeting, **namaskāra**, the word **namas** is the same but a personal pronoun is not present. The word **kāra** is derived from the verbal root **kṛ** (*to do; make; create; fashion*). Whilst **namaste** is, therefore, a salutation being offered to another, **namaskāra** is simply a statement that salutation is being made. This brings the reader to the point where an investigation of matters relating to verbs becomes incumbent, although not without a couple of exercises beforehand, by way of consolidation of the present chapter.

6.7 Exercises

6.7.1 Questions on declension

The reader is asked to attempt the following questions. The answers are given on the next page, for convenience's sake. It may be beneficial to attempt the questions twice: referring to the relevant tables on the first occasion and a second time from memory, to consolidate the information.

Questions

(i) What are the functions of the instrumental, dative, ablative and genitive cases?

(ii) Give the case and number of the following forms:

devaiḥ; **kamalasya**; **niśāyām**; **rātrībhyaḥ**.

(iii) Give the case and number the following forms **tat**-forms:

tam; **tām**; **tān**; **tāni**.

(iv) Two **tat**-forms do not begin with the phoneme **t**. Which ones are they?

(v) Give the case and number of the personal pronoun forms **vayam** and **tvayā**.

(vi) What are the personal pronoun forms for *my/mine* and *your(s)* (singular)?

(vii) What are the enclitic forms of the first person and for which cases are they available?

(viii) What are the enclitic forms of the second person and for which cases are they available?

Answers

(i) The instrumental signifies *with*; *by*; *by means of*. The dative is the case of giving. (Note that it is the English: *He gives this to you*, not the *to* of: *He goes to the town*). The ablative indicates *from*. The genitive indicates possession (*of; belonging to*).

(ii) **devaiḥ** Instrumental plural.
kamalasya Genitive singular.
niśāyām Locative singular.
rātrībhyaḥ Dative or ablative plural.

(iii) **tam** Accusative singular (masculine).
tām Accusative singular (feminine).
tān Accusative plural (masculine).
tāni Nominative and accusative plural (neuter).

(iv) **saḥ** (masculine singular) and **sā** (feminine singular).

(v) **vayam** Nominative plural of the first person.
tvayā Instrumental singular of the second person.

(vi) **mama** (*my/mine*); **tava** (*your(s)*, singular).

(vii) Singular: **mā** (accusative); **me** (dative); **me** (genitive).
Plural: **naḥ** (accusative, dative and genitive).

(viii) Singular: **tvā** (accusative); **te** (dative); **te** (genitive).
Plural: **vaḥ** (accusative, dative and genitive).

6.7.2 Sentences for translation

These sentences are aimed at activating the vocabulary that appeared in earlier chapters as well as the current one. In Sanskrit, the article (*a/the*) is implied by the context. New words (or reminders) are given in brackets. The appropriate verb forms are as stated.

No knowledge of sound changes (sandhi) is presupposed, since this has yet to be explored (Chapter 8). The translations on the following page nevertheless give both the unsandhified and sandhified versions of the sentences. It is recommended that the reader compare both versions to see if anything can be deduced, at this stage, regarding sandhi.

Sentences

(i) जनाः अन्नेन जीवन्ति ।

(**jana**: *person*. Masculine short **-a** stem)

(ii) बुद्धः ग्रामात् आगच्छति ।

(**grāma**: *village*. Masculine short **-a** stem)

(iii) ताः संस्कृतं पठन्ति ।

(**paṭhanti**: *they recite; are reciting*)

(iv) सा रामस्य पुत्राय कमलानि यच्छति ।

(**yacchati**: *he/she/it gives; is giving*)

(v) कृष्णः अर्जुनं युद्धे पश्यति ।

(**yuddha**: *battle*. Neuter short **-a** stem)

(vi) नगरस्य जनाः कृष्णं रामं च पूजयन्ति ।

(**pūjayanti**: *they worship; are worshipping*)

Translations

(i) **janāḥ annena jīvanti**
(With sandhi: **janā annena jīvanti**)
People live by means of food.

(ii) **Buddhaḥ grāmāt āgacchati**
(With sandhi: **Buddho grāmād āgacchati**)
(The) Buddha comes from (the) village.

(iii) **tāḥ saṃskṛtaṃ paṭhanti**
(With sandhi: no change)
They (feminine plural) *recite Sanskrit.*

(iv) **sā Rāmasya putrāya kamalāni yacchati**
(With sandhi: no change)
She gives lotuses to Rāma's son.

(v) **Kṛṣṇaḥ Arjunaṃ yuddhe paśyati**
(With sandhi: **Kṛṣṇo 'rjunaṃ yuddhe paśyati**)
Kṛṣṇa sees Arjuna in (the) battle.

(vi) **nagarasya janāḥ Kṛṣṇaṃ Rāmaṃ ca pūjayanti**
(With sandhi: no change)
(The) people of (the) town worship Kṛṣṇa and Rāma.

Note how an ending in **-aḥ**, when followed by a voiced consonant, changes to **-o** (sentence ii). When followed by a short **a-**, **-aḥ** changes to **-o** and the following **a-** disappears (sentence v). An ending in **-āḥ**, when followed by a voiced phoneme – be it a consonant or vowel – simply drops the visarga (sentence i) and there is no mutation of the long **-ā** to **-o**. These are visarga sandhi changes, as discussed in 8.2. Also, a voiceless consonant at the end of a word, if followed by a vowel, is voiced (sentence ii). This is consonant sandhi, discussed in 8.3.

7

THE SANSKRIT VERB

Conjugation

7.1 Preliminaries

The Sanskrit verb represents the most complex aspect of the language, and a full investigation of conjugation lies well beyond the scope of the present work. To attempt to present a synoptic view of conjugation would only serve to baffle the beginner. It is crucial, nevertheless, to understand how the verb functions. In the discussion which follows, the focus will be on exploring the Sanskrit verb in the present tense and the imperfect. There are many things to be said about the verb and a knowledge of formal grammar is not presupposed on the part of the reader.

To begin with, it is worth distinguishing between tense and mood. Tense is a description of when something is happening – the past, the present or the future. Mood defines the way an action is taking place. Sanskrit has five tenses: present (which includes the indicative, imperative and optative moods), imperfect, perfect, aorist, future. The present tense in the indicative mood represents the logical and sensible first step in the study of the Sanskrit verb. The indicative is used in the making of a statement or the asking of a question. *You go* is a statement; *are you going?* is a question. In both instances, the tense is the present.

Along with five tenses, Sanskrit also possesses an active, middle and passive voice. English makes the distinction between an active and passive voice but does not formally recognize a middle voice. An English speaker would not fail to identify a difference between the following sentences:

DOI: 10.4324/9780429325434-8

Peter washes the dog.
The dog is washed by Peter.

In the first sentence, the emphasis is placed on the one who is performing the action. It is Peter who is actively washing the dog. In the second sentence, the emphasis has shifted from Peter to the dog, who is being passively washed. The middle voice is more difficult to grasp, in that the emphasis may be on the one performing the action expressed by the verb, but the focus is on the action that is taking place. In the Sanskrit grammatical tradition, a distinction is made between the active voice, which is termed as *a word/voice for another* (**parasmaipada**), and the middle voice, which is *a word/voice for oneself* (**ātmanepada**).

There is something distinctly reflexive about the middle voice which, according to traditional Indic terminology, strongly indicates that the middle voice would originally have signified the personal attachment of the one performing the verb to its outcome. This can be captured by the following examples from English and French:

Peter washes [*the dog*]/*Pierre lave* [*le chien*] (Active voice).
Peter washes [*himself*]/*Pierre* [*se*] *lave* (Middle voice).

Whatever the original semantic distinction in Proto-Indic or Vedic between the active and middle voice, Sanskrit is deemed to have lost any such distinction. Classical Sanskrit retains the grammatical distinction all the same. A verb root, along with being allocated to a conjugational class, is also indicated as occurring in the active or middle voice. Very often, a verb root is identified as capable of being expressed in both voices. Most grammars and dictionaries of Sanskrit use the capital letters P (**parasmaipada**) and Ā (**ātmanepada**) to signify this, although some grammars and dictionaries prefer the capital letter U (**ubhayapada**: *a word/voice for both*) to indicate that the verb may appear in either voice.

As with the noun, the Sanskrit verb uses the concept of number. Verbs are performed in the singular (by one entity), the dual (two and only two entities) or the plural (three or more entities). Unlike the noun, case does not come into play in conjugation and there is no notion of gender. The third person singular of the verb *to go* (*he/she/it goes*) remains the same whether the entity is masculine, feminine or neuter. Whereas a noun undergoes declension according to its stem, the verb is a root from which a stem must be derived before it can be conjugated.

7.2 Root, stem and vowel mutation

In Sanskrit, verbal roots are classified as belonging to one of ten classes, usually indicated in Sanskrit grammars by Roman numbers. A verbal root forms a stem according to the strategies appropriate to the class to which it belongs. It is important to note that the stem represents a modification of the verbal root to which personal endings are applied, yielding the necessary grammatical information about who is performing the verb. Personal endings are not applied directly to a verbal root.

In English, only the third person tends to show what appears to be a personal ending, with personal pronouns being deployed to give the requisite information regarding the subject of the verb. Consider the following example:

Present simple (English)		
Person	Singular	Plural
First	*I go*	*we go*
Second	*you go*	*you go*
Third	*he/she/it go*<u>*es*</u>	*they go*

As the English example demonstrates, the third person singular ending is distinct; elsewhere, *go* is the conjugated form (This is the pattern in English, with the notable exception of the verb *to be*, where the first person singular also has a unique form: *I* <u>*am*</u>*; you are*; *he/she/it* <u>*is*</u>*; we are; you are; they are*). In the Sanskrit conjugation of the verb *to go*, by contrast to English, all endings are distinctive. This makes the personal pronoun redundant, given that each form can be identified by its ending:

Present indicative – active voice (Sanskrit)		
Person	Singular	Plural
First	**gacchāmi**	**gacchāmaḥ**
Second	**gacchasi**	**gacchatha**
Third	**gacchati**	**gacchanti**

Two things are worth noting about the Sanskrit conjugation of the verb *to go* in the present tense. First, English distinguishes between the <u>present</u>

simple (*I go*, *you go*, etc.) and the present continuous or progressive (*I am going*, *you are going*, etc.). When translating a sentence from Sanskrit to English, the appropriate form of the present tense must be selected. Second, Sanskrit often uses a personal pronoun, albeit that it is not necessary for meaning. On such occasions, one ought to be sensitive to the fact that this is indicative of emphasis: **gacchāmi** already means *I go/I am going*. If the appropriate personal pronoun is included (**aham**: *I*), a different reading suggests itself:

ahaṃ gacchāmi
I am the one who goes/is going.

Conjugation of a verb in Sanskrit does not rely on identifying the infinitive form of a verb, as is the case in English (see 7.5 for more on the infinitive). Instead, Sanskrit uses the verbal root to generate a stem. Some of these modifications involve vowel mutation, a phenomenon briefly discussed in 5.2, ix. Four of the ten verb classes are referred to as 'thematic', in that they share a common theme (Class I, IV, VI and X). The other verb classes (II, III, V, VII, VIII, IX) use different strategies to generate a stem. The present work will focus on the thematic verb classes. To do otherwise would be to present the reader with a mass of information on conjugation strategies, each of which would require investigation in the context of sound changes, irregularities, etc. The thematic group is always studied first, since it involves four of the ten classes at a stroke and accounts for substantially over half of all the verb forms encountered by the student of Sanskrit (Class I is unusually large and contains the lion's share of the most frequently occurring verbs).

The concept of vowel mutation (or vowel strengthening) states that a vowel may undergo changes according to 'grade'. This grade is effectively the fusion of a short **a** into the vowel in question, to produce a qualitative difference in the first instance (**guṇa**). With the strongest grade, a further short **a** is added to guṇa, which produces a quantitative distinction (**vr̥ddhi**). It will be noted that **e** and **o** are not simple vowels but complex ones. They appear in the table of vowel mutation as guna-forms, thereby reinforcing their classification by the Sanskrit grammatical tradition as vowels which were in some way less 'pure' than **a/ā**, **i/ī**, **u/ū**, **r̥/r̥̄** and **l̥**. The diphthongs, likewise, are present. They are vr̥ddhi-forms.

Simple vowel	a or ā	i or ī	u or ū	r̥ or r̥̄	l̥
guṇa	a	e	o	ar	al
vr̥ddhi	ā	ai	au	ār	(n/a)

Note that **a** does not change its quality at any point, but merely its length. This is because the strengthening agent is **a** itself. Only in the vr̥ddhi grade does short **a** change to long **ā**. As for r̥, r̥̄ and l̥, the pure vowel is replaced by the closest semivowel, since *ar̥, *ar̥̄ and *al̥ are not recognized as diphthongs in Sanskrit.

7.3 Thematic verbs

Verbs belonging to classes I, IV, VI and X share a common theme, as noted. Two of these additionally use vowel mutation in the process of generating the verbal stem. These are Class I and Class X (Classes IV and VI do not involve a mutation of the root vowel). Vowel mutation is best seen with reference to an actual example and, with this is mind, the verb root **bhū** (*to be*) is a good starting point.

√ **bhū** is extremely common in Sanskrit and therefore serves as an excellent introduction to the thematic group. It is an interesting example, since it is not entirely transparent as regards the process of vowel mutation. That said, once the principle is grasped, other examples of vowel mutation easily fall into place. The root vowel is subject to mutation and, since the vowel in question is neither **a** nor **ā**, strengthening produces something both audibly different to **ū**.

Applying guṇa to **bhū** produces *****bho**, which is not attested in the conjugational paradigm of the verb in the present tense. The form *****bho** would, in any event, lead to a violation in that the thematic strategy for a Class I verb is to add a short **a** after the modified root and before the personal endings. This would result, in principle, in the following:

*****bho + a + ti** (personal ending of the third person singular)

Clearly, something is required to prevent the violation *****oa** from taking place. This is resolved by the application of one of a set of rules relating to instances where a complex vowel or diphthong precedes a vowel <u>within a word</u>. Taking *****bho** as the example, the relevant rule is as follows:

Root with guṇa	Before a vowel	Stem
bho	bhav	bhava

The set of rules in question also transforms **-e** → **-ay**; **-ai** → **-āy**; **-au** → **-āv**. They prevent the creation of impermissible diphthongs, such as ***oa**, by changing the complex vowels and diphthongs into the segment: simple vowel + semivowel (with a long vowel, as regards the diphthongs).

The addition of **a** after the modified verbal root is the theme which creates the notion of a thematic group. Classes IV, VI and X also employ **a**, but not always by itself. In Class IV and Class X, the semivowel **y** is also present.

Thematic verbs (Class I): the present tense

√ **bhū** (*to be*) Class I

Strategy: **-a** is added to the root but the root undergoes mutation.

Stem: **bhava**

Active voice (**parasmaipada**)		
Person	Singular	Plural
First	**bhavāmi**	**bhavāmaḥ**
Second	**bhavasi**	**bhavatha**
Third	**bhavati**	**bhavanti**

Middle voice (**ātmanepada**)		
Person	Singular	Plural
First	**bhave**	**bhavāmahe**
Second	**bhavase**	**bhavadhve**
Third	**bhavate**	**bhavante**

Notes

1. The personal endings (**-mi**, **-si**, **-ti**, etc.) are added to the stem form of the verb. There are two exceptions to note. First, the final **-a** in the stem in lengthened to **-ā** in the first person (both singular and plural) except for the first person singular of the middle voice, where it is **-e**.
2. All of the middle voice forms end in **-e**, which replaces the final vowel in active voice forms ending in a vowel (e.g. **bhavati** → **bhavate**; **bhavanti** → **bhavante**). If the active voice form ends in visarga, the ending **-e** is simply added and the visarga changes to the aspirate

(**bhavāmaḥ** → **bhavāmahe**). There are two exceptions: **bhave** and **bhavadhve**.

3 The stem ***bhū** + **a** would violate the sound system of Sanskrit, which does not permit any diphthong other than **ai** or **au**. Vowel mutation takes place, resulting in **av** + **a** (i.e. **bhū** → **bhav** + **a** = **bhava**).

Thematic verbs (Classes IV, VI, X): the present tense

√ **nṛt** (*to dance*) Class IV

Strategy: **-ya** is added to the root. There is no vowel mutation.

Stem: **nṛtya**

Active voice		
Person	Singular	Plural
First	**nṛtyāmi**	**nṛtyāmaḥ**
Second	**nṛtyasi**	**nṛtyatha**
Third	**nṛtyati**	**nṛtyanti**

√ **likh** (*to write*) Class VI

Strategy: **-a** is added to the root. There is no vowel mutation.

Stem: **likha**

Active voice		
Person	Singular	Plural
First	**likhāmi**	**likhāmaḥ**
Second	**likhasi**	**likhatha**
Third	**likhati**	**likhanti**

√ **cur** (*to steal*) Class X

Strategy: **-aya** is added to the root, which undergoes vowel mutation.

Stem: **coraya**

Active voice		
Person	Singular	Plural
First	**corayāmi**	**corayāmaḥ**

Active voice		
Second	**corayasi**	**corayatha**
Third	**corayati**	**corayanti**

(Note that **cur** → **cor** merely takes the guṇa-form of vowel mutation.)

7.4 The imperfect

The imperfect is one of three tenses which Sanskrit employs to express past event: *I was; you were; he/she/it was;* etc. The other two tenses which do so are the perfect and the aorist. Unlike the perfect and the aorist, the imperfect uses the present stem to generate its forms. The same is true of two moods within the present tense, along with the indicative mood which has provided the examples so far (These are the imperative and the optative, where the former indicates an order or instruction, such as *go and look!*, and the latter has a wide range of uses including expressing a desire or wish for something to happen: *you ought to go and look*). The imperfect is extremely prevalent in Sanskrit, so it is useful for the learner to be familiar with it at an early stage.

As with the present tense, the imperfect requires a stem to be generated from a verbal root before personal endings can be attached and a finite verb form created (A 'finite verb' is one in which a person is indicated – first, second or third – in the singular, dual or plural number. A verb form that is not grammatically associated with a person is referred to as 'non-finite' or 'infinitive'). Unlike the present tense, the various forms of the imperfect all have a prefixed short **a**, known as the 'augment'. It is not helpful to think of the augment as a prefix, since Sanskrit has a considerable number of prefixes which are attached to the verbal stem and, in many cases, modify the meaning of the verb.

The augment signifies only one of a number of differences between the formation of the imperfect and that of the present. The singular endings of the present, in the active voice (**-mi**, **-si**, **-ti**), appear in the active voice of the imperfect as **-m**, **-h**, **-t**. In the plural forms of the active voice, the endings of the imperfect are not **-maḥ**, **-tha** and **-nti** but, rather, **-ma**, **-ta** and **-an** – not neglecting the augment. Because of the many differences existing between the personal endings of the present and the imperfect, these endings must be learnt separately. A simple 'transformation rule' is not at hand. The learner is advised to concentrate on the present tense, in both voices, and to look at the imperfect once the present tense endings have become second nature.

Sanskrit conjugation is not easy. The trick is to learn something thoroughly and to dovetail the knowledge of that thing into the acquisition of new information. Knowledge of the present tense should precede familiarity with the imperfect.

The imperfect (√ bhū)
√ **bhū** (*to be*) Class I
Stem: **bhava**

Active voice (**parasmaipada**)		
Person	Singular	Plural
First	**abhavam**	**abhavāma**
Second	**abhavaḥ**	**abhavata**
Third	**abhavat**	**abhavan**

Middle voice (**ātmanepada**)		
Person	Singular	Plural
First	**abhave**	**abhavāmahi**
Second	**abhavathāḥ**	**abhavadhvam**
Third	**abhavata**	**abhavanta**

Notes

1 Visarga is very often synonymous with the phoneme **s**. Bearing this is mind, there is a strong similarity between the singular, active voice endings of the present (**-mi**, **-si**, **-ti**) and the corresponding imperfect forms (**-m**, **-ḥ**, **-t**). A final short **-i** is absent in the imperfect endings.

2 The stem in the first person plural, in both voices, has a long **-ā**. This is precisely the case with the present tense endings. A long **-ā** is not, however, found in the first personal singular form of the active voice.

3 The first person singular of the middle voice patterns perfectly with the present tense (**bhave** with the augment: **abhave**). The patterning with the first person plural of the middle voice, whilst not exact, is not a far cry from the present tense form. Aside from the augment, only the final vowel differs: **bhavāmahe** (present); **abhavāmahi** (imperfect).

7.5 The infinitive

As mentioned in 7.2, Sanskrit does not use the infinitive to identify the base form of a verb prior to conjugation. The infinitive is not the simplest form of the verb, in Sanskrit, in that a suffix is necessary for its creation. The suffix in question is **-tum** or **-itum** added to the verbal root. From that point, there is no modification. The infinitive does not refer to any particular grammatical person, so personal endings are not applied. Its translation into English is straightforward. It is consistent with the English infinitive: the base form of the verb preceded by the preposition *to* (e.g. √ **han** → **hantum**: *to strike; slay; kill*). A grammatically well-formed sentence cannot just contain a verb root with an infinitive ending, and Sanskrit employs other strategies to indicate that an action is being, has been or is to be undertaken by the subject of the sentence. The most evident of these is the use of a finite verb.

Deciding whether a given verb root adds **-tum** or **-itum** in the formation of the infinitive is not always straightforward. The learner might suppose that a verbal root ending in a consonant would take **-itum** and that is indeed the case with √ **likh** → **likhitum** (*to write*). Sadly, that is not a rule which can in any sense be said to be widespread. With the verbs *to renounce; abandon* and *to go*, for example, the verbal root ends in a consonant but the infinitive suffix is **-tum**, not **-itum**. This causes a sound change to take place, avoiding a cluster which violates Sanskrit phonology:

√ **tyaj** → **tyaktum** (*to renounce; abandon*)
√ **gam** → **gantum** (*to go*)

With √ **tyaj**, the root ends in a sound that Sanskrit does not permit in word-final position. This is not a contradiction, since Sanskrit does not conceptually identify a root as a complete word. It is an element waiting to be shaped into a word. In the formation of a word, the element must accord with the rules of the language. Since neither **-j** nor **-m** can come together with a morpheme beginning with **t-**, a suitable adjustment must be made. In the case of **-j**, the palatal becomes a velar: **-k**. As regards **-m**, which is the labial nasal, it changes to the nasal of the class to which the following **t-** belongs: this is **-n**. Practically speaking, the student of Sanskrit learns the infinitives in their fixed form as and when they are encountered. There seems little point, under the circumstances, aiming for a set of rules which would be more of a burden than a benefit.

7.6 The gerund

The gerund is frequently used in Sanskrit and merits investigation. The term 'gerund' may not be too enlightening, even to those who are familiar with grammatical terminology. In English, it signifies a verb form which functions as a noun (e.g. *my coming to this party was a mistake; rage against the dying of the light*). It can be outrightly adjectival in nature, as can be seen in the phrases *driving instructor* and *singing lesson*. In Sanskrit, it is formed from a verbal root, as with the infinitive, and by the addition of a suffix. Often, the Sanskrit gerund is translated by the English present participle *having* (e.g. *having written; having renounced; having gone*). Unlike the finite verb, and in common with the infinitive, the gerund is not conjugated. This means that no personal endings are applied to the gerund. Once the appropriate suffix is added, the gerund is complete.

The gerund takes the form of the suffix **-tvā** or **-itvā**. As with the infinitive **-tum** and **-itum,** there may be an assumption that, where the verbal root ends in a vowel, one predicts the use of **-tvā** and, where the root ends in a consonant, **-itvā** is used. That is a useful rule of thumb, although there are too many exceptions for a more accurate set of rules to be postulated. If one takes the verbs explored in the infinitive (√ **likh**; √ **tyaj**; √ **gam**), one predicts the following gerunds:

√ **likh** → **likhitvā** (*having written*)

This is a correct deduction. The **-itvā** suffix is used. Note also that Sanskrit permits **lekhitvā**, where the vowel in the root appears to have undergone mutation to guṇa grade, although this is not a feature of the formation of the gerund. So too, **lekhitum** is also attested in the infinitive.

√ **tyaj** → **tyaktvā** (*having renounced; abandoned*)

By analogy to the infinitive, this is also a correct deduction. Note that the **-j** of the verbal root is velarized to **-k**, avoiding the cluster **-jt**.

√ **gam** → **gatvā** (*having gone*. Not ***gantvā**)

Here, the **-m** in the verbal root is dropped, resulting in **ga-**. The suffix **-tvā** is then added to this truncated root, yielding **gatvā**. Note that the **-m** is not dropped in the infinitive but, rather, subject to a sound change:

√ **gam** + **tum** → **gantum** (*to go*)

Irregularities aside, the gerund is an easy form to spot in Sanskrit. The ending – **(i)tvā** is distinctive. This is, however, complicated by the fact that the gerund takes the form of the suffix **-ya** when the verbal root contains a prefix. As noted in 7.4, a prefix can modify the meaning of a verb quite considerably:

Prefix **abhi-** + √ **likh** → **abhilikhya** (*having engraved; inscribed*)

The sense of writing has been maintained but refined to indicate a specific type of writing. The suffix **-ya** replaces **-itvā** because of the prefix.

Prefix **pari-** + √ **tyaj** → **parityajya** (*having left; quit*)

There is no change in the essential meaning of the verb because of prefixation. The appropriate **-ya** suffix is employed.

Prefix **ā-** + √ **gam** → **āgamya** (*having come*)

The verb has undergone quite a transformation as a result of prefixation. Note that the prefix **ā-** is not to be assumed as one which reverses the action of the verb. Prefixes are very often verb specific in terms of how they modify meaning. A proper understanding of prefixes must come with the reading of texts in Sanskrit. Attempting to give a bare meaning to individual prefixes would be a red herring.

The gerund can neither begin a sentence nor finish it. Its use is considerable with respect to giving information relating to the actions of the subject of the sentence prior to a finite verb making the sentence grammatically complete. Gerunds are best thought of as 'place holders' building up a body of information whilst remaining grammatically free of the subject or the object(s) of the sentence. Consider the following, stilted sentence in English, which mimics how the sentence would be structured in Sanskrit:

[*To the orchard having gone*,] [*apples having seen*,] [*these having eaten*,]
the mule was happy.

The first line in the example contains three gerunds, underlined. In all cases, the gerund is not at the start of the phrase (indicated by brackets) but follows either a noun or a pronoun. This is a requirement in Sanskrit. None of the phrases equate to a complete grammatical sentence. The second line of the example, containing the subject and the finite verb, is a grammatically complete sentence.

7.7 Exercise: sentences for translation

In preparation for tackling sentences in Sanskrit (Chapter 9) and to consolidate the current chapter, the reader is asked to attempt the following eight sentences, where sandhi has not been applied. New vocabulary is given under the relevant sentence. Translations, together with analyses of the sentences and a discussion of sandhi (where applicable), appear overleaf.

Sentences

(i) अहं पत्रं लिखामि ।

ahaṃ pattraṃ likhāmi
(**pattra** noun (n): *a letter*)

(ii) सूतः कमलानि चोरयति ।

sūtaḥ kamalāni corayati

(iii) कन्याः उद्याने नृत्यन्ति ।

kanyāḥ udyāne nṛtyanti
(**kanyā** noun (f): girl)

(iv) तम् अश्वं हन्तुं न धर्म्यं भवति ।

tam aśvaṃ hantuṃ na dharmyaṃ bhavati
(**dharmya** adjective: *righteous*)

(v) पाण्डवाः कुरुक्षेत्रं गन्तुम् इच्छन्ति ।

pāṇḍavāḥ kurukṣetraṃ gantum icchanti
(√ **iṣ**, Class IV → Stem **iccha**-: *to wish; desire*)

(vi) नगरं गत्वा कृष्णः पुत्रान् अवदत् ।

nagaraṃ gatvā kṛṣṇaḥ putrān avadat
(√ **vad**, Class I → Stem **vada**-: *to speak; address*)

(vii) तद् उक्त्वा रामः अगच्छत् ।

tad uktvā rāmaḥ agacchat

(viii) ग्रामं त्यक्त्वा/परित्यज्य जनाः संतुष्टाः अभवन् ।

grāmaṃ tyaktvā/parityajya janāḥ saṃtuṣṭāḥ abhavan
(**saṃtuṣṭa** past passive participle: *pleased; contented*)

Translations

(i) **ahaṃ pattraṃ likhāmi**
(No sandhi changes)
I am the one who is writing a/the letter.
It is clear, from the personal ending on the verb, who is doing the writing. The personal pronoun **aham** is not strictly speaking required. Sanskrit allows a pronoun to be dropped, unlike English, where the meaning of a sentence is clear. If the pronoun occurs, when it not required for grammatical purposes, this is usually indicative of emphasis. The point should be made, all the same, that Sanskrit verse often uses pronouns to ensure that there are the requisite number of syllables for the metre in question.

(ii) **sūtaḥ kamalāni corayati**
(No sandhi changes)
The charioteer steals (the) lotuses.
A straightforward sentence which has the preferred word order of an active construction in Sanskrit: subject – object – verb. Being heavily inflected, Sanskrit permits considerable freedom in word order. Nowhere is this more evident than in poetry, where word movement allows for metrical requirements to be met.

(iii) **kanyāḥ udyāne nṛtyanti**
(With sandhi: **kanyā udyāne nṛtyanti**)
The girls dance in the garden.
As with sentence (ii), this sentence is straightforward. Note that the word for *garden* (**udyāna**) is in the locative case, indicating where the action is taking place.
There is one sandhi change (**kanyāḥ** → **kanyā**). This will be investigated further in 8.2. Effectively, the ending **-āḥ**, when followed by a voiced phoneme (remembering that all vowels are voiced) results in the dropping of the visarga.

(iv) **tam aśvaṃ hantuṃ na dharmyaṃ bhavati**
(No sandhi changes)
It is not righteous to kill that horse.

This sentence contains an infinitival phrase (*to kill that horse*). The subject of the sentence is *it* (i.e. *it* is the thing which is not righteous) but a word for *it* is not present. Otherwise said, the subject is not overtly marked. The adjective, **dharmya**, qualifies the empty subject (*it is not righteous*) and accordingly takes a neuter ending. A pronoun can be dropped in Sanskrit whereas English does not permit such a thing. If there is an empty subject in English, a dummy subject is provided (e.g. *It is raining*). In this type of construction, Sanskrit deems the empty subject to be neuter.

(v) **pāṇḍavāḥ kurukṣetraṃ gantum icchanti**
(No sandhi changes)
The Pāṇḍavas wish to go to Kurukṣetra.
Note the position of the infinitive (**gantum**). It follows the place to which the Pāṇḍavas wish to go. The finite verb (*they wish*) is at the end of the sentence. The object (**kurukṣetra**) is between the subject and the verb. One does not use the dative case to indicate movement towards something or someone. That is a property of the accusative. The English preposition *to* is potentially misleading.

(vi) **nagaraṃ gatvā kṛṣṇaḥ putrān avadat**
(No sandhi changes)
Having gone to the town, Kṛṣṇa spoke to the/his sons.
As with the infinitive, the gerund does not come at the start of a sentence or phrase. The main sentence is **kṛṣṇaḥ putrān avadat**, and the finite verb is the third person singular imperfect, active voice. The sons – who may be Kṛṣṇa's, in the right context – are three or more in number, not just two (That would require the dual).

(vii) **tad uktvā rāmaḥ agacchat**
(With sandhi: **tad uktvā rāmo 'gacchat**)
Having said this, Rāma went.

As with sentence (vi), the gerund is not the first word in either the sentence or the gerundival phrase (**tad uktvā**). A tat-form is deployed to indicate the thing which has been uttered by Rāma. The thing is an *it*, rather than a *him* or a *her*, so the relevant **tat**-form is the neuter accusative singular.

A paradigm for the verb *to go* is given in 7.2, but in the present tense. Here, the verb form is in the imperfect (third person singular, active voice). If the augment (**a-**) is removed, together with the personal ending for the third person singular (**-t**), what remains is the stem: **gaccha-**. The stem is visible in all forms of the present tense and can be deduced by removing the personal endings.

The combination of a final **-aḥ** followed by an initial **a-** represents the most complex example of visarga sandhi. Sandhification takes two steps. First, the **-aḥ** does not simply drop the visarga but changes to **-o**; second, the initial **a-** of the following word is not pronounced. It disappears and its disappearance is marked with a sign called **avagraha** (see 8.2).

(viii) **grāmaṃ tyaktvā/parityajya janāḥ saṃtuṣṭāḥ abhavan**
(With sandhi: **grāmaṃ tyaktvā/parityajya janāḥ saṃtuṣṭā abhavan**)
Having forsaken the village, the people were happy.

There is a choice of gerund, with an unprefixed verb (in which case, the **-(i)tvā** suffix is used) or a prefixed verb (where the gerund takes the form of the suffix **-ya**). As with sentence (iii), the ending **-āḥ** in **saṃtuṣṭāḥ** drops the visarga when followed by a vowel, which is voiced. There is no dropping of the visarga in **janāḥ**, since it is followed by a sibilant – and all sibilants are voiceless.

A separate word needs to be said about the past passive participle which, whilst outside of the scope of the present work (along with a number of other participles that the language possesses), is very widely used in Sanskrit. It is formed from a verbal root and has the suffix – **(i)ta**. Quite unlike the gerund, it is subject to endings. These are not conjugational endings but declensional ones. In this respect, the past passive participle agrees with the noun with which it is associated. The past passive participle is most often adjectival in nature, as in the sentence in question: **saṃtuṣṭāḥ** qualifies the word **janāḥ**. The **-ta** suffix, as a result, agrees with respect to case, number and gender. It takes the nominative plural masculine ending, **-āḥ**: **-tāḥ**. This is subject to cerebralization (**-tāḥ** → **-ṭāḥ**) because it is preceded by the cerebral sibilant, **ṣ**. The past passive participle can also substitute for a finite verb, whilst a gerund and an infinitive cannot. Given its importance, the past passive participle will be explored in greater detail in the reading passages (9.3.1).

8

SOUND CHANGES

Sandhi

8.1 Preliminaries

Sanskrit places great emphasis on the sound system, as one might expect of a language in which recitation and the oral tradition have prevailed for millennia. The Devanāgarī aims to reproduce as faithfully as possible the sounds of the language, but all languages change over time and there are instances where the true nature of certain sounds are subject to an interpretation which, in due course, becomes 'traditional'. This is the case with **ṛ**, **ṝ** and **ḷ** as well as the articulation of visarga and anusvāra. Given the importance accorded to sound, a series of rules were posited in antiquity. These are collectively known as **sandhi**: an account of the adjustments which take place in sounds when they come together. The word itself is an example of what it addresses: prefix **sam-** (*with; together with*) + √ **dhā** (*to place; bring together*).

Sandhi is not unique to Sanskrit. Everyday English bristles with what are nothing other than sandhi features. The plural morpheme *-s*, for example, may either sound like a voiceless sibilant (the *'s'* in *snake*) or its voiced equivalent (the *'z'* in *zebra*). The words *cats* and *dogs* are examples of these sounds, respectively. From a phonological point of view, the distinction is an easy one: the voiceless *s* is heard after a voiceless sound (*ca*<u>*t*</u>) whereas the voiced sibilant occurs when it follows a voiced sound (*dog*). English spelling does not reflect this difference in sound, placing the emphasis on writing and leaving sandhi features to arise as they will. Even though

DOI: 10.4324/9780429325434-9

handbag contains a consonant cluster which reduces in everyday speech to **hanbag* and, from there, to **hambag*, English preserves the spelling. Consider, also, how unlikely one is likely to hear all the phonemes in the word *sixth* (i.e. *s* + *i* + *k* + *s* + *th*); yet the more representative spelling **sikth* would be deemed a spelling error.

In Sanskrit, sandhi features have an impact on spelling. They are pervasive and must be grasped by the learner, since no authentic example of Sanskrit is 'unsandhified'. Reducing or withholding sandhification for the learner is the natural and arguably the more sensible approach. With sandhi, words can (and do) change to the point where endings suddenly become invisible, leaving the learner confused and disorientated. An investigation of sandhi ought not, however, to be deferred for very long.

8.2 Visarga sandhi

Sandhi is best approached as a phenomenon which affects particular categories of sound. With regard to this, the methodical arrangement of the sound system is of considerable assistance. An example of a sound change was seen with the word **Buddha** (5.2), where voice was shown to be a trigger for the sound change in question. This is important to bear in mind, since the notion of voice is central to the phenomenon of sandhi.

A good place to start exploring sandhi is not as it affects consonants but as it affects visarga. Many declensional and conjugation forms end in visarga, and the first mention of sandhi was made as and when it was encountered in the sentence: **Rāmaḥ aśvaṃ paśyati** (6.2). This was subject to a sandhi change which resulted in **Rāmo 'śvaṃ paśyati**. Once the basis of visarga sandhi is understood, it becomes relatively easy to see why consonants change. Visarga sandhi is, therefore, the first port of call.

Visarga cannot occur at the start of a word, so it follows that visarga sandhi relates to the changes that take place at the end of words, as they encounter a following word. In essence, visarga sandhi states that a visarga is subject to change when it is followed by a voiced sound. It is crucial that the reader is now fully able to identify the sounds explored and classified in Chapter 3, since an understanding of which phonemes are voiced and which are voiceless goes to the heart of understanding sandhi. Consonants may be voiced or voiceless, but nasals are always voiced, as are semivowels. As for the sibilants, these are all voiceless. Vowels are voiced, without exception. If this much is understood, the majority of visarga sandhi outcomes can be rationalized. Returning to the sentence which appears in 6.2, one may now apply a visarga sandhi rule.

Before sandhi: **Rāmaḥ aśvaṃ paśyati**

The ending **-aḥ** is followed by a vowel (which is voiced). The visarga is subject to change. In this case, **-aḥ** is reduced to **-o** but there is a secondary effect, also: the initial **a-** of **aśvaṃ** disappears and is replaced by a sign called **avagraha**, resembling a handwritten capital *S*, which has no pronunciation. In the IAST, avagraha is indicated by an apostrophe.

रामोऽश्वं पश्यति

Rāmo 'śvaṃ paśyati

Rāma sees the horse.

What if **Rāmaḥ** had been followed by a word starting with a voiceless sound? The following sentence shows the outcome in this event, using **khara** (*mule*) rather than **aśva** (*horse*):

रामः खरं पश्यति

Rāmaḥ kharaṃ paśyati

Rāma sees the mule.

There is no change to the ending **-aḥ**, since voice is absent in the following phoneme (**kh**) and the trigger for visarga sandhi is missing. There are ten voiceless consonants in Sanskrit, not counting the three sibilants and the aspirate, all of which are voiceless. One might assume that, when followed by any of these phonemes, visarga sandhi would not come into operation. Whilst predicated on good logic, that is not the case.

Words ending in a visarga are subject to visarga sandhi changes when followed by voiced phonemes <u>or</u> by the following three pairs of consonants: **c-**, **ch**; **ṭ-**, **ṭh-**; **t-**, **th-**. Here, the following changes take place:

-ḥ + **c-**, **ch-** = **ś-**

-ḥ + **ṭ-**, **ṭh-** = **ṣ-**

-ḥ + **t-**, **th-** = **s-**

This is the case irrespective of whether the visarga is preceded by a short **a**, a long **ā** or a vowel which is neither of those (or indeed a diphthong). It is worth noting that visarga may <u>optionally</u> assimilate to one of the sibilants.

For example, in **Rāmaḥ sīdati** (*Rāma sits/is sitting*), the visarga may remain as it is or be assimilated to the following sibilant: **Rāmas sīdati**. The learner is more likely to see the former option being taken in textbooks aimed at the student of Sanskrit. The latter option is, nevertheless, to be borne in mind when Sanskrit texts are consulted in the original. Adjustment to the strategy of assimilation is not problematic.

If one now consults a table of visarga sandhi changes, the regularity of the application of visarga sandhi can easily be seen. Overleaf is just such a table, where visarga is grouped according to whether it is preceded by a short **a**, a long **ā** or any other vowel, for which a smiley symbol is used. The patterning between **-aḥ**, **-āḥ**, and **-☺ḥ** is identical in all cases where the following phoneme is voiceless. It is only when visarga is followed by voiced phonemes (i.e. the last two rows) that differences exist.

Visarga sandhi

-aḥ	**-āḥ**	**-☺ḥ**	Following phoneme
-aḥ	**-āḥ**	**-☺ḥ**	**k-, kh-, p-, ph-**
-aś	**-āś**	**-☺ś**	**c-, ch-**
-aṣ	**-āṣ**	**-☺ṣ**	**ṭ-, ṭh-**
-as	**-ās**	**-☺s**	**t-, th-**
-aḥ or – **aś/-aṣ/-as**	**-āḥ** or – **āś/-āṣ/-ās**	**-☺ḥ** or – **☺ś/-☺ṣ/-☺s**	**ś-, ṣ-, s-**
-o	**-ā**	**-☺r**[1]	Voiced consonants, semivowels and **h-**[2]
-a[3]	**-ā**	**-☺r**	vowels and diphthongs

Notes

1 When followed by **r-**, **-iḥ** and **-uḥ** drop the visarga and lengthen to **-ī** and **-ū**, respectively.

2 Although technically voiceless, the phoneme **h** acts as if it were voiced.

3 The rule applies to every vowel except a following short **a-**. Before short **a-**, **-aḥ** goes to **-o** and avagraha replaces the following **a-**.

रामः अवदत् → रामोऽवदत्

Rāmaḥ avadat → Rāmo 'vadat

Rāma spoke/said.

As seen with the pre-sandhified sentence, **Rāmaḥ avadat**, the visarga is dropped and the exposed short **-a** at the end of **Rāma** changed to **-o**. As the visarga sandhi table indicates, that is a strategy which is not adopted in other instances of visarga sandhi. Words ending in **-āḥ** have a simpler strategy in which the visarga is dropped, there is no mutation of the long **-ā** and no deployment of avagraha:

कन्याः अवदन् → कन्या अवदन्

kanyāḥ avadan → kanyā avadan

(The) girls spoke/said.

Note that the verb has changed, due to number (It is the third person plural of the imperfect, active voice, since **kanyāḥ** is in the nominative plural). With **-āḥ**, it does not matter if the phoneme which follows is a voiced consonant, a semivowel or a vowel (Remember that **h** acts as if it were voiced). In all cases where the following phoneme is voiced (or is **h**), the visarga is dropped and that is the end of it.

When the visarga is preceded by a vowel other than **a** or **ā**, the strategy is different again. Here, the rule is that the visarga changes to **r**.

अग्निः अवदत् → अग्निर् अवदत्

Agniḥ avadat → Agnir avadat

Agni spoke/said.

(The present work has not looked at the declension of short **i**-stems. Suffice it to say that the nominative singular ending for **Agni** is **Agniḥ**.)

There is an exception to this rule when the word which follows **-☺ḥ** begins with **r-** and this is subject to a note on the accompanying visarga sandhi table. This exception aside, **-☺ḥ** acts the same way in all cases where the following phoneme is voiced (or is **h**). The visarga becomes **r**.

It is important to note that sandhi is a mechanical operation in Sanskrit. Once visarga has been applied according to the rules specified, the output is fixed. There is no recombination after sandhi, however much it may appear that further modification is required. This point will become particularly relevant when vowel sandhi is investigated (8.4).

8.3 Consonant sandhi

As with visarga sandhi, the overarching criterion with consonant sandhi is the distinction between voiced and voiceless phonemes. There are remarkably few non-vocalic phonemes which may occur at the end of a word in Sanskrit. These are **-k**, **-ṭ**, **-t**, **-p**, **-ṅ**, **-n**, **-m**. Except for the nasals, they are voiceless sounds (Visarga may, of course, also occur at the end of a word. One may assume that visarga, although not usually subject to analysis in terms of voice, is a voiceless sound according to the changes made – and not made – with visarga sandhi). The final phoneme in a word, if voiceless, acquires voice through the application of consonant sandhi if it is followed by a word beginning with a voiced phoneme. A good example of this – pertinent, given the contents of Chapter 9 – is the word **Bhagavadgītā**, from **bhagavat** (*divine; holy*) + **gītā** (*song*). The **t** is voiceless and is in contact with the voiced **g** of the following word. This causes the voiceless word-final phoneme (**t**) to acquire voice (**d**).

Unlike the changes that take place with visarga sandhi, it is not suggested that the learner should memorize all the possible outcomes of consonant sandhi. Sandhi tables (or grids) exist for reference purposes. One ought, nevertheless, to know how to use a sandhi table and how to make sense of the data it contains. With **bhagavat** + **gītā**, the relevant information is found by identifying the word-final phoneme from the list of those which appear horizontally at the top of the table. The initial phoneme of the following word appears in the column to the right of the table. Where the entry in the top row intersects with the entry to the right of the table, the output is in the body of the table. The output for the **-d-** in **Bhagavadgītā** is stated under **t-**, on the third row (corresponding with **g-**, **gh-**).

A glance at the table reveals that, where a word ends in **-k**, **-ṭ**, **-t**, **or -p** (i.e. all the voiceless permitted final phonemes), these stay the same when followed by a voiceless phoneme, with only three exceptions: **-t** followed by **c-**/**ch-** is **-c**; **-t** followed by **ṭ-**/**ṭh-** is **-ṭ**; **-t** followed by – **ś** is **-c**. With word-final **-ṅ** and **-m**, the situation is even more straightforward. There are, in effect, no changes at all, beyond the first row (when they are followed by vowels). Anusvāra is present in all cases of word-final **-m** unless it is followed by a vowel. The situation is more complex with word-final **-n** and with word-final phonemes followed by **n-**/**m-**, **l**, **ś** and **h**. Practice in reading Sanskrit is the only way to become familiar with consonant sandhi forms which do not conform to a pattern.

Consonant sandhi

-k	-ṭ	-t	-p	-ṅ	-n	-m	
-g-	-ḍ-	-d-	-b-	-ṅ(ṅ)-[1]	-n(n)-[1]	-m-	Vowels
-k-	-ṭ-	-t-	-p-	-ṅ-	-n-	-ṃ-	k-/kh-
-g-	-ḍ-	-d-	-b-	-ṅ-	-n-	-ṃ-	g-/gh-
-k-	-ṭ-	-c-	-p-	-ṅ-	-ṃś-	-ṃ-	c-/ch-
-g-	-ḍ-	-j-	-b-	-ṅ-	-ñ-	-ṃ-	j-/jh-
-k-	-ṭ-	-ṭ-	-p-	-ṅ-	- ṃṣ-	-ṃ-	ṭ-/ṭh-
-g-	-ḍ-	-ḍ-	-b-	-ṅ-	-ṇ-	-ṃ-	ḍ-/ḍh-
-k-	-ṭ-	-t-	-p-	-ṅ-	-ṃs-	-ṃ-	t-/th
-g-	-ḍ-	-d-	-b-	-ṅ-	-n-	-ṃ-	d-/dh-
-k-	-ṭ-	-t-	-p-	-ṅ-	-n-	-ṃ-	p-/ph-
-g-	-ḍ-	-d-	-b-	-ṅ-	-n-	-ṃ-	b-/bh-
-ṅ-	-ṇ-	-n-	-m-	-ṅ-	-n-	-ṃ-	n-/m-
-g-	-ḍ-	-d-	-b-	-ṅ-	-n-	-ṃ-	y-/r-/v-
-g-	-ḍ-	-l-	-b-	-ṅ-	-ṃ-[2]	-ṃ-	l-
-k-	-ṭ-	-c-[3]	-p-	-ṅ-	-ñś-[4]	-ṃ-	ś-
-k-	-ṭ-	-t-	-p-	-ṅ-	-n-	-ṃ-	ṣ-/s-
-g-[5]	-ḍ-[5]	-d-[5]	-b-[5]	-ṅ-	-n-	-ṃ-	h-

Notes

1 If the vowel before **-ṅ** or **-n** is short, the nasal is doubled.

2 There is an optional change of **-ṃ** to a nasalized **-l** (**-l̃**). This appears in the Devanāgarī as the semivowel **l** with a symbol above it: लँ

3 The final **-t** changes to **-c**, and the following **ś-** changes to **ch-**.

4 There is an optional change to **-ñch-** (i.e. **ś-** changes to **ch-**).

5 The **h-** changes to **gh-**, **ḍh-**, **dh-** and **bh-**, which results in the clusters – **ggh-**, **-ḍḍh-**, **-ddh-** and **-bbh-**, respectively.

8.4 Vowel sandhi

Since all vowels are voiced, the issue of voice is not pertinent in vowel sandhi. Given that they are far less numerous than the consonants, the vowels are more straightforward as regards sandhi. Only two points need to be borne in mind since, between them, they provide the rationale for the greater number of vowel sandhi outcomes. First, vowels that have the same quality, irrespective of length, produce a long vowel of the same quality. For example, **-a**/**-ā** at the end of a word, followed by a word beginning with **a-**/**ā-** produces **-ā-**; and so on and so forth for all vowels (The diphthongs have a different strategy). Second, Sanskrit does not permit two vowels to be adjacent to each other. The second of these points contains a caveat, however. The operation of sandhi can result in a word ending in a vowel being followed by a word beginning in a vowel. This was seen with visarga sandhi in the example (8.2): **kanyāḥ avadan → kanyā avadan**. It is important to remember that once sandhification has taken place, whatever the outcome, there can be no recombination.

The first four columns of the vowel sandhi table are straightforward and predictable. Columns two, three and four contain a single stipulation: a vowel appears in its long form when followed by a vowel of the same quality and, where this is not the case, the relevant semivowel appears:

– i/-ī → -y-

– u/-ū → -v-

– ṛ → -r-

The first column greatly resembles the rules of vowel mutation discussed in 7.2. When **-a** or **-ā** is followed by the simple vowels **i-/ī-**, **u-/ū-** and **ṛ-**, one sees what are effectively the guṇa forms **-e-**, **-o-** and **-ar-**, respectively, with vṛddhi forms occurring when **-a** or **-ā** are followed by the complex vowels **e-** and **o-**, and the diphthongs. The fifth, sixth, seventh and eight columns contain the sandhi forms most likely to challenge the learner. There is, nevertheless, a pattern worth pointing out. As regards word-final **-e** and **-o**, except for where these are followed by a short **a-** (where avagraha is deployed), the vowel sandhi change is to a short final **-a**, which is then followed by the unmodified vowel of the following word. The Devanāgarī leaves a space between the words, as reflected in the IAST. Word final **-ai** copies this strategy but has a long final **-ā** in all cases. Word-final **-au** adds the phoneme **v** to the end of a final long **-ā** (**-āv**) although no space is left between the words on this occasion.

Vowel sandhi

-a/-ā	-i/-ī	-u-/-ū	-ṛ	-e	-o	-ai	-au	
-ā-	-ya-	-va-	-ra-	-e ’-	-o ’-	-ā a-	-āva-	a-
-ā-	-yā-	-vā-	-rā-	-a ā-	-a ā-	-ā ā-	-āvā-	ā-
-e-	-ī-	-vi-	-ri-	-a i-	-a i-	-ā i-	-āvi-	i-
-e-	-ī-	-vī-	-rī-	-a ī-	-a ī-	-ā ī-	-āvī-	ī-
-o-	-yu-	-ū-	-ru-	-a u-	-a u-	-ā u-	-āvu-	u-
-o-	-yū-	-ū-	-rū-	-a ū-	-a ū-	-ā ū-	-āvū-	ū-
-ar-	-yṛ-	-vṛ-	-ṝ-	-a ṛ-	-a ṛ-	-ā ṛ-	-āvṛ-	ṛ-
-ai-	-ye-	-ve-	-re-	-a e-	-a e-	-ā e-	-āve-	e-
-au-	-yo-	-vo-	-ro-	-a o-	-a o-	-ā o-	-āvo-	o-
-ai-	-yai-	-vai-	-rai-	-a ai-	-a ai-	-ā ai-	-āvai-	ai-
-au-	-yau-	-vau-	-rau-	-a au-	-a au-	-ā au-	-āvau-	au-

Notes

Avagraha (indicated in the IAST by an apostrophe) only ever replaces a word-initial, short **a-** when the previous word ended in either **-e** or **-o**. It does not occur elsewhere. If it is encountered in a Sanskrit text outside of this context, this is to be treated as manuscript or typing error. In the case of **Rāmo ’śvaṃ** (6.2; 8.2), the use of avagraha is triggered at the same time as the visarga change **Rāmaḥ** → **Rāmo**. It is not a change which takes place after sandhification but, rather, during it.

It is difficult to say which vowel sandhi changes are the most frequent. Certainly, it is not unusual for a word to end in **-a**/**-ā** (a gerund, for example, in the case of **-ā**) and to be followed by a word beginning with **a-**/**ā-**, **i-**/**ī-**, **u-**/**ū-** or **e-**. It is worth the learner spending a little time on the first column of vowels sandhi forms as a result.

8.5 Cerebralization

The exploration of sandhi so far has looked at the sound changes which take place when words come into contact with each other within a phrase or sentence. Sanskrit textbooks routinely refer to this process as 'external sandhi, in that these are complete words and sandhi affects word endings (and occasionally the start of the words which follow). There is also the phenomenon of 'internal sandhi', in which sandhification takes place within a word rather than at its edges. For a learner who is only starting his or her journey into the Sanskrit, an investigation of internal sandhi features can be deferred until external sandhi has, at least conceptually, been grasped. There are, nevertheless, two instances of internal sandhi which merit a mention at an early stage. These take the form of the cerebralization of the phonemes **n** and **s**. The phoneme **n** is the nasal of the dental series and **s** is, similarly, classified as a dental sibilant (That is technically not the case, since to pronounce **s** with the tongue touching the teeth would be to produce the English *th*-sound, as is the case in Spanish – at least in Castilian pronunciation – when *c* is followed by *i* or *e*).

If dental **n** and **s** are transformed by internal sandhi into cerebral sounds, that is to say that they change to **ṇ** and **ṣ**, respectively, without influence from the following word. When the declension of **niśā** and **rātrī** were introduced (6.4), the genitive and locative plural forms were cited: **niśānām**, **niśāsu**; **rātrīṇām**, **rātrīṣu**, respectively. The word **rātrī** contains both examples of cerebralization whereas **niśā** exhibits neither. The rules of cerebralization as regards the internal sandhi **s** → **ṣ** are not overly complicated; the same can certainly not be said of **n** → **ṇ**. For this reason, the learner is urged simply to acknowledge that they exist and can be referred to, as and when it becomes necessary to do so. On the following page, a set of rules is given for both instances of cerebralization, together with examples of nouns containing the instrumental singular ending **-ena** to test the rules relating to the cerebralization of **n**. This is aimed at pre-empting a question which arises quite early in the study of Sanskrit, the moment that a student is presented with an instrumental singular declension exhibiting the cerebral **ṇ**. Textbooks tend not to avoid giving sample paradigms which contain cerebralization. That said, it is good to know from the outset why cerebralization takes place. It suffices, by way of consolidation, to subject the declensions for **niśā** and **rātrī** (6.4) to the following sets of rules and to see why **rātrī**, in the plural, contains both instances of cerebralization and **niśā** does not.

Cerebralization: n → ṇ

The phoneme **-n-** changes to **-ṇ-** when three conditions are met:

1 **-n-** is preceded by **ṛ**, **ṝ**, **r** or **ṣ** at any point in the word.
2 There is no intervening phoneme which can inhibit the change.*
3 **-n-** is followed by any vowel, **n**, **m**, **y** or **v**.

* The intervening phonemes which block cerebralization are any of the palatal, cerebral or dental consonants, **l**, **ś** or **s**.

Example 1: **mārgeṇa**

The instrumental singular ending **-ena** is subject to cerebralization because all three conditions are met: **n** is preceded by **r**; **n** is followed by a vowel; **g** is not an intervening phoneme able to block cerebralization.

Example 2: **prabhāveṇa (prabhāva**: *strength; power*)

The instrumental singular ending **-ena** is subject to cerebralization because all three conditions are met: **n** is preceded by **r**; **n** is followed by a vowel; **bh** and **v** are not intervening phonemes.

Example 3: **aśvena**

The instrumental singular ending **-ena** is not subject to cerebralization. The first condition is not met by **ś**. Thus, even though **v** is not an intervening phoneme and **-n-** is followed by a vowel, the process of cerebralization does not take place.

Cerebralization: s → ṣ

The phoneme **-s-** changes to **-ṣ-** when two conditions are met:

1 **-s-** is immediately preceded in the word by **k**, **r** or any vowel other than **a** or **ā**.
2 **-s-** is followed by any phoneme other than **ṛ**, **ṝ** or **r**.

Example: **upaniṣad**

Although this word is derived from √ **sad** (*to sit*), the phoneme **s** meets both conditions the moment that the prefix **ni-** is added to it, hence it is cerebralized in the word **upaniṣad**. It is not subject to cerebralization in **sadana** (*seat; dwelling place*) since the first condition is not met.

8.6 Writing conventions

In the Devanāgarī, words may come together in five ways:

1. A word may end in a vowel and be followed by a word beginning with a consonant.
2. A word may end in a visarga and be followed by a word which begins with any phoneme (The following word cannot begin with a visarga).
3. A word may end in a consonant and be followed by a word beginning with a vowel.
4. A word may end in a consonant and be followed by a word beginning with a consonant.
5. A word may end in a vowel and be followed by a word beginning with a vowel.

In the first such case, the words are written separately. Also, when a word ends in a visarga, the rules of visarga sandhi apply. Consider the following:

नगरस्य जनाः अर्जुनं वदन्ति

nagarasya janāḥ Arjunaṃ vadanti

The people of the village address Arjuna.

The words **nagarasya** and **janāḥ** are written separately (A vowel is followed by a consonant). Furthermore, according to the rules of visarga sandhi, the ending **-āḥ** drops the visarga before a voiced phoneme.

नगरस्य जना अर्जुनं वदन्ति

nagarasya janā Arjunaṃ vadanti

Even though **janā** and **Arjunaṃ** put two vowels in adjacency, sandhi does not permit any recombination. Vowel sandhi is <u>not</u> subsequently applied to produce ***janārjunaṃ**. If one substitutes the word **jana** with **guru** (*teacher*), adjusting the verb to reflect a noun in the nominative singular instead of the nominative plural, one obtains the following, before application of sandhi:

नगरस्य गुरुः अर्जुनं वदति

nagarasya guruḥ Arjunaṃ vadati

The village teacher addresses Arjuna.

Applying the rules of visarga sandhi, **-☺ḥ** before a vowel becomes **-☺r**. This results in a semivowel at the end of the word **guru-**, which takes a virāma:

नगरस्य गुरुर् अर्जुनं वदति

nagarasya gurur Arjunaṃ vadati

Virāma does not, however, appear in authentic Sanskrit examples unless it is at the end of a sentence. Elsewhere, the writing conventions of the Devanāgari call for its removal. With **-r** as the word-final phoneme, the word combination is a semivowel followed by a vowel (The third possible writing combination, as identified on the previous page). The writing conventions are different to the rules of sandhi in that, if a combination is required, it is effected. Accordingly, the fully sandhified version of the sentence appears as follows:

नगरस्य गुरुरर्जुनं वदति

nagarasya gurur Arjunaṃ vadati

Note that the IAST does not indicate the writing together of words except in the case of vowel sandhi, where vowels become linked to the point where the sandhification affects both words rather than just one.

In the third combination, the Devanāgarī requires words to be written together. Consonant sandhi rules apply so, if a word ends in a voiceless consonant and is followed by a word beginning with a vowel, the consonant in question is voiced (The following example is from 6.7.2):

Before sandhi: बुद्धः ग्रामात् आगच्छति

Buddhaḥ grāmāt āgacchati

(The) Buddha comes from (the) village.

After sandhi: बुद्धो ग्रामादागच्छति

Before sandhi: बुद्धः ग्रामात् आगच्छति

Buddho grāmād āgacchati

So far so good, but the situation is more complex in the fourth and fifth combinations. Where a word ends in a consonant and is followed by a word beginning with a consonant, a conjunct is created. Additionally, a consonant sandhi may be required, if the word-final consonant is voiceless and it is followed by a word-initial voiced consonant:

Before sandhi: बुद्धः ग्रामात् वनं गच्छति

Buddhaḥ grāmāt vanaṃ gacchati

(The) Buddha goes from (the) village to (the) wood (**vana**).

After sandhi: बुद्धो ग्रामाद्वनं गच्छति

Buddho grāmād vanaṃ gacchati

Vowels do not create conjuncts. They are simply subject to vowel sandhi and to whatever adjustments are subsequently needed in the Devanāgarī. Take the following example, containing the emphatic (and occasionally restrictive) enclitic word **eva** preceded by a gerund:

Before sandhi: उक्त्वा एव

uktvā eva

having indeed been said/having just been said

After sandhi: उक्त्वैव

uktvaiva

The best way to accustom oneself to the conventions of the Devanāgarī is to see them in operation. With this is mind, the present chapter concludes with a mantra by way of a consolidating exercise. It is one of several peace mantras and arguably the best known of these. With any mantra, one ought to control one's breathing and to aim to pronounce each line with a single breath. At the end (**śāntiḥ śāntiḥ śāntiḥ**), the lungs are emptied, hence the drawing out of the final syllable – a thing that is not possible unless one articulates the echo vowel following the third and final **śāntiḥ** until the breath is exhausted. As with the sentences, the first version is unsandhified and the second one applies all the necessary sandhi features. The sandhified version is the one which is chanted.

8.7 Exercise: reading a mantra

Before sandhi

ॐ असतः मा सत् गमय ।
तमसः मा ज्योतिः गमय ।
मृत्योः मा अमृतं गमय ।
ॐ शान्तिः शान्तिः शान्तिः ॥

OM asataḥ mā sat gamaya
tamasaḥ mā jyotiḥ gamaya
mṛtyoḥ mā amṛtaṃ gamaya
OM śāntiḥ śāntiḥ śāntiḥ

OM. From non-being to reality, make me go.
From darkness to light, make me go.
From death to immortality, make me go.
OM. Peace, peace, peace.

Vocabulary

asat	noun (m)	*the non-existent* (ablative sg. = **asataḥ**).
mā	pers. pronoun	*me* (an alternative form for **mām**).
sat	noun (m)	*the existent* (accusative sg. = **sat**).
gamaya	verb (finite)	*cause to go* (second pers. sg. imperative).
tamas	noun (n)	*darkness* (ablative sg. = **tamasaḥ**).
jyotis	noun (n)	*light* (accusative sg. = **jyotiḥ**).
mṛtyu	noun (m)	*death* (ablative sg. = **mṛtyoḥ**).
amṛta	noun (m)	*immortality* (accusative sg. = **amṛtam**).
śānti	noun (f)	*peace* (nominative sg. = **śāntiḥ**).

After sandhi

ॐ असतो[1] मा सद्गमय[2] ।
तमसो[1] मा ज्योतिर्गमय[3] ।
मृत्योर्मा[3] अमृतं[4] गमय ।
ॐ शान्तिः शान्तिः शान्तिः ॥

OM asato mā sad gamaya
tamaso mā jyotir gamaya
mṛtyor mā amṛtaṃ gamaya
OM śāntiḥ śāntiḥ śāntiḥ

Notes

1 The words in question (**asataḥ** and **tamasaḥ**) both end in a visarga preceded by short **a** and are followed by a voiced phoneme (**m**). The rules of visarga sandhi relating to **-aḥ** apply: **-aḥ** → **-o**.

2 The word **sat** ends in an unvoiced consonant (**t**) and is followed by a voiced consonant (**g**). The phoneme **t** is sandhified, according to the rules of consonant sandhi, to its voiced equivalent (**d**). Since the resulting combination is **-dg-**, orthographic rules apply, generating a conjunct consonant which has the effect of joining the words together.

3 Both **jyotiḥ** and **mṛtyoḥ** end in a visarga preceded by a vowel other than **a** or **ā**. The rules of 'smiley visarga' apply, transforming the visarga to **r**. Since **r** is a semivowel and is followed by a consonant, a conjunct is produced and, as with **sad** + **gamaya**, the words are written together.

4 This is an interesting case of where both the rules of sandhi and writing conventions are compromised. Technically, one ought to see the long **ā** of **mā** and the following short **a** of **amṛtaṃ** being fused, according to vowel sandhi rules, to produce a single, long **-ā-**. This would yield ***māmṛtaṃ gamaya** – highly ambiguous in that it is not distinguishable in sound to ***mā mṛtaṃ gamaya** (*to mortality, make me go*). To avoid this, the Devanāgarī keeps the words **mā** and **amṛtaṃ** separate, thereby promoting a short pause between these words.

9

FROM SENTENCE TO TEXT

9.1 Preliminaries

Translating Sanskrit requires patience and great attention to detail. One must be prepared to acquire a good working vocabulary on top of a sound grasp of grammar whilst bearing in mind that, if reading the Devanāgarī rather than the IAST, writing conventions will challenge the eye. A knowledge of conjuncts is necessary, too, even if the text presented in the Devanāgarī uses virāma to keep words separate to avoid conjuncts arising between them. The great advantage of reading a text in the IAST is that, whilst it reflects sound changes brought about by sandhi, there are no conjunct forms. Phonemes which generate a conjunct in the Devanāgarī are kept separate in the IAST, allowing the learner to see more clearly how a sentence is constituted (This is not, however, possible with vowel sandhi). The readings in this chapter are verses taken from the first book of the Bhagavadgītā. The verses in question appear in the Devanāgarī and are fully sandhified. The IAST version is given immediately below the Devanāgarī, followed by a close translation. The vocabulary for the individual verses lists the words in their citation form, except for the verbs, since conjugation forms part of the analysis following each verse.

With respect to the IAST accompanying the Devanāgarī, capital letters are now avoided, reflecting the practice adopted by most Sanskrit scholars who use the IAST. The reader can identify, from the translation, the proper

DOI: 10.4324/9780429325434-10

nouns that would require a capital letter in English. There are a number of nouns which may be masculine, neuter or feminine. These have been identified as masculine (unless they are neuter only), largely because a feminine stem would require the final **-a** to be modified to reflect an ending suitable for a feminine stem. It is a minor point, in any event, and aimed at simplifying matters for the learner without violating any grammatical rules. Nouns are indicated with their gender in brackets: masculine (m), neuter (n) or feminine (f). Finally, personal pronouns are indicated as such but there are other pronouns: **kim** (Reading One, 9.3.1) and **yat/yad** (Reading Four, 9.3.4). These are discussed in the accompanying analysis. Being a work of poetry rather than of prose, the Bhagavadgītā does not always adhere to all the conventions discussed in the earlier chapters of the present work. Where that is the case, it is commented upon.

9.2 Reading Sanskrit

There are various steps to take when attempting the reading of a text in the Devanāgarī. One must first consult the appropriate vocabulary, assuming that one has been presented (This tends to be the case with most textbooks for Sanskrit, although by no means all). If vocabulary is not given and there is only a dictionary or lexicon to which the student is expected to refer, an alternative strategy suggests itself. For the learner, the text is best transliterated into the IAST. This allows for maximum transparency and allows conjuncts to be decrypted and checked in advance of investigating grammatical endings. Once the words comprising the sentence have been transliterated and separated out, the work of grammatical analysis can be undertaken.

It is often the case that a sentence in Sanskrit is 'back to front' when compared to the English equivalent. Sanskrit tends to place additional information relating to the sentence at the start, deferring the phrase which contains the subject and the verb to the end of the sentence. It is not advisable to adopt the habit of translating a Sanskrit sentence word-for-word in the sequence in which the words appear, expecting the result to make sense. The student should attempt to find out <u>who</u> is doing <u>what</u> to <u>whom</u> or <u>where</u>. This approach requires the identification of the subject of the sentence and the verb. A finite verb may not be in evidence, having been substituted by a participle (This is frequently the case with poetry). The subject, however, is not so easily omitted. Once the subject can be identified, the endings of the other nouns can then be checked to see what case functions are indicated. The best approach to translating Sanskrit is to attempt to group words into their respective phrases and to connect the phrases in question to each other in order to build up a coherent and logical sequence of units of meaning.

Certain words are useful in indicating the phrases which constitute a sentence. Pronouns are an obvious example of this. If the personal pronoun *your* or *my/mine* appear, one has then to establish the thing to which they are referring. The longer the sentence, the more likely it is that there will be a pronoun – either a personal pronoun or the demonstrative pronoun **tat/etat**. The sentence can be envisaged as a jigsaw of phrases and, to extend the analogy, the more one is able to identify the pieces, the easier they are to fit together to make the picture emerge. Attempting to connect words in strict sequence obscures the picture.

The readings which follow are challenging but intended to introduce the reader to authentic Sanskrit. The reader should not, as a result, feel dispirited if the sentences appear to be difficult. The Bhagavadgītā is not a text which would ordinarily be presented to the beginner with any expectation that he or she should be able to make sense of the grammar or the vocabulary. The verses presented serve as a good introduction to the richness and complexity of Sanskrit poetry. It should be borne in mind that the greater part of the texts which have survived in Sanskrit are works of poetry, not of prose. Early exposure to how Sanskrit patterns the sentence in poetry is, therefore, desirable.

The opening verse of the Bhagavadgītā (Reading One) is the most complex in terms of its structure and, accordingly, more space has been devoted to its analysis than is the case with the three subsequent readings. Being the first reading, certain features are identified and explained, such as the past passive participle, which appear elsewhere. The reader is presented with a surfeit of grammatical information with the first reading. Once the analysis of Reading One has been undertaken, the second and third readings fall easily into place. Reading Four is not much more difficult than Reading Two or Three, although it contains a compound, which is a phenomenon that has not so far been discussed.

It is recommended that the reader look at the text in the Devanāgarī to begin with, checking to see if his or her reading of this is accurate. If many mistakes are made in the reading of the Devanāgarī, this is an indication that a review of Chapter 4 is required. The IAST is used for all grammatical explanations, since little point is served by presenting the learner with grammatical concepts that are, in themselves, also exercises in reading the Devanāgarī. One task at a time is more than sufficient. If the reading of the Devanāgarī is accurate (albeit with the occasional hiccup) but declensional endings are the cause of confusion, the reader is directed back to Chapter 6. The visarga sandhi table in 8.2 is worth bookmarking, for ease of reference.

Reading Sanskrit is a rewarding experience, and it pays dividends for the learner to know something about a text prior to engaging with it in the original. With that in mind, Chapter 10 offers some suggestions as regards accessible publications relating to the Bhagavadgītā and, indeed, other literary works much cherished in the Indian cultural tradition.

9.3 Selected readings

9.3.1 Reading One

As seen in 4.4.3, this is the opening verse of the Bhagavadgītā, in which Dhr̥tarāṣṭra, king of the powerful Kaurava dynasty, asks his minister about the preparations for a battle that is about to commence in Kurukṣetra – literally, in a field or stretch of land (**kṣetra**) belonging to the descendants of King Kuru. Exact dates for King Kuru have not been established but, in the Indic cultural tradition, he is the remote ancestor of both the Kaurava and Pāṇḍava clans. It is likely that Kuru was an important chieftain in the Iron Age, between around 1200 and 800 BCE. There is no doubt that the story of the great war between the Kauravas and the Pāṇḍavas relates to an ancient conflict, although it has become a metaphor for the struggle to restore the rule of dharma to the world.

धर्मक्षेत्रे कुरुक्षेत्रे समवेता युयुत्सवः ।
मामकाः पाण्डवाश्चैव किमकुर्वत संजय ॥ १ ॥

dharmakṣetre kurukṣetre samavetā yuyutsavaḥ
māmakāḥ pāṇḍavāścaiva kim akurvata saṃjaya (Verse 1)

In the field of dharma, in Kurukṣetra, assembled and willing to fight,
What did mine (= my army) and the Pāṇḍavas do, o Saṃjaya?

Vocabulary

dharma	noun (m)	*dharma* (see 5.8, viii).
kṣetra	noun (n)	*field.*
kuru	noun (m)	*the name of a king/dynasty.*
samaveta	participle	*assembled.*
yuyutsu	adjective	*willing to fight.*
māmaka	noun (m)	*my/mine* (noun form of **mama**).
pāṇḍava	noun (m)	*descendant of King Paṇḍu.*
ca	enclitic	*and.*
eva	enclitic	*truly; indeed; really; only.*
kim	pronoun	*what; why.*
akurvata	verb (finite)	*they did.*
saṃjaya	noun (m)	*the name of Dhṛtarāṣṭra's minister.*

At the start of text, it is customary for Sanskrit to set the scene by locating the place in which an event occurs or when such an event took place. In this, the opening verse, the location is established with a locative singular ending (**kurukṣetra** → **kurukṣetre**). The first word of the verse does not so much establish a geographical location but a place in which justice is about to be done and dharma restored. Although it has the same grammatical structure as **kurukṣetre**, **dharmakṣetre** is figurative rather than literal. The rest of the half line of the verse, up to the single daṇḍa, is where one expects a grammatical subject to appear. Both **samavetā** and **yuyutsavaḥ** relate to the grammatical subject although the first of these is a participle and the second one is adjectival in nature.

Samavetā is a complex word. It is a participle composed of a verbal root with two prefixes and one suffix, as follows: **sam** (prefix) + **ava** (prefix) + √ **i** (*to go; come*) + **ta-** (suffix indicating a past passive participle). The resulting form, **samaveta**, is then subject to declension as if it were a short **-a** stem. Visarga sandhi obscures the fact that the ending, before sandhification takes place, is **-āḥ** (**samavetāḥ**). This indicates the nominative masculine plural ending of a short **-a** stem (see 6.3). As for **yuyutsavaḥ**, the student needs to be able to identify the word, before any grammar is applied, as one which ends in **-u** (The present work has not investigated **-u** stems, since that is not one of the first declensions to be studied by beginners). The ending **-avaḥ** also indicates the nominative masculine plural ending, albeit of an **-u** stem rather than an **-a** stem.

Both **samavetā(ḥ)** and **yuyutsavaḥ** encode the grammatical subject, which is masculine and plural, even if 'they' have yet to be identified. Before moving to the second half of the verse, however, it is essential to explore how a participle (**samaveta**) and what is effectively an adjectival word (**yuyutsu**) can function as if they were nouns, thereby capable of representing the grammatical subject. The past passive participle has already been seen (5.2, x and 7.7, viii). On the first occasion, it formed the noun **buddha**, albeit that the word in question contained a complex sandhi feature in which the suffixal ending **-ta** was voiced as a result of being adjacent to the voiced **-dh** in the verbal root **budh** and acquired the aspirate of the verbal root (i.e. **-ta** changed to **-dha**). As a noun, the word **buddha** is then subject to all the declensional changes associated with a short **-a** stem. This can be captured in the English translation of **buddha** as *the Awakened One*, which, as a noun, is subject to English morphology: *the Awakened Ones* (with the plural *-s* morpheme); the *Awakened One's* (with the *s* preceded by the genitive apostrophe). In this verse of the Bhagavadgītā, **samavetā(ḥ)** are *those who have come together*, the meaning being determined by the verbal root, modified by two prefixes. It is case-marked in the nominative plural, just as **buddha** could be made nominative and plural with the appropriate case ending: **buddhāḥ**, *the Buddhas/Awakened Ones* (three or more of them). It is important to point out, at this juncture, that two past passive participles can be placed together. Does this result in two grammatical subjects? No, since the first past passive participle functions to describe the second and thereby acts as an adjective. Consider the following sentence, which contains **samaveta** and **buddha**, both passive past participles in structure:

Before sandhi:	**samavetāḥ buddhāḥ vadanti**
After sandhi:	**samavetā buddhā vadanti**
	The assembled Buddhas speak/are speaking.

Importantly, the past passive participle can function as a verb as well as a noun and an adjective. It is not uncommon to come across a sentence in Sanskrit which has a past passive participle instead of a finite verb:

Before sandhi:	**buddhaḥ agacchat** (Imperfect, third person sg.)
After sandhi:	**buddho 'gacchat**
	The Buddha went.
Before sandhi:	**buddhaḥ gataḥ** (Past passive participle)
After sandhi:	**buddho gataḥ**
	The Buddha went.

The flexibility of the past passive participle is due to the fact that it is derived from a verbal root. It can generate a noun (as with *Buddha*) and substituting for a finite verb generated from the relevant verb root (**gata** from √ **gam**, with the appropriate declensional ending).

With respect to **yuyutsu**, acting as an adjective within the verse, that too can be identified as a noun. Nouns and adjectives are words which may relate to things or to descriptions of things. The word **yuyutsavaḥ** here describes the assembled men (**samavetāḥ**) but, on its own, would mean *those who are willing to fight*. It is the function within the sentence which distinguishes a noun from an adjective.

In the second half verse, the grammatical subject is specified. There are indeed two subjects: the army belonging to King Dhṛtarāṣṭra, referred to by a noun form, appropriately in the plural (**māmakāḥ**: *mine; those belonging to me*) and the opposing forces, described by Dhṛtarāṣṭra as the descendants of King Paṇḍu, the **pāṇḍavāḥ** (In point of fact, there are many allies on both sides also assembled on the battlefield). The ending of **māmakāḥ** is absolutely clear as it has not been subject to sandhi, given that the following phoneme is the voiceless **p-**. As for **pāṇḍavāḥ**, that undergoes a visarga sandhi change, as described in 8.2: **-āḥ** + **c-** → **-ś**. The enclitic **ca** (*and*) is a conjunction uniting both Dhṛtarāṣṭra's forces and those of the Pāṇḍavas (i.e. *X Y and*), with **ca** forming a vowel sandhi with **eva** to produce **caiva** (*Those of mine and, indeed, the Pāṇḍavas*).

The concluding part of the verse is a question: *what have they (the rival armies) done?* Dhṛtarāṣṭra, being blind, is reliant on the eyewitness testimony of someone capable of seeing how the armies have positioned themselves on the battlefield. Dhṛtarāṣṭra uses the customary way of asking a question: **kim**. It is a pronoun, as is **tat**, but more specifically the interrogative pronoun. Whilst it is the case that the interrogative pronoun is subject to declension across three genders, three numbers and seven cases (the vocative not being used), the learner can take heart that help is at hand. The declension of **kim** differs to **tat** in one respect: whilst **tat** is, strictly speaking, representing the neuter and accusative singular declensional forms, **kim** has the same restriction (i.e. it is the form for the neuter nominative and accusative singular). If one then substitutes **k-** for the initial **t-** of every **tat**-form (and, indeed, the initial **s-** of the masculine nominative singular **saḥ** and feminine nominative singular **sā**), the endings of **tat** and **kim** are identical. The demonstrative pronoun **tat** is, therefore, the key to knowing the declension of the interrogative pronoun **kim**. The finite verb form (**akurvata**) belongs to a conjugation that the present work has not explored. It is the third person plural of the imperfect for √ **kṛ** (*make; fashion*; *do; create* (see 5.2, vii)). It is the conjugation of a verb which does not belong to the thematic group of verb classes (√ **kṛ** belongs to Class VIII).

The final word in the verse is the most straightforward of all. It is the name of Dhṛtarāṣṭra's minister, **saṃjaya**, a name which has survived in the form *Sanjay/Sañjay*. Although the word does not appear to be case-marked, it is in the vocative singular which, for short **-a** masculine and neuter stems, is identical to the citation form.

9.3.2 Reading Two

The core of the Bhagavadgītā is the dialogue which takes place between the god Kṛṣṇa and Arjuna, one of the Pāṇḍavas and an archer without equal. Arjuna has been looking around at the combatants, Kaurava and Pāṇḍava alike, and is struck by the fact that he recognizes kinsmen and acquaintances on both sides. In his despair, he addresses Kṛṣṇa to say that his willingness to fight is deserting him. It will be down to Kṛṣṇa to advise Arjuna as to why he must take part in the fighting and what will be put into jeopardy if he fails to do so. Arjuna is not a coward. His courage is undoubted; but he is filled with pity, faced with the inevitability of participating in what he knows will result in the death of many.

सीदन्ति मम गात्राणि मुखं च परिशुष्यति ।
वेपथुश्च शरीरे मे रोमहर्षश्च जायते ॥ २९ ॥

sīdanti mama gātrāṇi mukhaṃ ca pariśuṣyati
vepathuś ca śarīre me romaharṣaś ca jāyate (Verse 29)

My limbs fail me and my mouth dries up
And my body quakes and my hair bristles.

Vocabulary

sīdanti	verb (finite)	*they sit; fall down.*
mama	pers. pronoun	*my/mine.*
gātra	noun (n)	*leg; limb.*
mukha	noun (n)	*face; mouth.*
ca	enclitic	*and.*
pariśuṣyati	verb (finite)	*he/she/it dries up.*
vepathu	noun (m)	*a quivering; trembling.*
śarīra	noun (n)	*body.*
me	pers. pronoun	*my/mine* (enclitic form).
roman	noun (n)	*body hair.*
harṣa	noun (m)	*a bristling; standing on end.*
jāyate†	verb (finite)	*he/she/it is born; brought forth.*

† The verb form is derived from √ **jan** (Class IV), stem: **jāya**. The stem is slightly irregular, in that one anticipates ***janya**. The ending is that of the third person singular of the present tense, middle voice (i.e. **-te**, not **-ti**).

There are two finite verbs in the first half verse (**sīdanti** and **pariśuṣyati**). The first of these has the third person plural ending of the present tense (**-anti**); the second has the ending of the third person singular ending of the present tense (**-ati**). The reader has only to figure out the meaning of the verb forms in question and to identify their subjects. With **sīdanti**, the root is **sad** (*to sit*: Class I, also occasionally, Class VI), the stem is **sīda**. The subject appears in the following nominal phrase, containing a personal pronoun (**mama gātrāṇi**: *my legs/limbs*). The noun is in the plural, suggesting limbs rather than two legs (which would require the dual), with a cerebralized **ṇ**, due to the presence of a preceding **r** in the word. The ending **-āni** /**-āṇi** indicates a plural form of a neuter short **-a** stem but can be either nominative or accusative. Since it identifies the subject of the verb *to sit*, the declension is in the nominative.

The remaining part of the first half verse contains the enclitic **ca**, which can be put to one side in the first instance, since it is the element which combines two things. This leaves the reader with **mukhaṃ pariśuṣyati** (*the mouth dries up*), which has the subject preceding the verb, as was the case with the sentences in 7.7. The noun **mukhaṃ** is, again, a neuter short **-a** stem, meaning that the ending can indicate either the nominative or accusative singular. Since it governs the verb, it is the nominative. As for **pariśuṣyati**, it is a prefixed verb: **pari** + √ **śuṣ**. It belongs to Class IV, which adopts the strategy of adding **-ya** to an unmodified root to form the stem. For a reminder as to the strategies for stem formation with thematic verbs, see 7.3: The Thematic Verbs (IV, VI, X).

The second half verse begins with an **-u** stem in the nominative singular (**vepathuḥ**) which is subject to visarga sandhi: **-uḥ** → **-uś**, as a result of the following **c-** in **ca**. Despite being a subject, it does not have an associated verb. One could argue that the verb *to be* has been dropped (i.e. *there is a quaking*); Sanskrit regularly drops the verb *to be* if the meaning of the sentence is clear enough without it. Equally, one could posit that it shares the finite verb at the end of the verse. As for phrase **śarīre me** (*in the body of me*), this is made up of a short **-a** stem (again, neuter) in the locative case, followed by the enclitic form of **mama**. Two words then come together to give a compound (of which more will be said in the analysis of Reading Four). This compound is treated as a masculine short **-a** stem in the nominative singular: **romaharṣaḥ**, which is sandhified for the same reason as **vepathuḥ**. This agrees with the finite verb **jāyate**, for which a note is provided in the vocabulary.

9.3.3 Reading Three

Gāṇḍīva is Arjuna's bow. It is a celestial weapon, given to him by the god Varuṇa, along with two quivers containing an inexhaustible supply of arrows. Arjuna is an archer whose arrows never miss their mark. Arjuna and Gāṇḍīva are, consequently, much feared by the Kauravas, even though the Kaurava army is greater in size than the Pāṇḍava forces arrayed against it. Arjuna has a divine origin, having been born because of a mantra uttered by his mother, Kuntī, calling on the gods to give her sons when her husband (Pāṇḍu) could not. Arjuna is the son of Indra, one of the most important deities of Vedic times, but he is human and is subject to human feelings.

गाण्डीवं स्रंसते हस्तात्त्वक्चैव परिदह्यते ।
न च शक्नोम्यवस्थातुं भ्रमतीव च मे मनः ॥३० ॥

gāṇḍīvaṃ sraṃsate hastāt tvak caiva paridahyate
na ca śaknomy+avasthātuṃ bhramatīva ca me manaḥ (Verse 30)

Gāṇḍīva slips from my hand and my skin burns
And I cannot stand and my mind wanders.

Vocabulary

gāṇḍīva	noun (m)	*the name of Arjuna's bow.*
sraṃsate	verb (finite)	*he/she/it slips; falls.*
hasta	noun (m)	*hand.*
tvak	noun (f)	*skin.*
ca	enclitic	*and.*
eva	enclitic	*truly; indeed; really; only.*
paridahyate	verb (finite)	*he/she/it is burned.*
na	negative part.	*not; no.*
śaknomi	verb (finite)	*I can.*
avasthātum	verb (infinitive)	*to stand; remain.*
bhramati	verb (finite)	*he/she/it wanders.*
iva	enclitic	*as if; like; in this manner.*
me	pers. pronoun	*my/mine* (enclitic form).
manas	noun (n)	*mind; intellect.*

The previous verse began with a finite verb which appeared to contradict what had been presented in 7.7. Sanskrit word order is flexible because of the detail contained in word endings. In addition, poetry permits word-ordering that is different to prose. In this verse, the finite verb is not at the very start of the verse but nevertheless follows the subject and precedes the object. In this respect, it accords with the word order of English: subject – verb – object. The enclitic **ca** helps to break the first half verse into two parts, as follows: **gāṇḍīvaṃ sraṃsate hastāt/ tvak caiva paridahyate**. Something happens and then something else happens. Sanskrit does not tend to state the obvious. The bow, **gāṇḍīva**, is a neuter short **-a** stem and therefore nominative or accusative singular. It falls (**sraṃsate**) – which makes it the subject and thereby nominative – from a hand (**hastāt**) which accordingly takes the ablative case. Arjuna does not say *my hand*, nor does he need to. The context makes it clear whose hand is involved. The finite verb **sraṃsate** (Class I), as with **jāyate** in the previous verse, is the third person singular, middle voice (present tense). The second part (**tvak caiva paridahyate**) again omits the personal pronoun *my* and uses a middle voice form (prefix **pari-** + √ **dah**: *to burn*). It is a Class I verb, for which **-ya** is not a stem formation strategy. This is a passive construction, created by adding **-ya** before the appropriate personal ending in the middle voice: *and truly (my) skin is burned.*

Using the enclitic **ca**, one is able, in the second half verse, to identify two parts: **na śaknomy+avasthātuṃ/bhramatīva me manaḥ**. The first of these has the finite verb form *I can* (√ **śak**, Class V: *to be able*), negated by **na** (*I cannot*). A noun or pronoun is not required, since the ending makes it evident that the subject is the first person. This is followed by a telltale infinitive, ending in **-tum** (prefix **ava-** + √ **sthā**, Class I: *to be; stand*). The prefix has the effect of refining the meaning of the verb to indicate *staying put* or *remaining in place*. The remaining part of the verse is straightforward. √ **bhram** (Class I: *to wander; ramble*) generates the stem **bhrama** to which the personal ending of the third person singular, active voice (present tense) is applied: **bhramati**. Because this ends in **-i** and is followed by a word beginning with **i-**, vowel sandhi takes place. The subject, in the nominative singular, is **manaḥ**: *mind* (an example of a consonant stem ending, which the present work does not investigate). Strangely, one does not find either **mama manaḥ** (*my mind*) or **mano me**, which would be the sandhified outcome of **manaḥ me**. The enclitic **me** appears before the noun to which it relates, which is not in accordance with grammatical rules. Here, poetic considerations take precedence.

9.3.4 Reading Four

Arjuna reflects on the matter of killing those who belong to the same clan. It is not far-fetched to suggest that this may reflect the ethical code of early Aryan society with respect to whom one may legitimately fight and slay. The Bhagavadgītā has strong echoes of an earlier age, which lends support to a suggestion that it derives from an earlier composition dating back to Vedic times. Arjuna obtains Gāṇḍīva from Varuṇa, Vedic god of the sky and of the oceans, having first approached the fire god Agni for assistance. Arjuna's birth is the result of an invocation to Indra, chief amongst the gods in the Vedic pantheon. With so many references to the Vedic Age, the world of the Bhagavadgītā is not that of the Common Era. It is an old tale recast in a later linguistic form.

अहो बत महत्पापं कर्तुं व्यवसिता वयम् ।
यद्राज्यसुखलोभेन हन्तुं स्वजनमुद्यताः ॥४५॥

aho bata mahat pāpaṃ kartuṃ vyavasitā vayam
yad rājya-sukha-lobhena hantuṃ svajanam udyatāḥ (Verse 45)

Oh, alas! We are resolved to do great evil
Which, by the desire for kingship, (we are) ready to kill our own people.

Vocabulary

aho	interjection	*o(h).*
bata	interjection	*alas.*
mahat	adjective	*great.*
pāpa	noun (m)	*evil; sin.*
kartum	verb (infinitive)	*to do.*
vyavasita	participle	*resolved; decided.*
vayam	pers. pronoun	*we.*
yat/yad	pronoun	*which.*
rājya	noun (n)	*royalty; kingship.*
sukha	noun (m)	*comfort; pleasure.*
lobha	noun (m)	*covetousness; desire for.*
hantum	verb (infinitive)	*to strike down; slay; kill.*
svajana	noun (m)	*own people; kindred.*
udyata	participle	*intent on; prepared.*

The verse begins with a frequently used interjection. Other common interjections are **he** and **bhoḥ**, which tend to be reserved for when the speaker is attempting to catch the attention of another. An additional interjection follows (**bata**) which, like **aho**, is not addressing someone in particular but simply lamenting a situation. The reader can put these to one side to concentrate on finding the subject in the first half verse. The subject cannot be **pāpaṃ**, since this is a masculine short **-a** stem and the declensional ending indicates the accusative singular. It is the object, preceded by a word which qualifies it (**mahat**). It is important to note that **mahat** can be both adjective (*great*) and noun (*a great person or thing*). It is a consonant stem, as is the case with **tvak** and **manas** in Reading Three. The declined form **mahat** represents the nominative, accusative and vocative singular. Here, one selects the accusative singular since, being adjectival, it agrees in terms of case with the thing it qualifies. This is a good example of how nouns and adjectives belong to the same category of word. It is their function within the sentence that determines whether they are, in a specific context, to be considered as nouns or adjectives. From this example, it is evident that the adjective precedes the noun which it qualifies.

The noun, adjectivally qualified (**mahat pāpaṃ**), is an object and cannot, therefore, govern a finite verb. The verb form which follows (**kartuṃ**) is an infinitive formed from √ **kṛ** (*do; make; fashion*; *create*). This still leaves the subject to find and, with few contenders now remaining, one focuses on **vyavasitā vayam**. If one's knowledge of personal pronouns is in place, **vayam** is instantly recognizable as the nominative plural form of the first person pronoun: *we* (see 6.6). Now that a subject is visible, all that remains is to identify its relationship with the word to the left of it. As with **mahat pāpaṃ** (adjective + noun), position establishes the relationship. The word **vyavasitā** acts adjectivally vis-à-vis the pronoun, but it is technically a past passive participle (Note that the form is **vyavasitāḥ** prior to sandhification). The word is complex, being composed of two prefixes, a verbal root with an irregular mutation and a suffix which is subject to declension: prefix 1 **vi-** + prefix 2 **ava-** + √ **śri** (Class I: *to fix on; turn towards*) → irregular form **si** + past passive participle **-ta** (with the relevant nominative plural ending for a short **-a** stem). The prefixes **vi-** + **ava-** are subject to vowel sandhi (**-i** + **a-** → **-ya-**). Complexity aside, the function of the past passive participle is straightforward. It describes a group of people whom Arjuna refers to as *we*, including himself within the group: *resolved/determined (are) we*.

The second half verse is significantly more resistant to translation than the first half. It contains a pronoun at the beginning (**yat/yad**) which is declined like **tat** (or, for that matter, **kim**), and it is the relative pronoun, expressing *which who(m)*, *whose*, etc. The reader is urged to put it to one side whilst scanning for the subject and – if one is indeed present – the finite verb. Regrettably, there is neither an overtly marked subject nor is there a finite verb. In such cases, it is suggested that one looks for a past passive participle, capable of substituting for the verb. One finds such a thing, in the form of **udyatāḥ**: prefix **ud-** + √ **yam** (Class I: *to give; support*) + -past passive participle **-ta** (Note that the **m** in the root is lost, as is the nasal in √ **jan**, when forming the stem **jāya**, in Reading Two). Since something verbal is required at the end of the verse, the past passive participle now adopts this role. Courtesy of the prefix **ud-**, the meaning becomes *to be intent on; be prepared.* As to the identity of those who are intent or prepared, that cannot be **svajanam** (*own people*; *kindred*), since that is a masculine singular noun marked in the accusative case. The subject is, in fact, recycled from the previous half verse. This is **vayam**.

Once **svajanam udyatāḥ (vayam)** are in place, one is left with the sense of a body of people prepared to do something to their kindred folk. If one then adds the infinitive **hantum**, from √ **han** (Class II: *to strike down*), the action is specified: *we are prepared <u>to kill</u> (our) own people.* This leaves only the long word **rājya-sukha-lobhena** to accommodate. The word is a compound containing three elements, all of which contribute to its overall meaning. Consider the English phrase *upper respiratory tract*. There are three elements encoding one concept which English expresses using three words. Sanskrit would combine all three words into a compound. In English, any morphology is applied to the final word in the sequence: *several upper respiratory tract<u>s</u>; the upper respiratory tract<u>'s</u> resistance to antibiotics.* This is also true of the Sanskrit compound. Of the three words comprising the compound in this verse, only the final element contains any grammar: **lobh<u>ena</u>** (the instrumental singular ending for a short **-a** stem). The other two words appear in their citation form. Taken as a whole, the compound yields the meaning *by/through royalty pleasure greed.* Sanskrit compounds are notoriously difficult to translate and very often ambiguous, in that the elements comprising a compound lack the grammatical endings that would serve to inform the reader as to their relationship to each other. The longer the compound, the greater the difficulty. As with all things related to the learning of Sanskrit, however, the more one reads, the more familiar things start to become.

10

TEXTS FOR THE STUDY OF SANSKRIT

The student of Sanskrit is strongly advised to read widely. Despite its strong and evident connections with other Indo-European languages, not to mention its pervasiveness in the languages and living cultures of India, Sanskrit is an ancient language and therefore separated from the modern era by millennia. To read Sanskrit is to read a language that was kept fixed by its custodians so as to reflect the unchangeable values of the tradition which it represented. To fail to read around the language is to divorce it from its historical and cultural base, with the result that it becomes little other than a linguistic curio. There is an abundant amount of scholarship on ancient India, on the linguistics of the Indo-European language family and on Sanskrit itself. There is also a lot of somewhat less creditable writing on such topics. Sanskrit is particularly prone to doubtful scholarship, given the alacrity with which it has been embraced by those who seek to elevate it to the status of the supernatural. Care must be taken to distinguish between sources which are well researched, balanced and reliable, on the one hand and, on the other, those which are impassioned but lacking critical judgement.

For those whose interests incline towards archaeology but who are not averse to dipping a toe into linguistics, both Mallory (1991) and Renfrew (1990) are to be recommended. These are solid and accessible texts, not aimed purely at archaeologists or linguists. They are balanced in their opinions, presenting the data relating to the thorny issue of Indo-European origins and allowing the data to speak for itself. For those interested in the

DOI: 10.4324/9780429325434-11

debate about the Aryans, Bryant and Patton (2005) is an excellent text, as also Trautmann (2005). For students of ancient history and those who wish to investigate the Indus Valley Civilization, a balanced and readable introduction to the subject is provided by Robinson (2015). The scholar who is the most authoritative, when it comes to the Indus Valley language and writing system, is Parpola (1994), with whose work those proposing to try their hand at deciphering the Indus Valley script should be familiar. Parpola (2015) also investigates possible cultural connections between the Indus Valley Civilization and early Hinduism. Works by authors claiming to have deciphered the Indus Valley script should be read with caution and only after Parpola has been explored. Such works are not mentioned amongst the following texts, since they cannot be recommended.

There are a number of textbooks currently in print for the student keen to learn Sanskrit. Some of these are accessible; others, less so. If the learner is not studying a course in Sanskrit for which a textbook has already been specified, the decision as which textbook to use is one that merits careful consideration. The learner has first to decide whether he or she prefers a solidly grammatical approach, where the language is presented purely as a linguistic system, or whether a more culturally oriented approach is likely to achieve the desired results. Sanskrit can be daunting for those not familiar with grammatical terminology. For such intending learners, the principal learning tool ought to be one in which cultural points are abundant and where there are frequent comparisons made between what happens in Sanskrit and in English. In this respect, the pedagogical tools of yesteryear are best kept as reference materials, with a more accessible textbook as the primary source.

Macdonell (1927) is excellent for reference. The approach is 'traditional' but none the worse for it. One of the greatest drawbacks to Macdonell is that legible copies are hard to find. The print quality tends to be poor, the font demanding on the eyesight. No such problems exist with Bucknell (1994), recommended for use as a resource alongside a coursebook. All explanations are given in the IAST, and there is no use whatsoever of the Devanāgarī. Bucknell will appeal to those who wish to see the grammatical bones of Sanskrit laid bare. For those who prefer more flesh on the bones, Burrow (1955), despite its age, has not lost any of its appeal. It is a beautifully written walk around the Sanskrit language. For a more contemporary approach, and a solidly linguistic one, Cardona and Jain (2003) is a work of great importance and distinctly 'guru'. It is knowledgeable and weighty, as one might expect for a text which exceeds a thousand pages.

Slimmer than Cardona and Jain (albeit not by much) is Maurer (2009). Not only is Maurer's introduction worth reading but his appendices contain much that will appeal to those whose primary interests in Sanskrit lie in linguistics, grammar and literature. The reading passages are annotated, allowing them to be accessible to the reader, and become increasingly more complex as the reader's knowledge of grammar, syntax and vocabulary develops. As an all-round coursebook, and despite being brisk in the earlier chapters, Maurer represents a solid choice for the intending Sanskritist. Maurer's appendices are a mine of information on such matters as the Indo-European languages, as well as grammar.

For students who are interested in pursuing a literary exploration of Sanskrit, a number of texts can be recommended. Vedic literature is not accessible to the beginner, since the language is quite far removed from classical Sanskrit. A good starting point is the Bhagavadgītā, in that it is compact and can be tackled in easy stages. For those who would like to approach the Bhagavadgītā in English, to make themselves familiar with its contents prior to attempting the text in Sanskrit, Mascaró (1962/2003) can profitably be read. The 2003 edition, containing an excellent introduction by Dr. Simon Brodbeck, Reader in Religious Studies at Cardiff University, is worth obtaining. For a translation containing the original Devanāgarī text, Feuerstein (2011) is heartily recommended. Feuerstein has the additional benefit of containing nine introductory essays, firmly establishing the Bhagavadgītā in its literary and cultural contexts. Sanskrit students tend to gravitate towards Sargeant (2009) which, in terms of permitting a close reading, is unmatched. The Devanāgarī text of the Bhagavadgītā appears on the left-hand page, together with both a literal and more polished translation. The right-hand page contains an explanation of all the words which appear on the facing page. For the reader who is also studying Sanskrit, this is ideal. An exploration of the Bhagavadgītā in its wider literary context requires familiarity with the **Mahābhārata**, for which the reader is directed to van Buitenan (1980).

As regards literature other than the Bhagavadgītā, Lanman (1884), despite its age, continues to be useful. Most reading passages are taken from wisdom literature, akin to Aesop's fables in tone (the **Hitopadeśa**), and the much early **Ṛgveda**, even though the latter represents Vedic rather than classical Sanskrit. Copious notes accompany the reading passages, and Lanman contains a substantial Sanskrit to English vocabulary so that the reader is not required to refer constantly to a dictionary. The Hitopadeśa represents an accessible text, in that the stories are engaging and of manageable length. They offer an insight into the folk wisdom and moral precepts of ancient

India and have remained popular in contemporary India, where they are often cited. An excellent introduction to the Hitopadeśa is available through the Clay Sanskrit Library series (Törzsök, 2007), a series which, at the time of writing, is out of print. Any number of copies of the various books in the series continue to be available secondhand, and they are a useful resource for the Sanskrit learner. Texts in the Clay Library Series are bilingual editions, with the Sanskrit (in the IAST) on the left-hand page accompanied by a close translation on the right-hand page.

A more comprehensive collection of wisdom literature than the Hitopadeśa is the **Pañcatantra**, older in terms of composition and widely known in antiquity wherever Indic culture and a knowledge of Sanskrit were spread. The reader interested in exploring in more depth this important genre within Sanskrit literature is directed to the original text (again, in the IAST) and scholarly analysis by Egerton (1924). This is not a translation of the work but a detailed investigation of the text based on extent versions. For a readable and accurate translation, Egerton (1965) is recommended. Egerton (1924) is a work best approached with both a translation and a dictionary to hand.

On the subject of dictionaries, there is only one that fits the bill, as far as the student of Sanskrit is concerned. This is Monier-Williams (1899), the constant companion of every Sanskritist, teacher and student alike. Care should be taken to inspect a copy of the dictionary prior to purchase, if possible, since the quality of the print can often be extremely poor in places. It is a marvel of European scholarship in Sanskrit, and it is difficult to envisage a point where Monier-Williams would become obsolete. The dictionary is available online and the learner is strongly encouraged to take the time to find out how its contents may be accessed. The Harvard-Kyoto Convention, as discussed in 2.3, is extremely useful in this respect.

A final word is needed regarding a work which is both immensely readable and able to put the study of Sanskrit into a context where it can fully be appreciated as one of the world's great cultural languages. The work in question is Ostler (2005). Ostler explores the spread of various languages, such as Akkadian, Aramaic, Greek and Latin. A chapter is devoted to the 'cultured career of Sanskrit' (Chapter 5), seeing how it was taken to Southeast Asia and, with Buddhism, to central Asia and to East Asia along the Silk Road. By its very nature, Sanskrit contained the seeds of its eventual decline, despite its spread. It was the language of the few; a language acquired through years of careful study; the language of Hinduism and Buddhism and, ultimately, linked to the progress (or decline) of Hindu and Buddhist thought. As other languages flourished, either through trade, conquest or the spread of new ideas, Sanskrit fell away. Ostler's 'charming creeper' was cut back, retreating to South Asia, where it continues to face the challenges of the modern age. The fate of Sanskrit, as indeed of all languages, depends on the relevance it has for learners and users. Despite the march of globalization, Sanskrit has not yet reached the end of its life cycle.

Indo-European studies

Mallory, J. P. (1991) *In Search of the Indo-Europeans: Language, Archaeology and Myth*. London: Thames and Hudson.
Renfrew, C. (1990) *Archaeology and Language: The Puzzle of Indo-European Origins* (New Ed.). Cambridge: Cambridge University Press.

Indo-Aryan studies

Bryant, E. F. and Patton, L. L. (Eds.) (2005) *The Indo-Aryan Controversy: Evidence and Inference in Indian History*. Abingdon, Oxon: Routledge.
Trautmann, T. R. (2005) *The Aryan Debate (Debates in Indian History and Society)*. New Delhi, India: Oxford University Press.

Indus Valley Civilization

Parpola, A. (1994) *Deciphering the Indus Script*. Cambridge: Cambridge University Press.
Parpola, A. (2015) *The Roots of Hinduism: The Early Aryans and the Indus Civilization*. New York: Oxford University Press.
Robinson, A. (2015) *The Indus (Lost Civilizations)*. London: Reaktion Books.

Sanskrit language

Bucknell, R. S. (1994) *Sanskrit Manual: A Quick-reference Guide to the Phonology and Grammar of Classical Sanskrit*. New Delhi, India: Motilal Banarsidass.
Burrow, T. (1955) *The Sanskrit Language*. London: Faber and Faber.
Cardona, G. and Jain, D. (Eds.) (2003) *The Indo-Aryan Languages*. Abingdon, Oxon: Routledge.
Macdonell, A. A. (1927) *A Sanskrit Grammar for Students* (3rd Ed.). Oxford: Oxford University Press.
Maurer, W. H. (2009) *The Sanskrit Language: An Introductory Grammar and Reader* (Rev. Ed.). Abingdon, Oxon: Routledge.
Ostler, N. (2005) *Empires of the Word: A Language History of the World*. New York: HarperCollins Publishers Inc.

Sanskrit literature

Egerton, F. (1924) *The Panchatantra Reconstructed (Volume 1: Text and Critical Apparatus)*. New Haven, CT: American Oriental Society.
Egerton, F. (1965) *The Panchatantra: Translated from the Sanskrit*. London: George Allen and Unwin Ltd.
Feuerstein, G. (2011) *The Bhagavad-Gītā: A New Translation*. Boston, MA: Shambala Publications, Inc.
Lanman, C. R. (1884) *A Sanskrit Reader: Text, Vocabulary and Notes*. Cambridge, MA: Harvard University Press.
Mascaró, J. (1962/2003) *The Bhagavad Gita*. London: Penguin Books.
Sargeant, W. (2009) *The Bhagavad Gītā* (25th Anniversary Ed.). Albany, NY: Excelsior Editions, State University of New York Press.
Törzsök, J. (2007) *Friendly Advice by Nārāyaṇa & King Vikrama's Adventures* (Clay Sanskrit Library. General Eds. R. Gombrich and S. Pollock). New York: New York University Press and the JJC Foundation.
van Buitenan, J. A. B. (1980) *The Mahābhārata. 1: The Book of the Beginning* (New Ed.). Chicago: University of Chicago Press.

Sanskrit dictionary

Monier-Williams, M. (1899) *A Sanskrit-English Dictionary*. Oxford: Oxford University Press.

The University of Cologne (Universität zu Köln) has created a digital archive (Cologne Digital Sanskrit Dictionaries) which contains all the major dictionaries for Sanskrit as well as Monier-Williams. The vocabulary for Lanman's *Sanskrit Reader* is included within this archive. It can be accessed by typing 'IITS Koeln' into one's preferred search engine.

GLOSSARY

Ablative The fifth of eight cases in Sanskrit, equating to the English preposition *from* (e.g. *The mouse came out from its lair*).

Accusative The second of eight cases in Sanskrit, representing the object of the sentence. The object does not control the verb but is the recipient of it (*Sītā addresses the guru*). The accusative also indicates movement towards a place (*You go to the village*).

Adjective A word which describes a noun (e.g. *dark* horse; *small* house). In Sanskrit, an adjective agrees with the noun, so that it is case-marked in accordance with the case-marking on the noun. If a noun is masculine nominative and plural, the adjective has the same ending. Adjectives are often expressed using compounds or the past passive participle.

Adverb An adverb describes the way a verb is taking place (e.g. to go *swiftly*; to speak *angrily*). Most adverbs in Sanskrit are not declined, meaning that they have a fixed form. They do not have the same ending as the finite verb form, since finite verb forms have a personal ending.

Affricate The description of a phoneme in terms of its manner of articulation. An affricate contains features of both a stop, where the air builds up in vocal tract but is allowed to hiss out. In Sanskrit, there are four affricates: **c**, **ch**, **j** and **jh** (These are palatal consonants). In all cases, the tongue touches the top of the mouth and moves to allow a *sh*-sound to follow.

AMT (See *Aryan Migration Theory*.)

Anusvāra This is the dot, in the Devanāgarī, placed above a consonant, semivowel or sibilant to indicate that the immediately preceding vowel is nasalized. In the IAST, it is indicated by a dotted *m* (e.g. **kiṃ**). Anusvāra cannot occur before a vowel or right at the end of a sentence. It is common practice to pronounce anusvāra as the nasal belonging to the same place of articulation as the following consonant, semivowel or sibilant.

Apabhraṃśa The phase of an Indic language, transitional between the Old and Middle Indic stages, as represented by Sanskrit and the Prakrits, and New Indic, which is the term applied to the modern languages of India. In Sanskrit, the word **apabhraṃśa** means *falling away* – a name which indicates a language variety in the process of losing endings associated with declension and conjugation in the Old and Middle Indic languages.

Articulation The production of a phoneme. This is often described as pronunciation, although articulation refers to the actual creation of a sound rather than to anything relating to its quality.

Articulators The parts of the oral tract (i.e. the soft palate, the roof of the mouth, the hard palate, the teeth, the lips, the tongue).

Aryan A controverted term, given its political misuse, but prevalent in writing concerned with the language and settlement of speakers of the early Indic languages. In Sanskrit, the term **ārya** means *honourable* or *esteemed person*. To what extent the term was used in antiquity to distinguish between ethnic groups is debatable. It is more likely that it indicated adherence to a particular cultural tradition associated with the Vedas. The terms 'Aryan', 'Indo-Aryan' and 'Indic' all relate to the non-Iranian languages of the Indo-Iranian branch of the Indo-European family.

Aryan Migration Theory (AMT) Often conflated with the earlier Aryan Invasion Theory, this is the term used to refer to a hypothesis which posits that the original speakers of Vedic Sanskrit entered South Asia bringing the language with them. The greatest objection to the AMT is that it is claimed to represent an extension of outmoded and colonial thinking. The opponents of the AMT promote the Out of India Theory (OIT).

Aspirate A sound in Sanskrit which is represented by an individual phoneme (**h**) and is present in ten consonantal phonemes: **kh**, **gh**, **ch**, **jh**, **ṭh**, **ḍh**, **th**, **dh**, **ph** and **bh**. It is a forceful exhalation which needs to be audible in Sanskrit, since it distinguishes aspirated phonemes from unaspirated ones. The IAST represents the aspirate with the letter *h* in all cases.

Avagraha The sign which resembles the handwritten, uppercase English letter *S*, restricted to indicating the absence of the initial short **a-** when preceded by a word that ends with either **-e** or **-o**.

Avestan The oldest known Indo-Iranian language on the Iranian side. It is the language in which the earliest Zoroastrian scriptures were composed and is the closest in structure to Sanskrit, outside of South Asia.

BJP The Bharatiya Janata Party, currently in power in India. It supports Hindu nationalist views and holds Sanskrit in great esteem due to its central role in the preservation of Hindu culture.

Borrowing Linguistic borrowing refers to the adoption of a word from another language, which then undergoes a process of 'nativization' so that the loan word is consistent with the sound system of the borrowing language (Chinese loan words are borrowed into English without their tone, for example). A borrowed word may potentially come from any language. The relatedness of languages is not a key factor in this respect.

Brāhmī The parent writing system of all Indian languages (both Indic and Dravidian) except for those employing the Perso-Arabic script, such as Urdu. The Brāhmī is the first attested writing system of India, with the exception of the Indus Valley script, and is the script used in the pillar inscriptions of Aśoka (c. 250 BCE). A direct connection with the Indus Valley script has not been established. Although the Brāhmī is the oldest-known writing system known for the Indic languages, there is currently no evidence to suggest that it was used for Sanskrit. The origin of the Brāhmī remains contested.

Case In Sanskrit, case is marked as an ending to a noun, indicating the relationship of the noun in question to the rest of the sentence. There are eight cases, traditionally numbered in Sanskrit (i.e. *first*, *second*, etc.) but for which a Latin-based terminology is usually employed in textbooks. The eight cases, in order, are as follows: nominative, accusative, instrumental, dative, ablative, genitive, locative and vocative. It should be noted that the Indic grammatical system did not acknowledge the vocative case.

Cerebral A place of articulation represented by a series of consonant phonemes (**ṭ**, **ṭh**, **ḍ**, **ḍh**, **ṇ**) and allocated to the semivowel **r** and the sibilant **ṣ**. Cerebrals are often referred to as 'retroflex', although that is not so much a place of articulation as a description of what happens to the tongue tip in articulating the phoneme in question.

Citation form The form in which a word appears before any declension or conjugation has been applied. With nouns, it is the stem form; with verbs, it is the root. The term is synonymous with 'dictionary form'.

Cognates (See also *Borrowing*.) Cognates are words which show evident similarities in form across languages, leading to a supposition that the similarity is due to the fact that the languages in question are related. This is distinct from borrowing, which does not indicate any necessary genetic relatedness between languages. Distinguishing between cognates and loan words is not always easy. Borrowing can (and does) take place between languages that are related, as evidenced by the massive influx into English of words from Latin and French – the latter being a descendant of Latin.

Compound Not to be confused with conjunct, the term relates to a fusion of words to produce a composite word, often with a sense which is not the sum of its parts. In English, for example, a *bigwig* is not a person who necessarily has to wear a false hairpiece. Compounds occur frequently in Sanskrit.

Conjugation This applies to verbs, not to consonants, and refers to the process of adding endings to a verb stem to indicate who is performing the verb.

Conjunct Conjuncts represent the coming together of any combination of consonants without an intervening vowel. There are various strategies used in the formation of conjuncts and they represent the greatest challenge in learning to read the Devanāgarī.

Consonant In Sanskrit, the consonants are represented by a group of thirty-three phonemes (thirty-five, if anusvāra and visarga were to be included), arranged according to five places of articulation. Consonants are sounds which require articulators to be in contact.

Daṇḍa The only punctuation mark used in Sanskrit. It has the form of a single vertical stroke, not connected to any letter and not bearing a horizontal stroke at the top. A single **daṇḍa** indicates a full stop in English. A double **daṇḍa (dvadaṇḍa)** indicates either the end of a text or the end of an individual verse of poetry. The word means *stick* or *staff*.

Dative The fourth of eight cases in Sanskrit, indicating the recipient or beneficiary of an action. The English prepositions that correspond to the dative are *to* and *for* (e.g. *The teacher reads the book to his students*; *the army fights for the king*).

Declension This relates to the process of adding endings to nouns and to adjectives to show their function within the sentence. Declension indicates gender, case and number.

Definite article In English, the definite article is the word *the*. Sanskrit does not possess a definite article but may indicate that something is being referred to by using the relevant declension of the word **tat** (a demonstrative pronoun).

Demonstrative pronoun Words such as **tat**, **etat** and **idam** are used in Sanskrit to indicate *that one*; *this one*; *those*; *these*, etc. They are demonstrative pronouns and refer to something or someone mentioned elsewhere in the text.

Dental A place of articulation represented by a series of consonant phonemes (**t**, **th**, **d**, **dh**, **n**) and allocated to the semivowel **l** and the sibilant **s**.

Devanāgarī The writing system associated with Sanskrit. The Devanāgarī is also used to write Hindi and Marathi. It is the most widespread of all Indian writing systems within India and Nepal. The meaning of the word Devanāgarī is *(of/from) the city of the god(s)*. The Devanāgarī is descended from the Brāhmī script.

Diacritic/diacritical mark Any sign added to a letter in the Roman alphabet to indicate its pronunciation. Typically, this is a dot or a slash but there are several diacritical marks, and these vary from one language to another.

Diphthong A fusion of two audibly distinct vowel sounds. A diphthong may not necessarily be represented by two letters in all languages. In Sanskrit, there are two diphthongs and these have their own letter within the Devanāgarī. Importantly, diphthongs are deemed to be single phonemes.

Dravidian The name of a language family of southern India which includes four languages with long literary traditions and which are official state languages of India: Tamil, Telugu, Kannada and Malayalam. Although heavily influenced by Sanskrit, especially with respect to borrowing, these languages are not Indo-European or Indic.

Dual The term which relates to grammatical number and refers to two – and only two – participants. Dual forms exist in the noun (e.g. *two hands*; *two horses*) and in the verb (e.g. *They [the two of them] go*).

Enclitic A word which follows another and indicates something about the preceding word. In Sanskrit, an enclitic can indicate a connection between two words (**ca**), emphasize a word (**eva**; **iva**) or represent a shortened form of a pronoun (**me**; **te**, etc.). A common enclitic is **tu** (*but; however*).

Finite verb This is a verb which appears in a conjugated form, which means that someone is identified as performing it (e.g. *I speak*, *you* *speak, he/she/it speaks*). When no person is identified in the verb ending, it is in the infinitive (*to speak*).

Fricative This describes the manner of articulation of a phoneme, where air is hissed out rather than being held. The tongue is positioned in a way in which the airflow can be sustained over a number of seconds; the sound does not need to be released immediately. The fricatives in Sanskrit are **ś**, **ṣ**, **s** and **h**. These are the three sibilants and the aspirate.

Gender In Sanskrit, all nouns are either masculine, neuter or feminine. Often, the gender of a noun is determined by its biological characteristics. *Horse* is masculine, *mare* is feminine; *cow* is feminine, *bull* is masculine, etc. With things that do not possess obvious gender or are abstract (*knowledge*; *fear*; *thought*), the gender must be learnt as it cannot be assumed.

Genitive The sixth of eight cases in Sanskrit, indicating possession (e.g. The horse's mane). Although English possesses a genitive apostrophe (*Mark's book*), it does not always need to use it. In the sentence: *this is the house of your sister*, the preposition *of* indicates the genitive function. Often the genitive function is indicated adjectivally in English (e.g. *The town road* – meaning *the road of the town*).

Germanic A branch within the Indo-European language family representing languages such as English, Dutch, German and the Nordic languages (Icelandic, Norwegian, Swedish, Danish).

Gerund In Sanskrit, a gerund is a word which gives verbal information but does not involve conjugation. It is composed of a verbal root, which often undergoes some form of modification, to which **-(i)tvā** is added, or **-ya**, if the verb is prefixed (In a handful of cases, **-na** is added rather than the predicted **-(i)tvā**). A possible way of translating a gerund is to use the English formula: *having + past participle*, such as **tyaktvā** (*having forsaken; renounced*). The gerund **tyaktvā** contains the verbal root **tyaj**, with a mutation affecting the final consonant (**-j** to **-k**), plus **-tvā**.

Guṇa A form of vowel mutation in which a primary vowel other than **a** undergoes a change in quality (**i/ī** → **e**; **u/ū** → **o**; **ṛ/ṝ** → **ar**; **ḷ** → **al**).

Guttural (See *Velar*.)

Harvard-Kyoto Convention A transliteration system for the Devanāgarī which is keyboard-friendly and widely used with computer applications.

Indefinite article In English, the indefinite article is the word *a* (or *an*, before a vowel). Sanskrit does not possess an indefinite article but may indicate that a singular something is being referred to by using the word **eka** (*one*).

Indic This word is not to be conflated with 'Indian'. 'Indian' indicates something as originating from India, whereas 'Indic' specifically draws attention to a group of related languages. The Indic languages are those belonging to the Indo-Iranian branch of the Indo-European family. The term is often used in preference to 'Aryan', to avoid unwanted historical overtones.

Indo-European The term for the language family to which both English and Sanskrit belong. It is the most geographically widespread of all the language families of the world.

Indo-Iranian A branch within the Indo-European language family which some linguists consider to be too broad, preferring to split the branch into two component parts: Iranian in the west and Indic in the east. Other branches of Indo-European include Romance (or Italic) and Slavonic (or Slavic). English is from the Germanic branch.

Infinitive A verb form which does not have a personal ending (e.g. *to speak*; *to go*; *to live*). In Sanskrit, infinitives end in **-(i)tum**. In the sentence: *he wants to speak to her*, the verb form *wants* is conjugated, and therefore finite, and the verb form *to speak* is in the infinitive. Note that infinitives in English are preceded by *to*. Dictionaries of English list verbs in their infinitive forms, whereas dictionaries of Sanskrit list verbs according to their root.

Instrumental The third of eight cases in Sanskrit, representing the means by which something is taking place. In English, the prepositions *by* and *with* reflect the Sanskrit instrumental (e.g. *she travels <u>by</u> train; she always visits <u>with</u> her brother*).

Interjection A word which represents an exclamation, such as *oh!* or *ah!*

Labial A place of articulation represented by a series of consonant phonemes (**p**, **ph**, **b**, **bh**, **m**) and allocated to the semivowel **v**. Labials are strictly speaking 'bilabials', since the term 'labial' can also indicate phonemes that are not attested in Sanskrit (e.g. ***f**).

Language branch A division within a language family which identifies a group of language more closely related to each other than to other members within the family in question. For example, Italian and Spanish are closer to each other than either of them are to Polish or Russian.

Language family A concept which groups languages on the basis that are deemed to have descended from the same ancestral form. With Indo-European, the ancestral language form is the hypothesized (and reconstructed) Proto-Indo-European. Other language families of Europe and Asia include Finno-Ugric, Altaic, Semitic, Dravidian, Sino-Tibetan and Austroasiatic. Languages belonging to these families may have been profoundly influenced by languages from other families, making the process of determining family affiliation a problematic one.

Locative The seventh of eight cases in Sanskrit, giving information on the location of something within the sentence (e.g. *on the ground*; *through the street*; *in the shade*).

Macron This is a diacritical mark which takes the form of a horizontal line written over a vowel to indicate that the vowel is long (e.g. **ā**; **ī**). The diacritical mark for indicating a short vowel is known as a 'breve' (e.g. *ĕ*; *ŏ*). The breve is not used in Sanskrit to indicate a short vowel. Vowels are short unless indicated to the contrary. There are two exceptions to this: **e** and **o**. Both are long in Sanskrit and do not have short equivalents.

Manner of articulation Distinct from place of articulation in that it describes how a phoneme is pronounced rather than where. Voice and aspiration are manners of articulation. The term 'sibilant' is another example of manner of articulation, since it indicates airflow. In Sanskrit, a sibilant is palatal (**ś**), cerebral (**ṣ**) or dental (**s**), according to its place of articulation.

Mantra A short composition aimed at concentrating the mind by placing the focus on sound rather than meaning.

Mātrā The horizontal topline which is found over most letters in the Devanāgarī. This is the last stroke to be written in the formation of a letter. The word **mātrā** means *measure*.

Mood Often conflated with tense, mood indicates the way a verb is being undertaken rather than if the action is taking place, has taken place or will take place.

Morpheme A unit of meaning which can be a word itself or a small part of it. The word *cat* is a morpheme, since it cannot be split into anything smaller and still retain its meaning. The words *cats*, *cat's* and *cattish*, however, contain additional morphemes which add to the meaning. In the first of these, the noun is put into the plural with the addition of the plural morpheme *-s*; in the second, the genitive apostrophe is used (*'s*), indicating that something belongs to the cat; in the third, the morpheme *-ish* is added, indicating similarity or equivalence.

Morphology The identification of a word according to the units of meaning contained within the word in question. Morphemes can be individual words (e.g. *cat*) or things added to a word to add to its overall meaning (*uncatlike*).

Nasal In Sanskrit, five consonantal phonemes are identified as nasal: **ṅ**, **ñ**, **ṇ**, **n**, **m**. With these consonants, the air must be allowed to travel through the nose as well as the mouth when they are pronounced. This passage of air through the nose is what makes them nasals (see also *Anusvāra* and *Manner of articulation*).

Nominative The first of eight cases in Sanskrit, representing the subject of the sentence. The subject controls the verb (*Sītā speaks to the guru*).

Noun A thing as opposed to an action. Nouns may be proper nouns (as with the names of people, or places), concrete nouns, representing things which may be touched or detected by the senses (e.g. *soil*; *a garden*; *scent*) or abstract nouns (*wisdom*; *time*, etc.). In Sanskrit, a noun can function as an adjective. It is not so much the form of a noun but its position within a phrase or sentence which indicates whether it is functioning as a noun or as an adjective.

Number With respect to grammar, number indicates whether a noun or a verb involves one person or more than one. English has two numbers: singular and plural. Sanskrit has three: singular, dual and plural (see also Dual). Number needs to be considered alongside person, where verbs are concerned. In the phrase *third person singular*, person and number are indicated and identify a specific conjugational form.

Object The person or thing who/which is the recipient of the action of a verb, assuming that the sentence is an active construction (e.g. *The dog chases the cat*). In a passive construction, the situation in English is more complicated, in that the recipient of the verb is placed in subject position, before the verb, but is still the recipient of the action: *The cat is chased by the dog*. Since word order is more flexible in Sanskrit than in English, Sanskrit uses case endings to distinguish the object from the subject. The subject must be indicated by the nominative case, whereas the object may appear in any of the other cases (except the vocative).

OIT (See *Out of India Theory*.)

Old Indic A term used to designate the earliest attested Indic languages: Vedic, Sanskrit and classical Sanskrit. Prakrits tend to be classified as Middle Indic languages but have a long history and contain features which connect them closely to Vedic in terms of antiquity.

Out of India Theory (OIT) A hypothesis suggesting that Sanskrit originated in South Asia, along with its ancestral form. This posits the Indo-European homeland as South Asia, given that Sanskrit is an Indo-European language. Opponents of this hypothesis point to the fact that is it is not supported by linguistic and archaeological data.

Palatal A place of articulation represented by a series of consonant phonemes (**c**, **ch**, **j**, **jh**, **ñ**) and allocated to the semivowel **y** and the sibilant **ś**.

Paradigm A pattern or model exemplifying a particular phenomenon. Typically, it is used in language learning to indicate a table of declension or conjugation.

Participle In Sanskrit, a participle is a word formed from a verbal root which serves a number of functions. The past passive participle is an example of how broad such uses can be: it can substitute for a finite verb or can be purely adjectival in nature. It is better for the learner to put participles to one side until a firm grasp has been achieved on declension and conjugation.

Person As with English, Sanskrit grammar acknowledges three persons: the first (*I/we*); the second (*you [singular]/you [plural]*); the third (*he, she, it/they*). It is important to remember that, whilst English and Sanskrit agree as to this grammatical concept, person is to be seen within the context of number. With respect to number, English and Sanskrit differ.

Personal ending The addition to a verbal stem which creates a finite verb. For example, the verbal root **bhū** (*to be*) generates the stem **bhava-**, to which a personal ending is added to create a finite verb form (e.g. **bhavati**, *he/she/it is*). The knowledge of personal endings is what allows the student of Sanskrit to make sense of conjugation.

Phoneme A sound which is recognized by the sound system of a language. The word 'sound' has its uses when attempting to capture similarities between languages but, within the context of describing Sanskrit, is too vague. The classification of phonemes in the Indic tradition is precise and comprehensive. A phoneme has only one outcome, unlike the letters of the Roman alphabet as it is used for English. For example, the plural morpheme *-s* in the word *cats* is the same as the initial phoneme in the word *snake*. It is an unvoiced sibilant. In the word *dogs*, however, the sibilant is voiced and sounds like the English *z* in *zebra*.

Phonology The description of the sound system of a language from the point of view of how the sounds in question interact with each other. Investigating sounds is, technically speaking, the science of phonetics; but sounds can undergo change due to a number of factors. Note the difference in sound in the plural morpheme *-s* in the words *cats* and *dogs*. The difference is due to a phonological process.

Phrase A phrase is a component within a sentence, not a grammatically complete sentence. *My hamster* is a noun phrase whereas *my hamster is cute* is a complete sentence (It contains both a subject and a finite verb). Phrases account for a large number of sayings and expressions which do not qualify as complete sentences, such as *my country, right or wrong*.

PIE (See *Proto-Indo-European.*)

Place of articulation Sanskrit identifies five positions within the oral (or vocal) tract that account for the production of its consonants, semivowels and sibilants: the velum (or soft palate), producing velar sounds; the hard palate, which accounts for the palatals; the cerebrum (the highest part of the hard palate, presumed to be closest to the brain – hence its name), producing the cerebral sounds; the top teeth, with which the tongue is in contact to produce the dentals; the lips, which must be in contact with each other to create the labials. These five positions are the places of articulation.

Plural The term which relates to grammatical number and, in Sanskrit, refers to three or more participants. Plural forms exist in the noun (e.g. *several hands*; *several horses*) and the verb (e.g. *They [three or more of them] go*).

Prakrit(s) There is ample linguistic evidence to show that the Prakrits are not the descendants of Sanskrit but, rather, ancient vernacular languages of India, used for everyday purposes whilst Sanskrit was reserved for religious and scholarly purposes and literary composition. In due course, some Prakrits became literary languages, such as **Pāḷi**. The Prakrits precede the Apabhraṃśa phase, which represents the transition between Middle Indic and New Indic languages. There is no distinct cut-off point between phases; these represent a convenient linguistic fiction, albeit justified in terms of representing language change.

Prefix A morpheme added at the start of a word to modify its meaning. Nouns may be prefixed in Sanskrit (e.g. **vidyā**, *knowledge*; **avidyā**, *ignorance*), but it is with verbs that prefixes are at their most complex. Before verbs, they may drastically modify the root meaning of the verb (e.g. √ **gam**, *to go*; with prefix **ava-** [**ava-** + √ **gam**], *to understand*).

Pronoun A word that relates to something or something which occurs in the same sentence or wider text (either spoken or written). One may refer to *him*, *her* or *it*; but without a clearer indication as to who or what is being discussed, the pronoun does not shed any light. It is a place-holder for a noun and relies on the speaker or reader to deduce the noun in question. Consider the sentence: *That dog is overweight, so it's slow*. The pronoun *it* refers to *that dog* – not to another dog or to its owner.

Proto-Indo-European (PIE) The hypothesized ancestor of the Indo-European languages. The term 'proto' is used to refer to any language variety for which there are no literary records, as such Proto-Germanic, the putative ancestral form of the Germanic languages. Proto forms must be reconstructed.

Punctuation (See *Daṇḍa.*)

Retroflex (See *Cerebral.*)

Romance A branch within the Indo-European language family representing languages such as Italian, Spanish, French and Romanian. All members of the Romance branch are descendants of Latin.

Root The core form of a verb which carries the meaning. A root, in Sanskrit, is not a complete word but requires an ending. Roots usually undergo modification to generate nouns or verbal stems (see also *Stem*).

Sandhi A Sanskrit word adopted by linguistics to indicate a sound change which takes place in the process of articulation (It is triggered by phonological phenomena). In Sanskrit, the rationale behind sandhi is that it is deemed to reflect what happens in natural pronunciation and its effects have an impact in spelling. This tends not to be the case in English, where spelling is preserved irrespective of actual pronunciation. For example, in rapid speech, one might hear the phoneme *r* in the phrase *India (r)and its neighbours*, but it would not be written.

Schwa This is another term for the indeterminate vowel, frequently heard in English, which occurs in an unstressed syllable (e.g. *insider*). Sanskrit does not possess an indeterminate vowel. The inherent vowel in Sanskrit (**a**) is not to be confused with the indeterminate vowel.

Semivowel In Sanskrit, these are the phonemes **y**, **r**, **l** and **v**. They are a group of sounds contained within the larger category of consonants but do not have the feature of aspiration. All semivowels are voiced.

Sibilant Literally, a *whistling sound.* Sanskrit possesses three sibilants: **ś**, **ṣ** and **s**. The aspirate **h** can be convenient placed alongside the sibilants, for the purposes of analysis, since it is technically a fricative – a category which includes all the sibilants (see also *Fricative*).

Singular The term which relates to grammatical number and refers to one – and only one – participant. Singular forms exist in the noun (e.g. *a hand*; a *horse*) and in the verb (e.g. *She goes; I go*).

Stem A form which is derived from a verbal root. As with the root, the stem is not a word in itself but requires an ending to be complete. With nouns, the ending is the relevant case ending; with verbs, it is a personal ending, resulting in a finite verb form.

Subject The person or thing who/which controls a verb, assuming that the sentence is an active construction (e.g. *The dog chases the cat*). The subject of an active construction is indicated by the nominative case.

Suffix A morpheme added to the end of a word to modify its meaning. Participles are examples of suffixes. Infinitives and gerunds are also created by the addition of a suffix.

Syllable A unit of sound which may contain a vowel by itself or in combination with a consonant, semivowel or sibilant (or more than one). In all cases, a syllable requires a vowel. Syllables are best thought of as beats. Consider the sentence: *Cry 'Havoc!' and let slip the dogs of war*. There are ten beats to that sentence. Otherwise said, the sentence contains ten syllables.

Tense Often conflated with mood, tense indicates the time in which a verb is taking place, has taken place or will take place.

Transliteration A transliteration system aims at a one-to-one correspondence from one writing system to another, in an attempt to capture the pronunciation of an unfamiliar script. Transliteration systems for Sanskrit are many but the IAST is the system of choice for Sanskritists.

Velar A place of articulation represented by a series of consonant phonemes (**k**, **kh**, **g**, **gh**, **ṅ**) and allocated to the aspirate **h**. Velars are often referred to as 'gutturals', a term which is wider than it needs to be, given that it includes sounds which are not attested in Sanskrit.

Verb Often defined as a 'doing word', which is a pithy and accurate description. In Sanskrit, one needs to distinguish between roots, stems and finite verbs. When giving a full description of a finite verb, one cites the following: root, stem, verb class, person, number, tense/mood, voice.

Vocative The eighth of eight cases in Sanskrit, used to indicate a calling out to someone or something (e.g. *Hey, Sid!*; *oh, God!*; *o cruel fate!*). In Sanskrit, the vocative case ending is applied to the person or thing being addressed. Often, the word marked in the vocative is preceded by **aho**, **bhoḥ** or **he**.

Voice Voice has a twofold meaning in Sanskrit. When investigating a phoneme or a sound change, voice relates to when the vocal cords vibrate during the articulation of the phoneme in question. As regards conjugation, voice indicates if a finite verb form is active, middle or passive. In English, *you eat the cookie* is active, whereas *the cookie is eaten by you* is passive. The consensus is that there is no real difference in meaning between the active and middle voice in Sanskrit and that it is a purely grammatical phenomenon: some verbs specify for the active voice; others, the middle.

Vowel In Sanskrit, vowels may be short or long. Long vowels are indicated with a macron, except for **e** and **o**. Unlike consonants, semivowels and sibilants, vowels do not involve any touching between articulators.

Vowel mutation A process by which the vowel of a verbal root undergoes a change prior to forming a stem. This process is also known as 'vowel gradation', 'vowel strengthening' and 'ablaut'. English employs vowel mutation in *man* → *men* and *mouse* → *mice* in the creation of irregular plural forms.

Vr̥ddhi A form of vowel mutation in which a vowel undergoes a change with respect to length or diphthongization (**a** → **ā**; **e** → **ai**; **o** → **au**). See *guṇa*.

INDEX AND LIST OF VERB ROOTS

CPSIA information can be obtained
at www.ICGtesting.com
Printed in the USA
LVHW081928061022
730134LV00015B/878

9 780367 343859